DICKIE BIRD'S
BRITAIN

DICKIE BIRD'S
BRITAIN

Dickie Bird
with Keith Lodge

with photographs by Derry Brabbs

Hodder & Stoughton

P H O T O G R A P H I C   A C K N O W L E D G E M E N T S

The author and publisher wish first to thank Derry Brabbs for contributing over 150 superb photographs to the book during his extensive travels with the author. They would also like to thank the following for their excellent photographs: Patrick Eagar, pages 75, 78, 79, 84, 85, 91, 93, 99, 128, 133, 135, 139, 165, 180, 184, 189; Allsport, pages 37, 38, 41, 43, 109, 148, 164, 184, 186–9, 228–33, 238, 239, 241–3, 245–7; npower, page 14; Susan Greenhill, page 31; *Barnsley Chronicle*, pages 45–7, 219.

First published in Great Britain in 2002 by Hodder and Stoughton
A division of Hodder Headline

ISBN 0 340 82143 4

Typeset in Stone Serif

Printed and bound in Great Britain by
Butler & Tanner Ltd, Frome & London

Hodder and Stoughton
A division of Hodder Headline
338 Euston Road
London NW1 3BH

CONTENTS

ACKNOWLEDGEMENTS

I would particularly like to thank Roddy Bloomfield, not only for coming up with the idea of the book, but also for masterminding my round Britain trip with such patience, expertise and good humour.

Also vital to putting this book together has been Keith Lodge, the distinguished former editor of the *Barnsley Chronicle* and a friend and neighbour of mine throughout my life. Keith was at my side on almost all of the journeys so that he could put my spoken words into written form. He is a master at reflecting my voice, and he has never let me down. Thank you, Keith.

Then, of course, there is Derry Brabbs, who has gone beyond the call of duty to provide such magnificent photographs.

There have been so many people whose friendly help has been invaluable on my travels: Quentin Seddon, the Somerset smallholder who put me right on vegetable matters; England's most respected football manager Sir Bobby Robson; The Duke and Duchess of Devonshire; record-breaking Olympic rower Sir Steve Redgrave; Robin Easton, manager of Simpson's in the Strand, and Sarah Manser at The Ritz, whose combined contribution to the book was simply food and drink; cricket historian John Ford; *Wisden* editor Graeme Wright; Lord's museum curator Stephen Green; Christians in Sport director the Reverend Andrew Wingfield Digby; Scottish journalist Jack Webster, who was my guide north of the border; David Hardy, manager of the Blair Athol distillery; Lizzie Gilks, who showed me round Arundel Castle; bat-maker Eric Loxton; former television racing commentator Julian Wilson and York racecourse manager/secretary and clerk of the course John Smith; Welsh rugby legend Cliff Morgan; Welsh vicar Eldon Phillips, who was such a good-natured courier on my return trip to 'The Land of My Fathers'; Millennium Stadium Public Relations Officer Rob Cole; The Gallery's Don Masson; Alex Hill from the London Weather Centre; Graham Child, divisional director of BMB Menswear Ltd; Paignton station manager Barry Cogar; Brixham harbourmaster Paul Labistour; Bridget Cobbald, the director of Weston Park Hospital's Cancer Appeal; Eileen Higgins, who set up the Macmillan cancer nursing service in Barnsley; Claire Strachan, the Yorkshire regional fund-raising manager for the National Autistic Society; pigeon expert Keith Hodgson; golfing guru John Jacobs; and Bruce and Robert Ropner of Camp Hill. Finally a thank you to the designer of my splendid-looking book, Bob Vickers.

PREFACE

WHEN my publisher, Roddy Bloomfield, rang to suggest that I write another book I was rather taken aback. There was, I thought, little left for me to say. My fund of stories had been exhausted in *My Autobiography* and *White Cap and Bails*. Surely my days as an author had come to an end, along with my career as a Test umpire.

But he was insistent. He said the Bird supporters wanted more from me, and he told me that he had come up with an idea for a travel book with a difference. It is true that after travelling the length and breadth of Britain to fulfil cricket appointments, I often talked about the marvellous places and fascinating people that I had been lucky enough to encounter. I have always been very proud to be British, so he said why don't I write about this country as I see it, and take a photographer with me as I go on my travels.

Reflecting on this proposition, I could see that here was a chance to write about people I regard very highly. I thought I could also include chapters on some of the great houses and gardens of England, and on some of the great British institutions, such as bank holidays, bed and breakfast establishments, fish and chips, the weather, and of course our great sporting heritage. Then there was food and drink. I love my food! What were my likes and dislikes? Where were my favourite dining-out places? And where would I like to go, given the opportunity? Well, Scotland for a start. I could highlight the Scottish traditions that I admire, such as the Highland games. And in Wales there are the chapels, male voice choirs and rugby, which I have always so much respected.

The more I thought about it, the more I warmed to the idea. I have often got fed up with people knocking Britain. I have travelled all over the world and every country has something to offer, but British is best as far as I am concerned. I have never wanted to live anywhere else. Of course we have problems here – you only have to pick up your newspaper any day of the week to realise that – and we need to sort them out, but at the same time, I believe we should revel in the achievements and history of this country. We should have a sense of pride. It occurred to me that a book like this would give me the opportunity of reminding people of all the good things that are there for us all to enjoy in Britain.

Wheels were consequently set in motion and for nine months I had a wonderful time journeying from Devon in the south of England to Tyneside in the north, from the valleys of Wales to the Highlands of Scotland. I revisited places I knew and discovered others where I had never been before, and in the process, renewed old friendships and made new ones.

Almost everywhere I went I was accompanied by the well-known photographer Derry Brabbs, who has produced over 150 magnificent photographs to illustrate the text. I also travelled with my good friend Keith Lodge, and for some of these lovely trips his wife Pat came too – quite a touring party. It was Keith who so patiently helped me to put my thoughts down in writing for my previous two books. I was honoured to have him working with me again.

So, come with me on my travels in celebration of the Britain I know; the Britain I love.

P.S. I would have liked to include Ireland, but my knowledge and experience of that wonderful country is far too limited to do it justice. I have paid just two visits. One was while I was playing with Yorkshire; I remember scoring 64 in Belfast. The other visit was with Leicestershire, and it proved a bit of a disaster for me. The ferry crossing from Liverpool was so rough that I was violently seasick and I spent the whole four days of that trip in my hotel room feeling very much under the weather and dreading the return journey!

To my late Mum and Dad
for giving me such a happy start to life
and instilling in me the true Christian values
of right and wrong, and also to my sister Marjorie
for her love and support through the years.

CHAPTER 1

BESIDE THE SEASIDE

Scarborough Castle has stood guard over the town since the twelfth century. It's a bit of a climb but, if you've any puff left, the view is breathtaking.

Left: A beautiful beach, a bustling harbour and an ancient castle – Scarborough has all you need for a bank holiday outing.

WHEN I was a little lad the whole of Barnsley used to close down for seven days in August while families took their annual Feast Week holiday. Other towns throughout the north had their own special weeks when thousands upon thousands of people traipsed off to the seaside – Blackpool, Southport, Morecambe, Rhyl, Scarborough, Bridlington, Filey, Whitby and such places. The annual exodus was a great British tradition, along with bank holiday Mondays.

Having chosen cricket as a career, I was denied those bank holiday treats. I was always either playing cricket for Yorkshire or Leicestershire, or umpiring.

So it was that in the summer of 2001, now retired and a man of leisure, I decided to turn back the clock and take a holiday in Scarborough during the famous Cricket Festival in the week leading up to the August bank holiday Monday. It turned out to be a far more memorable visit than I could ever have imagined because not only did Yorkshire clinch the county championship for the first time in thirty-three years with victory over Glamorgan, but also it was announced that I was to be the next president of the Scarborough Cricket Festival, from January 2002. It was a tremendous honour to follow such great names as Sir Leonard Hutton, Sir Donald Bradman, Sir Paul Getty – and my old pal Michael Parkinson. I felt humble yet so proud – and all the better that I would be starting my term of office at a time when Yorkshire were the reigning champions.

Scarborough provides a wonderful setting for cricket. The cliffs overlooking the glorious North Bay are nearby on one side of the ground, although not visible to spectators. It was here that Bill Bowes, one of the best bowlers Yorkshire and England have ever had, was so humorously misquoted when covering a match for the Yorkshire Evening Post after he had retired from playing. He was faced with the usual problem of telephoning his reports from the ground to the sports desk back in Leeds, and during one Festival Week he sent the following piece of copy: 'After a quiet spell, Parfitt went down the wicket to Illingworth and edged him over the slips and into the deep for three.'

Unfortunately, the young lady on copy-taking duty that day had no interest whatsoever in cricket, and was therefore completely in an east coast fog when it came to talk of bowling maidens over, short legs, silly mid-ons and suchlike. She was, however, fairly well acquainted with the seaside resort itself. So, struggling to overcome the additional difficulties posed by a bad line, she typed out, 'After a quiet spell, Parfitt went down the wicket to Illingworth and edged him over the cliffs and into the deepest part of the sea.'

One of my most memorable – and painful – umpiring experiences at the ground came during a Yorkshire v Essex game when I was struck at square leg by a ball hooked with tremendous power. I went down as if pole-axed. The Essex twelfth man rushed on with a stretcher, one or two of his colleagues bundled me on to it and they carried me off the field post haste. When they got to the boundary's edge they tipped me off. 'Leave him there,' I heard one of them mutter, 'serves the bugger right.' Obviously one or two of my decisions had not met with complete Essex approval. At that time, Essex were not only a very good

Scarborough's beautifully placed cricket ground, where in 2001 Yorkshire clinched the county championship for the first time in thirty-three years, and where I once got stretchered off and dumped over the boundary.

side, they also liked to have a bit of fun on the field, and that was a typical example. The players enjoyed the game, had a laugh and a joke, yet still gave a hundred per cent in their desire to win matches. That's how it should be, and it was often the case in those days, but not so much now. The game has changed, and not for the better in some respects. A lot of the fun has gone out of it and that's a crying shame.

Still, that did not prevent 14,000 people from packing into the ground on the final day of that 2001 championship decider with Glamorgan, and it was a sight well worth seeing – such a crowd at what is, after all, only a club ground. What delighted me in particular was to see so many kids there on the boundary edge with their bats and balls. I could not help but think to myself that this surely must be a good sign for the future of Yorkshire cricket.

For those who have followed my career it will come as no surprise when I tell you I had a lump in my throat and tears in my eyes watching my team carry off the championship again on that memorable August day. The last time Yorkshire had won the title, in 1968, I was still coaching at Plymouth College and playing for Paignton Cricket Club before taking up a new career as a first-class umpire the following year. Now here I was, four years into retirement. That's how long it took to bridge the gap.

I have to admit that some of my predictions do go a bit haywire – I said England would beat the Australians in the 2001 Test series over here and we were walloped 4–1 – but I was spot on with my Yorkshire forecast. As early as June I said that Yorkshire would win the championship. And having seen them do so, I was convinced that they would go on to win it more than once again during the next five or six years because they were far and away the best side; however, there again, 2002 did not go their way at all.

Yorkshire, I noted, had a good depth in the squad, including some fine young players with the best days of their careers ahead of them. Pace bowler Steve Kirby burst on to the scene in the championship season; off-spinner Richard Dawson brought more balance to the side; up-and-coming wicket-keeper Simon Guy was given a taste of county cricket towards the end of the campaign; and Matthew Wood began to realise his batting potential.

It was good to see Wood beginning to blossom after a couple of lean years because the lad is so keen. He has cricket in his blood. His father played for Emley, near Huddersfield, where his mother made the teas and his sister was scorer. He is also a very dedicated fan of Emley Football Club, whose manager is former Barnsley FC legend Ronnie Glavin. When they had a good run in the FA Cup a few years ago, Matthew flew back home from New Zealand, where he was coaching,

Yorkshire's secret training weapon – I help administer Yorkshire puds to the current crop of England stars (from the left) Craig White, Michael Vaughan, Matthew Hoggard, Darren Gough and Ryan Sidebottom.

to watch a tie with Lincoln City, then took the next flight back to New Zealand. There's loyalty and dedication for you. That's the kind of attitude he has shown for Yorkshire, coming through after a dodgy spell to play a big part in the county championship triumph.

At the other end of the age scale, there is a left-arm bowler called Albert Holgate who was still, at the time, playing for Scarborough's third team at the age of eighty-two, and he was determined, he told me, to carry on until he was a hundred. It was amazing that Albert should still be playing a reasonably good standard of cricket at that age. It made me wonder why on earth I had to retire from umpiring as a mere spring chicken of sixty-five.

It was, of course, a tremendous team performance by Yorkshire, who were without England-contracted star bowler Darren Gough for the vast majority of the campaign. The success was thoroughly deserved. I was so pleased for captain David Byas. In his six years as captain he had come so close and had so many disappointments. To clinch the title on his home ground – he played for Scarborough in the Yorkshire League – make a century and take the championship-winning catch was Roy of the Rovers stuff. It didn't really surprise me when he announced his retirement at the end of the season. After all, it could hardly get better than that. I was, however, stunned to hear the following March that he had decided to come out of retirement to play for Lancashire. I couldn't believe it. I thought someone was pulling my leg. If he was making a comeback, it should have been with Yorkshire, certainly not with the arch rivals from across the Pennines. For a Yorkshireman, there is only one rose to wear and its colour is white.

You have got to give a lot of credit for Yorkshire's success to Aussie coach Wayne Clarke, who instilled self-belief into the squad. Another Aussie, Darren Lehmann, also played a tremendous part, not only for the runs he scored, but for the advice and support given to the captain out there on the field. He gets big scores and gets them quickly, which means that the fine array of young bowlers – Matthew Hoggard, Chris Silverwood, Richard Dawson, Ryan Sidebottom and Steve Kirby – have a target at which to bowl. Darren Lehmann captain of Yorkshire himself for 2002 is probably one of the best overseas players to have featured in county cricket, and any future Yorkshire successes may depend on whether or not they can hold on to him.

As a Yorkie through and through, and of the old school, I have always believed that we should pick Yorkshire players and coaches born in the county. However, when other counties began to import top-quality stars from overseas, it soon became apparent that we would have to do the same if we were to compete on equal terms. There is no doubt that recruiting Clarke and Lehmann has provided a marvellous boost for Yorkshire cricket. The much maligned committee also deserve a pat on the back. I have not always seen eye to eye with them, but they came up trumps in bringing in Lehmann and then Clarke, who was not a universally popular choice. A lot of people were against his appointment as coach but he has proved the committee right.

I was also pleased for the members and public of Yorkshire, who had supported the county through thick and thin. No one deserved the success more than they did.

During the Festival, I took the opportunity to renew my acquaintance with Karen and Jayne Holmes. These lovely lasses run the Small Fry fish and chip shop in North Street, near to the ground, and I have

Karen and Jayne Holmes, the lovely lasses who run Small Fry, the tiny fish and chip shop with the big reputation.

Left: Fish and chips always taste better out of the paper, especially on a bank holiday in Scarborough.

Below: The Confederate flag flies in the Castle grounds during a re-enactment of the American Civil War. I'm more used to the Wars of the Roses myself.

been going there for donkey's years. It is only a small place, as the name suggests, but it has a big reputation. Visiting cricket teams go there, and Yorkshire members nip down during the lunch break – saves them packing sandwiches, you see. I have taken many cricketers there, including Derek Randall who liked the fish and chips so much that he had another two lots – and then went out to batter the Yorkshire bowling with a century.

Originally I used to eat my fish and chips out of the paper in the traditional manner, but when the Holmes sisters bought the little café next door, I started to dine in comfort. I always look forward to going there whenever I'm in Scarborough because Karen and Jayne serve up some of the best fish and chips I've ever tasted.

They are particularly busy during Cricket Festival weeks, especially when the weather is good, but because they are a little bit out of the way, they do rely on word of mouth recommendation.

Thinking about an early morning paddle before the crowds descend on Scarborough sands.

What with all the cricketing success, the subsequent celebrations – and the fish and chips – I was in the best of spirits when it came to joining the thousands of other holidaymakers for the traditional bank holiday Monday by the sea. An early morning paddle freshened me up and after breakfast I paid a visit to Scarborough Castle. As I have repeatedly argued, there is nowhere in the world to touch the British Isles when

Above: Background music at the Spa Pavilion and a chance to chat to other cricket lovers about Yorkshire's championship success.

Left: I always say an ice cream takes some licking.

Now for a bit of donkey work, but it is a pleasure to see the kids enjoying themselves in traditional bank holiday fashion.

you get the sort of glorious weather I enjoyed that day. I've seen all there is to see in the world, but when the sun shines and the sky is blue and you are gazing out over a panorama like the one at Scarborough from the famous castle, it is simply breathtaking. You can't beat it.

After lunch I relaxed at the Spa Pavilion, listening to the resident musical trio and chatting to other cricket lovers still revelling in Yorkshire's success. Then it was time for an ice cream and a stroll on the sands, where I joined in a game of beach cricket and helped the girl in charge of the donkeys lead her plodding four-legged team on their circular tour of duty, carrying chattering boys and girls of assorted sizes perched precariously on their swaying backs.

Thankfully, the Scarborough donkeys proved better behaved than one of my earlier acquaintance which decided to deposit what seemed a ton of natural manure on to the newly washed sands and then refused to budge an inch further. It was then that I came to understand the phrase 'stubborn as a mule'.

After all that, I needed a doze in a deckchair before tea and a stroll along the prom-prom-prom. There was no brass band and tiddly-om-pom-pom on this occasion, but thoroughly enjoyable for all that.

And there you have it – the great British bank holiday. Now I know just what I've been missing all these years. Roll on the next one.

CHAPTER 2

HOW DOES YOUR GARDEN GROW?

Eye-catching gladioli on parade for the judges.

LOOKING west from Chatsworth House over the rolling Derbyshire countryside, the Duke of Devonshire said to me, 'Do you know, Dickie, when the sun's shining like it is now, I don't think there is anywhere better in the whole world.'

Well, I have travelled around most of it and I have to admit he had a point. Chatsworth House is impressive enough, but the true worth lies in the beauty within which it is set – so many different shades of green, hills and dales, sheep and cattle grazing, rivers and lakes, church spire just visible over the trees. Here is an absolute jewel in the crown, and so typically British. It is an enchanting place that manages to combine great natural beauty with a magnificent house and outstanding works of art.

The home of the Cavendish family for nearly 450 years, having been built in 1555 by Bess of Hardwick, the Elizabethan house is richly furnished and decorated with painted walls and ceilings, woodcarvings, elaborate inlay furniture and wall hangings of tapestry and leather. It has a magnificent library and a collection of paintings, drawings, sculpture, silver, porcelain and curiosities that is world famous. It is very much a part of our national heritage.

It was the gardens, however, that most interested me. While not a gardener myself – I have never had the time, nor, to be honest, the inclination – my garden at White Rose Cottage has, like Chatsworth, been featured on television, although I have to confess to a little jiggery-pokery. The artist Alan Hydes had been commissioned to do a series of paintings on television showing the gardens of well-known personalities, including me.

Now it may well be that I got just a little bit carried away when Alan rang beforehand to suss out the lie of the land and asked if I had plenty of flowers. 'Oh, yes,' I enthused. 'Loads of 'em.' I have to admit to a slight exaggeration. Apple trees, plum trees and a lawn – plus a marvellous view over the Pennines – yes, indeed. But maybe just a petal or two short of an award-winning entry for the Britain in Bloom contest.

So poor old Alan ended up painting my pride and joy – a Yorkshire rose – surrounded by an array of plants hurriedly trundled in from a

Left: Chatsworth is one of the finest houses in England, a jewel perfectly set in the Derbyshire countryside.

At Chatsworth with the delightful Devonshires, as I will always remember the Duke and Duchess.

local garden centre. It made a lovely painting – and brought a rare splash of colour to my garden borders.

Alan would have no problems finding something to paint at Chatsworth – at any time of the year. There is a continual round of work for the twenty-one full-time gardeners. The Duchess was justifiably proud of the traditions of long service in this department – and no wonder. It is quite exceptional. The last three head gardeners have each worked there for fifty years, which must surely qualify for a mention in *The Guinness Book of Records*.

Their Graces allowed me the privilege of walking round the West Garden, which is not open to visitors, although they can see it from the window of the State Dressing Room on a tour of the house. Designed by the sixth Duke, it is most unusual, with raised beds on stone bases, which used to be filled with bedding plants. The Duchess told me this was never very satisfactory and she is much more pleased with the new scheme of sharp geometrical patterns of golden box – 3,350 of them. The nurseryman was amazed when he received that order. Nobody had wanted them since 1914. The Duchess added that the design had to be looked down on from above to get the full effect. 'At ground level it appears quite meaningless – except for children to steeplechase over.'

Looking beyond the West Lawn towards the skyline, it is possible to see the Millennium Rock, which was placed there by the Devonshires in the year 2000. They transported it from the grounds around the house. The first one they chose cracked when they tried to move it, so they had to find another. Said the Duchess, 'We wanted to do something different for the millennium and thought this was a good idea. The rock can be seen from Andrew's [the Duke's] study.'

The study is where I sat and had a pleasant chat with this most charming couple – the delightful Devonshires is how I remember them – and this was another aspect of my visit which caused my eyebrows to raise. My sister Marjorie is for ever chiding me for leaving my study in such an untidy state. 'Looks like a bomb's dropped in here,' she'll complain. Well, all I can say is that it must have been an atomic one that had hit His Grace's study.

One of the most popular visitor attractions is the Cascade, and it really is a most unusual and fascinating water feature. It fair takes your breath away. Intrigued as to how it had come about, I read up a little bit of its history and it proved very interesting. The length of the paving stones over which the water flows, and the numbers and widths of the twenty-four groups of steps, are all different, so the sound of the falling water also varies. At the base of the Cascade the water disappears underground, passes through a pipe and works the Seahorse

Water features, whimsical or ambitious, abound at Chatsworth. Here the Seahorse Fountain dominates the south lawn.

Fountain on the South Lawn in front of the house before going underground again to work the fountain in the West Garden below the house. It is then finally piped into the river. Now, I could never have thought of a scheme like that, not in a month of Sundays. It is an ingenious piece of engineering.

I had been told where all the water went, but I did not have the foggiest idea where it all came from. So I asked. Well, you never learn anything if you don't ask, do you? It is, I was informed, supplied by natural pressure from four large reservoir lakes, all man-made, on a plateau above the wood that provides a backdrop for the Cascade. They, in turn, are fed from miles of conduits that drain the surrounding moor. The waterworks are turned on only when the garden is open to visitors, and even then, in dry summers, the hours they play are rationed.

It is a long climb up to the Cascade House to look down on the whole length – 208 yards – of the steep, watered stairs running down the hill, but it is well worth it. There, stretched out before you, are the Salisbury Lawns and the imposing house, with the river Derwent and the hills of the park to the west, farmland and woods above, and Edensor Spire dominating the valley beyond. Britain at its finest.

Another water feature that both delights and surprises visitors is the Willow Tree Fountain, which was first built in its own little secluded dell in 1692. It has been replaced twice and was last restored in 1983. Of course, this is no ordinary tree. The original was made of copper and

Impressively ancient vines provide natural shade in the display greenhouse.

The Duchess's rare breed hens have the run of the grounds and she feeds them herself every day.

lead, and it squirts water from its branches and leaves, showering unsuspecting visitors. In winter it looks so much like the other leafless trees that this trick of wetting the unwary comes as an even greater surprise, even a nasty shock. It is recorded that this 'squirting tree' delighted Princess Victoria when she visited Chatsworth as a thirteen-year-old.

There is more spouting water at the Ring Pond, this time from the mouth of an ancient lead duck. It was moved there from its original home on another pond – known, for obvious reasons, as the Sick Duck Pond – where it began life in 1696.

The Duchess told me, 'I believe that a garden the size of Chatsworth needs movement as well as plants, trees and buildings, and the water in all its facets – fountains, cascades and ponds – goes a long way towards adding this variety.'

The timid woodland creatures are seldom seen in the daytime, but I saw waterfowl on the ponds and some unusual poultry round the greenhouses. It is well known that the Duchess takes a keen interest in the hens and she told me that she had looked after them ever since she was a little girl. The Duke whispered to me that, for his wife, feeding the chickens was the most important part of the day.

'We had them all through the war, you know,' the Duchess informed me. 'And I couldn't imagine being without them now. I love having something alive around. As I'm too old for horses, the hens are just right. You'll see them on the loose. We must have the only head gardener in England who allows hens to go loose like that. They wander all round the grounds and the car parks.'

The Duchess feeds the hens every day – they also get plenty of extra titbits from left-over picnics – and she collects the eggs. Sometimes, if there are children around, she will take them with her to watch. 'Do you know,' she confided, 'there are boys and girls who have never seen where eggs come from?' I bet it comes as a bit of a shock when they find out, I thought to myself.

The Duke is very fond of cricket, an affinity going back to his grandfather, who was a regular attender at Derbyshire matches. The present Duke recalled the day when his grandfather's Rolls-Royce was struck by a six-hit which shattered the windscreen. A young batsman, looking absolutely terrified, sought out the Duke afterwards to offer a profuse apology. 'Apology be damned,' said the Duke. 'That was an absolutely magnificent shot.' And handed him a ten-pound note as reward.

Just before I left, the Duke told me, 'No visitors to Chatsworth are more welcome than those who, like you, come to the gardens. Over the years many of my happiest hours have been spent in the gardens here, and I like to think that all those who visit go away with similar memories of their walk round Chatsworth's 1,200 acres.'

Well, I can assure the Duke that here is one visitor who did just that. Now where's my spade? I must get my own little bit of Britain at White Rose Cottage sorted out.

Admiring the rose garden, just one corner of Chatsworth's 1,200 acres.

Part of the private West Garden, showing the design in golden box copied from Chiswick House, London.

Talking of spades, I have the greatest admiration for the spadework done by those gardeners who produce the remarkable exhibits you find at the traditional horticultural shows. I have never seen anything in my life like the ones at the Harrogate Show. It must give those people so much pride and pleasure to be able to grow carrots and leeks of that size. I thought it a pity they did not give me a sample to take home. But I would have been disappointed if they had. Meeting Somerset smallholder Quentin Seddon put me right on that one, and a number of other vegetable matters.

He explained, 'They must have been wonderful to look at, but not so good to eat, I suspect. As the name of the event implies, they are produced for show rather than taste. My guess is that those serious competitors started out in the village shows, because you have one or two classes in the local veg and flower events, which point the way. You have all the standard classes for onions and for shallots and cabbages and whatever, but you also have categories for such things as the most unusually shaped vegetable.'

And that, Quentin mused, was nearly always the most suggestively shaped vegetable. In fact, ninety-nine times out of a hundred, the most suggestively shaped vegetable was the winner of the most unusually shaped vegetable competition.

He warmed to his theme. 'Then you have the competition for the biggest marrow, and the biggest marrow really is something to behold. You know the old music-hall song, "Ooh, what a beauty, I've never seen one as big as that before." It's all about a marrow, of course, but again, it's very suggestive. Then you have a competition for the longest stick of rhubarb – and everybody knows where that's pointing. It's all part of the fun. Nobody takes that section of the event seriously. And, in general, those local shows focus on the fun aspect.'

Some competitors decide to take it a step further, and look for more serious competition at the bigger shows. 'And when they do that,' Quentin confided, 'they begin to do very strange things. For example, they will buy a big piece of drainpipe, quite wide and about four feet long; fill it up with good commercial compost; tweak it up with their own compost and manure; add special ingredients known only to themselves; and finally drop a single parsnip seed in the top. After that comes the watering, manuring and feeding.'

Said Quentin, 'Just imagine, the lone parsnip in there with no competition, and nowhere to go except down. So it goes down fast. And gets longer and longer. They've got all sorts of tricks up their sleeves have these people, and once you get into that sort of company, it's very, very competitive.

I have such admiration for the dedication of gardeners who can produce exhibits like these displayed in the North of England Horticultural Society's annual show at Harrogate.

Dahlias at Harrogate, straight from the beauty parlour, bloomin' marvellous.

More prize-winning exhibits at Harrogate.

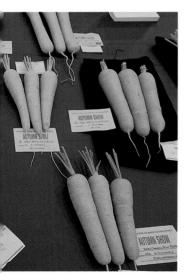

'It's a different class, quite literally, from the village shows. People like me grow veg to eat. We love doing it. It's very enjoyable work and it's great to have all your own fresh veg. It's also lovely to enter the village show. But if we were to go in for the bigger competitions, we would be completely outclassed. We would have to buy those drain-pipe things and suchlike. It's a completely different operation.

'I think it's just as funny an old game as football because everybody knows that the best vegetable is the little young sweet vegetable. Once it gets bigger and older it starts getting woody. The flavour is lost, so is the sugar, and that's what counts. The show-stopping prize beauties may look magnificent, wonderful, amazing, but appearance is every-thing. There's not much taste and flavour in most of them.'

Appearance, he observed, also counted for a lot in the village shows. While judges taste the jams and the chutney, and cut the cakes open to see the texture – in other words they are very concerned with taste and succulence – with the vegetables, the art is to produce three, four, six, or whatever the number is, of identical-looking entries. They need to be as alike as peas in a pod. It is no good producing one huge carrot and two not quite so big.

Quentin and his wife, Rowena, once grew what they considered to be a giant pumpkin. Rowena could not pick it up. They could hardly

get it into the boot of the car. So they decided to enter it for the 'Biggest Pumpkin' category at their local show.

'We were very, very pleased with it. Very proud. But as we drove off to the competition we saw tractors with fore-loaders taking along pumpkins that made ours look puny by comparison. The upshot was that we never opened the boot. We didn't even make it to the show. We did a sly U-turn and drove straight back home. Do you know, Dickie,' he went on incredulously, 'they grow pumpkins up to a third of a ton in weight. Imagine that. They have to have a special variety of seed, the right environment, and a drip-feed capability with water and fertiliser. In fact, I'm not sure if they don't feed them by direct injection, appropriately enough, pumping the stuff in. And, my word, there are some giants.'

For all his disappointment with the pumpkin, Quentin said there was nothing more enjoyable than the local vegetable and flower shows. 'They are terrific. They're right at the heart of the community. There is a tiny competitive edge to it, but they're much more collaborative than the big shows, much more fun, and such an important part of village life.'

I remember such events being held in the North Gawber Colliery Miners' Welfare Hall and the Village Hall in Staincross. Many of the miners had allotments where they used to grow their own vegetables,

Makes your eyes water lifting these onions, never mind peeling them.

not to sell, but for their families to eat – it was much cheaper than buying the stuff in the shops and money was tight. Any left over was given away to families who were not so lucky. The best of the crops they would put on one side for the annual horticultural show or harvest festival at the chapel. The pride on the faces of anybody lucky enough to win any of the classes at the show had to be seen to be believed. As for the overall winner, he became a local hero, and much admired. He was, however, also a target. All the other competitors were determined to knock him off his perch the following year.

There are not so many allotments around in the mining communities now, and the show is no longer held. It is sad to see something that has been such a feature of village life disappearing like that. They say it is progress but I wonder.

The Seddons' smallholding is in East Somerset, not far from Wincanton, a really lovely part of the world on the edge of Salisbury Plain. Quentin ventured, 'Although I hesitate to say this in the presence of a Yorkshireman, Dickie, I think Somerset is one of the most beautiful counties in England.'

'Aye, well,' I conceded, 'it's fair ter middlin'. Just so long as it remains one o' t' best.'

Quentin has suggested that the people around about should consider having a little co-operative of local gardeners who would be able to take any spare produce into the nearest town and sell it. He feels there would be a market for it. It would be very informal, but he was sure it would be a success.

I wondered if I could do the same with my plums and apples from the trees in my garden. At the moment I give away as many as I can. People come with their bags and take what they want. The rest just rot on the ground. Quentin suggested that I should make some plum brandy. He used to know a chap in the Forest of Dean who had a traditional orchard with huge old beautiful trees – not these little ones, the real McCoy. He grew apples, pears and plums. He sold a lot, but always had a load left and people would come and pick their own. Even then, he could never get rid of all the plums. One day a fellow with an Eastern European accent came and said he would take most of what was left.

'That's fine with me,' said Quentin's friend. 'You pick as many as you like.'

A year later, the guy came back for some more.

'Go ahead,' came the reply. 'I'm glad you liked them so much.'

With that, the plum-lover produced a bottle of plum brandy he had made after his previous visit and presented it to the orchard-owner, who later told Quentin that it was the most disgusting thing he had ever tasted.

Somerset smallholder Quentin Seddon knows his onions and he put me right on vegetable matters.

When Quentin and Rowena have a meal at night, nothing is picked until five o'clock in the afternoon. You can't get fresher than that. Quentin enthused, 'It makes all the difference. There are endless arguments about how you grow your vegetables, whether high tech or organic, or whatever, but the most important thing is that they are fresh. Pick 'em and eat 'em, that's the motto, because as soon as you've picked the veg, it's all downhill from there. It stops growing from that moment. It's dead. It's had it. It loses freshness, succulence and vitamins by the minute. Pick it, put it in the pot, and eat it. That's the one-two-three ruling.'

I asked Quentin about my favourite veg, the turnip, and was told that he grows them only one year in three. 'Trouble with turnips,' he explained, 'is that they have to be picked very young, and sometimes they get away. As soon as they've got away, they've had it. They go woody.'

I wondered what Quentin's favourite was, and his instant reply was, 'All of 'em.'

One thing that does annoy him is people who prepare the ground, put the seeds in, hoe and weed, water if necessary, keep off pests and diseases – and then never get round to harvesting the crop. 'You've got to honour the harvest. If you've been a farmer you know that. Farming is for the harvest. But there are vegetable growers who sadly let their crops run to seed.'

The Seddons have no livestock on their smallholding. There is, however, a wild cat who wanders in and out. Apparently, Quentin's missus gave it a drop of milk one day and now it is a regular visitor. It has even learned how to open the kitchen door. Said Quentin, 'It jumps up and knocks the handle until the door opens. It's becoming quite an expert. So either we keep the kitchen door locked the whole time or become resigned to the fact that whenever we go back in we'll find the cat sitting by the stove, fast asleep and a picture of contentment.' The cat that got the cream, obviously.

They used to have a cat of their own, and the best thing this bizarre feline ever did was when the VAT-man came to call for the first time. Quentin related the story.

'We were a bit nervous as he went through all the procedure, checking the books, studying the figures, frowning and making notes here and there, and we weren't sure if we'd done everything right. We were giving answers to his questions, not quite knowing if they were the right ones. We were in a bit of a state to be honest. And the guy didn't look all that happy. Then, all of a sudden, our cat ran up his back and sat on the top of his head. Now, cats sometimes jump and sit on your lap, even on your shoulder. But this was something else. Quite hair-raising really.'

On a dark night, one of these might be classed as an offensive weapon.

Quentin remonstrated with his pet. 'Snail,' he said, 'what on earth are you doing on that poor man's head?' No answer. Not even the slightest mew. Just a contented purring and a stretching of claws. Said Quentin, 'The VAT-man looked extremely disturbed, as well he might. He must have wondered what was going on. And he obviously dreaded to think what this pesky cat was going to do next.'

They finally managed to persuade Snail to leave his precarious perch, and barely two minutes later the VAT-man snapped his books shut, picked up his hat and coat and grunted, 'Right, everything's fine. I'd better be on my way.'

Quentin chuckled. 'Believe it or not, that day when the VAT-man came to call was the only time Snail ever took it into his head to do such a thing.'

Just shows, of course, if you want to sort out your tax problems, it pays to go right to the top.

CHAPTER 3

FOOTBALL
FANTASY

A view of Barnsley FC ground from one of the old colliery slag heaps, which have now been grassed over.

IT IS the dream of all starry-eyed young sportsmen and women to play for their country one day. I was no exception, but I had my sights set on turning out for England at both cricket and football.

I was generally recognised as being a better footballer than cricketer in those days and, after playing for the Barnsley Schools' team, I signed amateur forms with Barnsley Football Club, along with my school pal Tommy Taylor. Tommy went on to play for Manchester United and England before being so tragically killed in the Munich air disaster in February 1958. I have seen some of the greatest English centre-forwards, from Tommy Lawton to Alan Shearer, and, for me, Tommy Taylor was the best of all.

My own dream of an international football career was shattered when I had to have a cartilage operation at the age of fifteen. Barnsley's Northern Intermediate League fixture at Hull was postponed because of a waterlogged pitch, so youth-team coach Jock Steele, who later went on to become manager, said I could go and play for the YMCA in a Barnsley League game at Dodworth. It was there that I crocked my knee. There was no keyhole surgery in those days and I was laid up in bed for four weeks. Even then, the operation was not a complete success. I have had five operations since, and that knee has always been a problem. It put paid to my football career and I was devastated at the time. But the good Lord moves in mysterious ways and cricket has provided me with a wonderful life.

Northern Intermediate League matches were played on first-team pitches in those days and I had the privilege of appearing in a fixture at St James's Park, the home of Newcastle United. It was a big ground to us back then in 1949, but, of course, it bore no comparison to the magnificent stadium it is today, with an all-seater capacity of nearly 53,000. When I went back there, I was highly impressed with the set-up.

I was also highly impressed with the manager, a certain Sir Bobby Robson. I had been forced to retire from umpiring at sixty-five, yet here was Bobby, the same age as me – sixty-nine – still going strong as the boss of a side challenging for the Premiership title – and still as

Left: The new Millennium Bridge on Tyneside, near St James's Park.

passionately enthusiastic as ever. So what, I asked him, had kept him going when he could have been putting his feet up and enjoying a well-earned rest?

He told me, 'I tried putting my feet up for three months, and I didn't like it. You loved being out there in the middle, didn't you, Dickie? You loved the excitement of it all. You loved to be making those crucial decisions. And I've no doubt you would have carried on if you had been able to do so. It's exactly the same with me. I don't need the money. I work because I want to, not because I have to. I just can't give football up.

'Three years ago, when I left PSV Eindhoven, I thought that maybe that was it. So I did my garden, I played a bit of golf, I took the wife on holiday, and when I'd done that I sat at home, completely at a loss. For the first time in almost fifty years, when the eighteenth of August came round, I wasn't at a football match. And I knew then that I had to try to get back into management. With due respect, I didn't want to go to Southend, or Crewe, or places like that, so I looked at all the top jobs. But none were available.'

At that stage, Bobby could not see himself getting the kind of job he wanted. After all, Premiership managers are usually the best in the game, so they don't shift all that often. But then Newcastle made an awful start to the season. They were bottom after eight matches, and Ruud Gullit resigned.

Said Bobby, 'I thought, that's just the job for me, so I made it known at the club that I was available. Okay, I was sixty-seven, but I had just come from a successful spell with PSV, and the people at Newcastle knew the vast experience I had.'

He heard nothing in ten days and had almost given up hope, but then he got the call, and he can hardly believe what has happened since.

'It's like turning over another page. Finish that and you go on to the next one. You've just got to keep working at things – a page at a time.'

Like me, Bobby fell in love with football and cricket at a very early age. He started as a young lad kicking a ball about in the back streets in Durham and, after playing representative schoolboy soccer, at the age of seventeen he signed professional forms. Surprisingly, however, it was with Fulham, not his beloved Newcastle, and to this day he can barely understand why. His father, steeped in the black and white, could certainly not understand it at the time.

'I suppose,' mused Bobby, 'I was swayed by the fact that the Fulham manager, a man called Bill Dodgin, came to see me personally. Newcastle just sent one of their scouts. And that was a lesson I learned. If you want to sign a young kid, go and see him yourself. Don't send somebody else. Basically, kids sign not just for the club, but also for the

There's no mistaking Newcastle fans when you see them.

manager. Kids signed for Bill Shankly, or Don Revie, or Brian Clough, and so on. Bill Dodgin took the trouble to meet me and I liked him immediately.'

Another consideration was that, at the time, Newcastle appeared to be a buying club. Local lads rarely seemed to get a chance, so Bobby felt he might be given an earlier first-team opportunity at Craven Cottage, and so it proved.

Incidentally, Bobby knows Micky Stewart well from his days at Fulham, where the former Test cricketer was a regular visitor. Bobby and his wife would sometimes visit Micky and Sheila on Saturday nights, and watch in disbelief as Micky's little lad Alec, who was about five or six years old at the time, set about hitting a tennis ball all over the lounge – dad bowled to him and Sheila looked on unconcerned. It turned out to be time well spent because that little lad went on to captain Surrey and England although I dread to think what it cost in damages.

As Bobby's life in football went on, the game began to mean more and more to him, and it is a love affair that burns as fiercely as ever today. It has brought him the rewards of wonderful travel, success at home and abroad – and also the prestigious job of England manager.

He chuckled, 'You have to love football to stick it out in that role because the press are unbelievable. They don't seem to appreciate that they play very good football in Spain, in Italy, in France, in Romania, and all those places. Their stance seems to be that we invented the game so we are the masters, but the fact is that the pupils have over-taken us. We have no divine right to win. We will only win if we have better players than the other team. It's the same in cricket. People have to realise that the Australians and the South Africans play very good cricket. It's no disgrace to lose to them although, of course, we should always do our best to win.'

Bobby loves cricket and it has always been an ambition of his to follow England on a tour to Australia or the West Indies. He very nearly achieved it six years ago, when he lost his job at Sporting Lisbon. In the January, when he was kicking his heels in Portugal, a journalist rang to ask if he would like to go to see England play in the West Indies. He would be sponsored by the *Daily Telegraph* to take charge of a group of people and talk about football. What's more, his wife could go with him.

The man who just can't give up football – Newcastle United and former England manager Bobby Robson watches intently from the dugout.

'I'd been sacked, I couldn't get a job, it was an awful time. So this offered the perfect pick-me-up. I'd worked hard all those years, I would now have a little sabbatical.'

So there he was, on 12 January, waiting for the three-month tour to begin, when the chairman of Porto FC paid him a visit to try to persuade him to take over as manager.

Said Bobby, 'I thought how nice that would be. I loved Portugal and I had been very successful there. But it would mean missing out on the cricket tour. What was I to do?'

Deep down, however, he knew there was only one decision he could make. So Porto it was. I told him he would have had a great time on that cricket trip because it was the kind of thing that I had done for the *Daily Telegraph* myself, and that made him all the more determined to fulfil his ambition one day. 'Before I die, I'll do it,' he said. 'I will.'

Bobby feels he has gone through a double phase in his managerial life. For twenty-two years he had only two clubs – fourteen years with Ipswich and eight with England. Then he went abroad and he had five clubs in ten years. He spent two years with PSV, two with Sporting Lisbon, two with Porto, two with Barcelona, then one more back at PSV. Whereas in England you look for stability, that is how they operate on the continent.

There was success all along the line, with his time at Barcelona emerging as the high point. 'Barcelona are the biggest club in the world, so just being asked to become their manager was a wonderful honour. It's not just a football club, it's a nation. Barcelona is the capital of Catalonia and the club is the nation's army. When they go to Spain, it's a battle, a fight. They are warriors. So the pressure there is unbelievable. Every day you are besieged with fifty or more journalists from newspapers, radio and television. But I thoroughly enjoyed my time there.'

Under Bobby, Barcelona won the European Cup-Winners' Cup, the Spanish Cup and the Super Cup, but when they finished runners-up to Real Madrid in the League, he was 'moved to another position'. They had played fourteen games more than their rivals because of their cup commitments, but the club wanted to bring in Louis van Gaal, who was leaving Ajax. 'Two years – time for a change, you see.'

Bobby basically believes that stability in the job is preferable to this constant change, but at the same time, he 'didn't half enjoy his time abroad'. He went on, 'What a great education it was for me, as well as being a great experience. I was dealing with a different mentality, a different culture, a different style of football. In Spain, it's slow, possession, cat and mouse. Here in England, it's so quick and frenetic. If you stick five passes together in midfield, the supporters start shouting, "Oi, get it forward for goodness sake". Or words to that effect.'

Managing England was another wonderful honour for Bobby. It was, he said, the highest accolade anyone could have, like being the prime minister in football terms. But it also brought his biggest disappointment when they went out of the World Cup at the semi-final stage in 1990, beaten by old rivals Germany on penalties.

He recalled, 'We had a good team by this time. The team had evolved during the tournament, getting better and better. During the four weeks prior to the World Cup and the three weeks of the competition, we had built up morale, understanding and team spirit. We were the better team over the ninety minutes. We were still the better team in extra time but it went to penalties. I was still confident because our first five penalty takers were brilliant, every one. Our best was Stuart Pearce, so we put him at number four. Every kick is important, but if it's 3–2 or 3–3 and you score the fourth, it's very often decisive.

'Three-three it was on the day. Pearcey steps up. He never misses. The ball went one way, the 'keeper went the other. As he dived across, horizontal, the ball hit his foot and flew over the bar. I couldn't believe it. None of us could. Then Chrissie Waddle, who could run up to the ball in training, close his eyes, and still score, hit one miles over the top. It was like missing a full toss in cricket with only a boundary needed to win.' Or running yourself out on 99, I thought, from painful personal experience.

Another low point came with Bobby's sacking at Sporting Lisbon. He recalled, 'We were top of the League at the time, and the club hadn't been in that position for fifteen years. Benfica were second, Porto third, but we were top of the pile in December. Then we travelled to Ostend on a bitterly cold Wednesday night, lost 2–0, and were knocked out of the UEFA Cup in a tough match. The next day they sacked me. It was the first time in my life I had been given the boot and I couldn't believe it. After just one defeat. But the chairman was a man who didn't deserve to be chairman. He was the worst chairman I have ever worked with. Thankfully, everywhere else I have had decent people you could talk to in a sensible way.'

One chairman he will always remember with affection is John Cobbold of Ipswich. Bobby was teetotal when he first went to Portman Road, but the chairman always had a glass of sherry for him after every home match and insisted that he drink it. If Ipswich had lost, John would tell his manager, 'Bobby, you have to lose sometime, so that the other people can have the pleasure of winning.'

Bobby used to look at him and think, 'Is he all right? Is this fellow for real?' But he meant it. He was a typical Old Etonian, with that Corinthian spirit of 'If you win, you win; if you lose, you lose. To the victor the spoils.' He would accept victory or defeat with equally good grace.

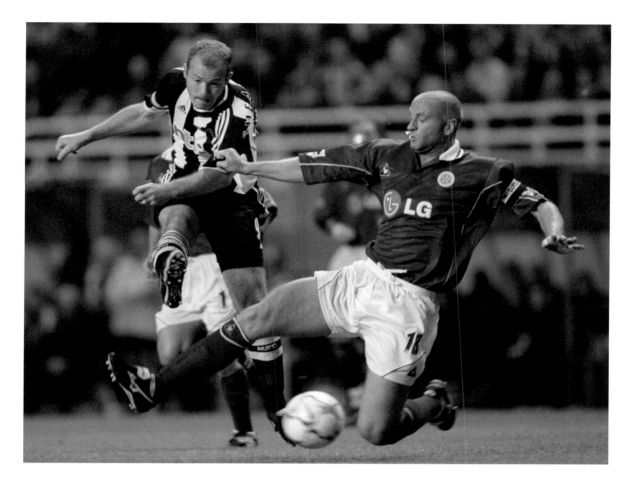

Magpies' star striker Alan Shearer gets in a shot at goal despite a desperate challenge from Leicester City defender Matt Elliott.

There was one occasion when the Tractor Boys had lost four in a row and John said to Bobby, 'Are you worried?' Bobby replied, 'No, but I am concerned.' The chairman boomed, 'Fine. That's all right then. As long as you're concerned,' and there and then offered to extend his manager's contract by a further two years.

Said Bobby, 'I was staggered. But he meant it. He did it. Eventually he put me on a ten-year contract. And when England came in for me in the middle of that ten years he offered me another ten years on top of that to stay.'

It seems that the tradition is being carried on at Portman Road. With Ipswich bottom of the Premiership at Christmas, and no team having survived relegation after being in that situation, current manager George Burley said he felt under no pressure because he knew that his job was safe, even if the team was relegated. He knew he had a loyal chairman – cast in the mould of John Cobbold – in David Sheepshanks.

It has taken Bobby fifty years to return to Newcastle. He has done a full circle. He left in 1950 at the age of seventeen and never went back, apart from holidays, family visits, or to play cricket, until the call came on the resignation of Ruud Gullit. Since then, he has shifted out thirty-two players and brought in about nineteen, saving substantially on the wage bill because some of those who departed were high-flyers.

He reflected, 'Some had to go, some wanted to go, some needed to go. Then we bought well. Craig Bellamy, for example, is twice the player that he was when we signed him. In cricketing parlance, we had a player capable of scoring fifties regularly, but that was about his whack. Now we have a player capable of hitting hundreds. He has doubled his capacity, just by playing for a bigger club, with better players, better coaches and better training. We've also brought in Andy O'Brien – he's a fantastic kid – and so on.'

On the day I was there, United were completing the signing of Nottingham boy-wonder Jermaine Jenas for about £5 million, but Bobby was quick to point out that was peanuts compared with what teams such as Manchester United, Leeds United, Arsenal and Chelsea had been forking out.

'I had to plead with the chairman for the £5 million to buy Jenas, who is still only nineteen and learning his trade. Compare that with Manchester United. They won the championship again last year, yet this season they have spent a further £53 million on Forlan, Veron and Van Nistelrooy. That's the difference. It's huge. And that is what we are up against here. Money doesn't buy success, but it doesn't half help.'

Newcastle had not won anything for a long, long time and Bobby said he was desperate to bring some success for the sake of the fans, who were so marvellous. 'We have 53,000 for every home game. It's always a sell-out. You can't get a ticket. That kind of support deserves success. Our fans have been disappointed for a number of years, it would be wonderful if we could give them something to celebrate.'

At the time of my visit, United were still competing on two fronts. They were in the chasing bunch closely behind Manchester United in the title race and in the fifth round of the FA Cup. The latter, Bobby reasoned, was the better bet. 'To carry off the Cup, you have to win six matches. To be champions, you have to win around thirty. So you could say that winning the FA Cup is much easier than winning the title.

'I really do not think that we will win the championship this season, but we will stop people who think they can. If you set out to climb a mountain, the first bit is relatively easy. It's the last bit that's the most difficult and the most important. At the moment, we have climbed the first bit. Now we face the hardest part. And, of course, Manchester United, Arsenal, Liverpool and the like have all been there, done it, got the T-shirt, in recent times. We have not.'

Bobby is a great admirer of Manchester United. 'Their secret,' he told me, 'is that the players are still hungry for success. Money doesn't come into it. They've already got their Porsches. You watch Beckham, Scholes, the Neville brothers, Keane. It's quite clear they want more success. Keane is a multi-millionaire, yet he's in there, digging it out every match, fighting, battling, working his socks off, because he wants to win. It's difficult to keep on wanting to win when you've done just about all there is to do, but the United lads seem to want to do it again and again and again. You need players like that. If you don't have them, you've got to get them out and start again.

'What you should always look for in a player is quality, plus character, plus determination. That's the key combination. It's the same with cricketers. One ball will get you out. In football, one mistake can cost you the match.

'Some may say, how on earth do you motivate a millionaire? And it is a problem. Even the lads here at Newcastle are earning in a week what most people earn in a year. But the secret is to buy not just good players, but good people. If you buy a good person and the character is right, you have a chance. I can judge whether a lad can play or not, what his potential is, but you also need to know what his character is like, on and off the pitch. I never buy anyone unless I have made a thorough investigation into the character of that player. I always seek out those who have known him, played with him, and employed him.'

Bobby admitted that he told Sir Alex Ferguson to snap up Van Nistelrooy. 'I had him for a year at PSV. I had to spend every day with him on the pitch. I knew what a player he was going to be, and I also knew he had the right character. He was a winner. So when Alex asked about him, I told him not to miss the chance, to trust him, and he wouldn't be disappointed. I'd have loved to have bought him, but I haven't got anywhere near £19 million to spend.'

Bobby's footballing philosophy is simple. 'One goal more. You score one more than the other side and you win. You can't beat that, can you?'

And he really does like to see his teams attack. He loves to play with wingers. He had John Barnes and Chris Waddle in the England side to support Gary Lineker and Peter Beardsley, and he has wingers at Newcastle in Nol Solano and Laurent Robert. He also has players of extreme pace and vision such as Kieron Dyer and Craig Bellamy.

'You have to get results, so you know you can't be flamboyant all the time. In cricket, a batsman knows he can't flash the bat at everything, otherwise he's going to get out. It's the same in football. You have to work at it. You have to hustle. You have to graft. You've got to win the ball, then you've got to get it forward, then you've got to get it in the box, then into the net. Football is built up of three segments – strong defence, creative midfield and a penetrating attack. You need

Danny Wilson, the popular manager who rose to fame by taking Barnsley into the Premier League.

character, and you need pace. If you get all that right, you have a chance.'

Bobby told me that, for him, being the manager of Newcastle United was 'a job made in heaven' and he could hardly believe the transformation that had taken place since he took over – from a team struggling at the bottom and fearful of relegation to one challenging for the championship. His only disappointment is that his father is no longer around to see it. 'He went to the 1932 FA Cup final when Newcastle beat Arsenal. He brought me here in 1946 after the war, and he would have loved to be here now. He was black and white and he would have been so proud. But that's life. At least my brothers come.'

Bobby is renowned for his gaffes, particularly in mixing up names. He is said to have once addressed Bryan Robson as Bobby, the former Manchester United and England captain reminding him gently, 'No, you're Bobby. I'm Bryan.'

He also comes out with some classic quotes, and, sure enough, there was one in the post-match press conference when I was up there for the Bolton game. Summing up Newcastle's title chances he said, 'You can't start counting your chickens before they are hatched, otherwise they won't lay the egg.'

Well, you can see what he meant, can't you?

In any case, it just adds to the aura surrounding the man. He had already had a wonderfully successful career and here he was, at the age of sixty-nine, performing miracles on Tyneside. As for his philosophy of one goal more, that day Newcastle were twice behind, but came back to beat Bolton 3–2. Need I say more?

I really enjoyed that day, and it got even better when I learned that Barnsley had come back from 4–2 down at Portsmouth to draw 4–4 as they continued their fight to climb away from the First Division relegation zone. I have always remained a big supporter of the Reds and, once my globe-trotting days were over and I could get to more matches, I became a season-ticket holder.

One of the proudest days of my life was when I sat with Michael Parkinson in the stand at Oakwell on Saturday, 26 April 1997, and watched them beat Bradford City 2–0 to clinch promotion to the Premier League for the first time in their 110-year history. We sat there side by side, Parky and I, two Barnsley lads, tears in our eyes, and proud as punch. I had a real lump in my throat at the end of that game, with fans swarming all over the pitch, the players coming back out to receive the applause, and everyone singing 'You'll Never Walk Alone' and 'It's Just Like Watching Brazil'.

I was so pleased for all those fans, especially the 2,000 or so who had followed the Reds all over the country when they were bottom of the old Fourth Division and struggling to stay in the Football League. I hoped

Two Barnsley lads, my old mate Parky and I, watch our team beat Bradford City to clinch promotion to the Premier Division for the first time in their 110-year history.

there were still a few of them alive to see that memorable day when top-flight football came to town. There had been great games, great players and wonderful moments, but nothing to match that afternoon.

A close second, however, must be our first visit to Wembley for the First Division play-off final at the end of the 1999-2000 season. Nearly 35,000 Barnsley fans made the trip, and I was delighted to be one of them, travelling down by coach with a group of people from the local newspaper, the *Barnsley Chronicle*. It was just like a dream walking up Wembley Way to watch my team play in a final. It was something I had always hoped for, but never really thought would happen. Now here we were and I felt as though I was walking on air.

Things did not go quite according to plan for the rest of the day. I was privileged to have been invited by Nationwide to sit in the royal box, but during the game I suddenly felt a bit of a drip – on my head at first, then another down the back of my neck. I thought, surely it can't be raining in the royal box, of all places. Is there no escape for me? But it wasn't raining rain at all, nor even vi-o-lets, as the old song goes. What had happened was that one of the sinks in the toilets above us – at least, I hope it was one of the sinks – had sprung a leak and we were right in the drop zone, or should that be drip zone? Well, you know what people are like. When they spotted what was happening, they yelled up to me, 'Better bring 'em off, Dickie, it's raining.'

It was amazing that the water fell only on me and the chap from Nationwide. Everybody else escaped. I got so wet that I had to leave the box to dry off with a towel. Thankfully, they had plugged the leak by the time I returned – but I missed Ipswich's third goal, scored by Marcus Stewart. Sadly, you see, our defence sprang a leak on the pitch as well. Craig Hignett gave us the lead with a stunning goal, but Ipswich fought back to equalise and then Darren Barnard had a penalty kick saved just before half-time. That was the turning point. Ipswich went on to win 4–2 to claim their place in the Premiership, while we had to face another season back down in the First Division.

To make matters worse, I couldn't find the coach afterwards. When I finally located it, you can imagine the reception I got from the other fans who had been sitting there for nearly an hour, eager to get back to Barnsley for the last half-hour drinking time to drown their sorrows.

Even so, it was a great day. If we had to lose to anybody, Ipswich were the team. As in Bobby Robson's day, they are still trying to play football the right way and their supporters are among the best in the country. You never hear of Town fans involved in any trouble. They are super. As far as rival fans are concerned, that Wembley final must have been one of the friendliest ever.

I also remember us beating Newcastle United in the FA Cup by 3–0

I've always been faithful to the Reds, and now my globe-trotting days are over I'm a season-ticket holder at Oakwell.

at Oakwell to go through on aggregate after losing the first leg 4–2 at St James's Park, and I have seen some of the best players in history play at our ground. Stanley Matthews and Stan Mortensen were in the Blackpool team that knocked us out of the Cup one year, with Morty hitting the winner from a Matthews cross. Then there was the winger I rated even better than Matthews, Tom Finney, who scored five against us one day. The best Barnsley player I ever saw was another winger, Johnny Kelly, a typical Scot. He was two-footed and could go inside or outside the full-back, cross with his right foot, cross with his left foot – a tremendous player and a real crowd pleaser.

I have a lot of fond memories like these, but when we beat Bradford City to join the big boys, that was something else. That was special. It was an historic day, and there has never been anything to match that. Maybe there never will be again. In the Premiership campaign, the Reds knocked holders Manchester United out of the FA Cup with a 3–2 win in an Oakwell replay, but not even that wonderful performance could compare with the dramatic, emotional day in 1997 when Barnsley Football Club became Premier League.

Everybody had kept saying that Barnsley would never go up, some even claiming that they did not want to go up, but we showed them. We did it and no one can take that away from us.

Everywhere I went during that memorable Premiership season, people kept telling me that they did not want Barnsley to go down. The club had captured the imagination of all England with the way it had conducted itself. Despite early heavy defeats, the team continued to try to play good football. The Reds did us proud, even though it was just beyond their resources to stay up in the end.

Unfortunately, I did not see too many of their Premiership matches because I spent a lot of time in Australia and the West Indies that winter, but the games I did see gave me a lot of pleasure. I was there for the last game of that special season when Barnsley entertained Manchester United, who had lost their title to Arsenal. It was another experience I will never forget. The Barnsley supporters were simply marvellous. It was very emotional seeing them give such a fantastic reception to a team that had been relegated, and once again I had a lump in my throat as they sang 'You'll Never Walk Alone'.

Barnsley can look back on that season with justifiable pride. It was good for the town, too. That year in the top flight gave the whole place a lift. It set everyone buzzing and raised the spirits of an area that had been so badly hit by the closing of the pits. They even started showing us on 'Match of the Day'.

Who will ever forget the wonderful fans chanting 'We're going to win 6–5' when the Reds were trailing 5–0 at Old Trafford. Crazy? Maybe. Bobby Robson will understand.

CHAPTER 4

FOOD FOR THOUGHT

The brass plate which signified the creation of 'Simpson's Divan Tavern' in 1848.

Left: Pennine summit conference, at Val's Café on the windswept Woodhead pass. If all the truck drivers stop there, you know you are on to a good thing.

I LOVE food but I have to rely on other people cooking it for me. I'm hopeless. So I always go out for hot meals, unless my sister Marjorie comes in and prepares something for me. I can just about manage to open a tin, so I have quite a lot of salmon or tuna, together with fresh tomatoes and salads. We also have a village butcher who knows exactly what I want and cuts me some lovely pieces of cold meat. Sometimes I pop into Staincross to get some fish (without batter) and chips from the local chippie, and I also eat a lot of fruit. So, you see, I don't stick fast. A typical day's menu would be something like this:

BREAKFAST: raisins, All-Bran, Cornflakes and a banana.
DINNER: chicken, fish or red meat, with roast potatoes and plenty of vegetables, plus a glass of red wine.
TEA: cold meat (usually chicken) or salmon/tuna, tomatoes, salad, brown bread (no butter), tea (no milk) and a couple of dates.

That's it. I don't touch anything else then. Of course, that healthy diet goes haywire when I'm invited out for dinners, either as a guest or to speak, or I'm on my travels – and I also have a weakness for chocolates. I have to keep away from them. I could go through a whole box watching television, just like that, as my favourite entertainer, Tommy Cooper, used to say.

I don't drink coffee because I believe it's bad for you. But, then again, there are some people who say tea isn't good for you. I do wonder sometimes. I take tea without milk. My dad was the same. Lots of miners didn't like milk in their tea when they took their flasks down the pit. It was how I was brought up. But if you look in my cup after I've drunk the tea, you will see a stain. That's what makes me think. If it's doing that to my cup, what might it be doing to my insides?

Marjorie plays hell with me when she sees the stains in my cup, but I say, 'What's the problem? I'll have that off in a jiffy.' And I do. You know that stuff you have to clean dentures? Well, I put some of that inside the cup and the stain disappears overnight.

I don't drink beer or whisky or anything like that, but I have the occasional Guinness on doctor's advice, and I do like a glass of red wine, which a heart specialist in Australia said was good for my circulation. Cleared the blood round the arteries, he told me. He actually advised two or three glasses a day, but I don't drink anywhere near as much as that. Apparently, Denis Compton, one of the greatest batsmen I've ever seen, was also told to have two or three a day, but he thought the doc meant bottles.

I don't smoke, either. It's all down to my dad. When I was a young lad, he advised me, 'Keep off cigs, don't drink – and steer clear of women in nightclubs.'

For thirty-five minutes every morning I do exercises on a mat in my bathroom, so, basically, I have a pretty healthy lifestyle.

I buy food on a day-to-day basis, which means I never have anything much in the house, and this, coupled with my inability to cook, does pose problems when visitors come to call – as Roddy Bloomfield, from my publishers Hodder and Stoughton, found to his cost. Usually we arrange to go out for lunch, but on one occasion, when he was forced to pay a flying visit to my cottage, this was not possible. Having travelled up from London by train on a particularly bleak November morning, he was, no doubt, just a tad disappointed to discover that I had nothing to offer him in the way of food although he had a choice of liquid refreshment – red wine or tea. Our meeting lasted for about four hours, covering what would normally have been his lunchtime, so he left White Rose Cottage with his belly thinking his throat was cut.

The next time he called in to see me he was on his way back to London from somewhere or other, and he was fully prepared. After our business had been concluded I said, 'Right then, Roddy, I'll make us a cup of tea.'

He looked at me with a mischievous glint in his eye and replied, 'Before you do, Dickie, I've got a surprise for you.'

With that he delved into his briefcase and pulled out packets of crisps, biscuits, bread rolls, butter – and a delicious-looking meat and potato pie.

'There you are,' he grinned. 'Lunch. All you need to do is warm up the pie while I butter the rolls and then we can tuck in.'

I squirmed in embarrassment, and it took a real effort to admit, 'I'm sorry, Roddy. But I've got this new oven and I just don't know how to work it.' So we ate the pie cold.

*

Putting the world's biggest meat and potato pie to the sword in Denby Dale. Anyone for seconds?

However, I did manage to enjoy a piping hot pie in the summer of 2000. In the village of Denby Dale, just a few miles down the road from where I live, they decided to celebrate the millennium by baking the world's biggest meat and potato pie. They thought that if it was not possible to have four and twenty blackbirds in it, they would do with the next best thing. So they invited this little Bird to go along and cut it open.

It was one of the oddest jobs I have ever been asked to do, made odder by the fact that I was given an ancient sword to carve the first mouth-watering slice. But I was delighted to go along because I love a nice piece of pie – and, because it was so big, I was able to have four or five helpings.

As you will gather, this was no ordinary pie. It weighed in at twelve tonnes, was twelve metres (forty feet) long, 2.5 metres (eight feet) wide, and 1.1 metres (forty-four inches) deep. It used the electricity generated to power nine houses. If you fancy giving it a go, here is the 'secret' recipe:

INGREDIENTS:
5,000kg diced prime quality British beef
2,000kg potatoes
1,000kg onions
3,900kg water
100kg John Smith's Best Bitter
200kg beef bouillon, mixed herbs and gravy
salt and pepper to taste
3,465kg shortcrust pastry

METHOD:
1 Have plenty of helpers ready.
2 Divide all ingredients into equal parts.
3 Have all water in pie dish ready to add meat and onions.
4 Bring to a temperature of 90°C and cook gently for approximately eight hours.
5 When cooked, add potatoes and thicken with gravy mix, stirring occasionally.

This was by no means the first record-breaking pie produced by the villagers. The tradition started in 1788 to celebrate the recovery of King George lll from mental illness. There is no record, however, of him having a slice.

The second pie was made in 1815 to celebrate the resounding defeat of 'Old Bony' and his French troops at the Battle of Waterloo, but this was not a particularly big one, containing merely 'two sheep and twenty fowl, with half a peck of flour being used for the crust'.

Queen Victoria's Golden Jubilee on 17 August 1887 gave the Denby Dale villagers another excuse for a pie. This one was even bigger – eight feet in diameter, two feet deep, and baked in a specially made metal dish, fourteen feet square. The pie comprised a variety of game, poultry, rabbits, veal, mutton, pork and beef – and forty stone of potatoes. Sadly, however, it was a disaster. The meat was not quite as fresh as it might have been – to put it mildly – and reports say that 'the resulting obnoxious smell overpowered the crowd. With due ceremony, the offending pie was carried to the nearby wood and buried with generous quantities of quicklime.' The pie dish itself was auctioned several times, raising £79 for forces charities in the Second World War, and it was finally melted down for munitions in 1940. So some good still came out of it.

Due to rationing, no pies were baked to celebrate either the end of the Second World War or the Coronation of Her Majesty Queen Elizabeth ll, but on 5 September 1964, the village witnessed another bake to commemorate four royal births. The Pie Hall in the village is a lasting monument to the success of that occasion. Outside the hall you can still see the dish in which that pie was baked, now used as a planter.

For the bicentenary of the first pie, in 1988, visitors again flocked from far and wide to enjoy a slice of the giant, world-record breaker, plus a whole weekend of festivities ranging from a Radio One road-show to a display by parachutists. Then came the millennium and it was my turn to put a finger in the pie. That particular one not only continued the long-standing tradition of record-breaking, but also raised money to provide a football field in Denby Dale and to refurbish the village youth club. I can't wait for the next one – if I'm still around.

My favourite meal locally is the Barnsley chop, which has been served to me for years at the Brooklands Restaurant, near the M1 intersection. Remarkably, the same man – head chef John Smith – has cooked it for me ever since I started going there, and it really is a meal fit for a king – well, a prince, at least. The first Barnsley chop was prepared for the Prince of Wales when he opened Barnsley Town Hall in 1933 – the year I was born.

Head chef John Smith prepares my favourite, the legendary Barnsley chop, which is cut from a whole saddle of lamb to make a dish unique to Brooklands restaurant.

The Barnsley chop weighs in at about two pounds. Once I've got outside one of these, I don't need to eat much else for the next three days!

People often ask me, 'What exactly is a Barnsley chop?' Obviously more than meets the eye, but not being particularly well up on that kind of thing, I can only tell them it is a big piece of lamb. So I asked John to fill me in on the details.

'We buy whole saddles of lamb, then cut straight across the back of the saddle, which provides us with three or four joints of meat. We roast for about an hour and a half, with rosemary and seasoning, and serve with fried mushrooms, tomatoes and the juices from the meat itself.' He'll also throw in some onion rings for good measure, if I ask him nicely.

Each piece of meat weighs about two pounds, so it really is a chop and a half, and it takes some eating, I can tell you. I usually manage to polish it off, but only if I don't have anything else to eat that day, and

I don't really want much for two or three days afterwards either. Most people find a starter and a dessert – or even just the one – out of the question.

The motto of the restaurant, written large on a mural for all to see, is 'Within these portals it is no sin to ask for more; it will be freely given.' Said John, 'That means if anybody wants another chop, they can have one. But there have not been many takers.' Not many? I'm amazed there have been any at all.

There are other hotels and restaurants that serve so-called Barnsley chops, but nowhere have I come across any as big as the ones at Brooklands.

John explained, 'A lot of places split the saddle the long way and then cut it. It used to be done that way in the top restaurants in London and Glasgow, then grilled with a kidney inside. Very tasty it may be, but that's not a Barnsley chop, it's a Crown chop. The way we prepare and serve the dish is unique to Brooklands.'

Simpson's-in-the-Strand hasn't been around quite as long as the Denby Dale pie, but once it got going as a restaurant in 1848, there was no looking back. It started as Samuel Reiss's Grand Cigar Divan, a meeting room for gentlemen to smoke cigars, drink coffee and play chess. Not much good for me, then. I don't smoke, don't drink coffee and have never played chess, but obviously one of my well-to-do ancestors did. On a plaque just inside the entrance, among a list of the top players of the day, there is displayed the name of H.E. Bird.

Simpson's originally opened in 1828 and became known as the home of chess. Anybody who was anybody played there; but there was not a lot of money to be made from it, and in 1848 Reiss invited caterer John Simpson to become his partner. That was when the Grand Cigar Divan was renamed Simpson's Grand Divan Tavern and the chess room was moved upstairs to allow the downstairs room to reopen as a restaurant.

They have been serving roast beef there ever since but now, as manager Robin Easton pointed out, they have a 'proper oven'. He explained that they used to do the roasts over open fires. In fact, Richard, the head chef, is one of only four in the country entitled to call themselves 'Master Cook', wearing a small black cap instead of the traditional white. Apparently, this came about because, when their ancestors cooked over an open fire, all the soot and smoke made a right old mess of their white caps, with the result that the owners had a bit of a beef about the laundry bill. So they came up with the brilliant idea of producing a black cap to mask the effects of all the dirt.

It was also at that time that they introduced the practice of wheeling in the large joints of meat to the tables on silver trolleys – a custom that continues to this day. William Gladstone and Benjamin Disraeli were regular diners and Charles Dickens used to have lunch there three or four times a week when he had his offices in Wellington Street.

Simpson's was later acquired by Richard D'Oyly Carte, of Gilbert and Sullivan fame, who, in Robin's words, 'opened the bed and breakfast café next door' – he was referring to The Savoy. Simpson's reopened in 1904 under the name it bears today. It continues to uphold the very best of British dining traditions, as I found on my latest visit when I enjoyed asparagus and buttered leeks in crisp pastry, followed by roast rib of Scottish Aberdeen Angus beef with Yorkshire pudding, roast potatoes and Savoy cabbage, and a pudding of treacle sponge with custard.

As you might expect in such an establishment, it is not cheap to eat there. That little lot cost £33.95. Had I decided to have broad beans as well as the cabbage, it would have knocked me back an extra £2.95. However, upstairs you can get a three-course meal for £19.95 or a two-course meal for £15. Still a touch more expensive than the two-for-a-fiver offers you get in pubs around Barnsley, but, as the saying goes, you get what you pay for and at Simpson's you get an excellent meal.

Having said that, you still have to go a long way to beat the all-round quality of another of my favourite local eating places, The Three Acres at Emley. I don't have to go a long way, do I? I dine there quite regularly. You get a super meal. Don't take my word for it. Just look at this impressive list of awards: 1990, Egon Ronay Runner-up Pub of the Year; 1996, Egon Ronay Sandwich Pub of the Year; 1998, Readers of the *Yorkshire Post* Restaurant of the Year; 2000, *Yorkshire Life* Runner-up Restaurant of the Year, *Yorkshire Evening Post* Oliver's Restaurant of the Year, and *Good Pub Guide* Fine Dining Pub of the Year; 2001, Les Routiers Inn of the Year, *Which? Guide to Country Pubs*, one Rosette. No doubt there will be more.

But whether it's The Three Acres or Simpson's, I stick to my guns about the sauces. The beef at Simpson's is usually served with horse-radish, and I was also offered some redcurrant jelly, but I told the waiter, 'Not for me, thank you. I'm not going to spoil that lovely beef by putting anything on it.' The poor chap was obviously somewhat taken aback, and one of my dinner companions, former Sussex captain John Barclay, intervened. 'But it brings out the flavour, Dickie.' I was not to be swayed. When I have meat I want to taste the meat, nothing else, and nobody is going to persuade me otherwise.

There is a different taste to the beef served at Simpson's, and I was told that this is because they hang their meat for twenty-eight days rather than the customary ten days maximum. Robin explained, 'The longer meat is hung the better the flavour, the texture, the tenderness, although there is, of course, a limit. When we first started hanging our beef for longer, I was concerned that people might feel there was some-

The ceremonial carving of the joint on its silver trolley, a Simpson's tradition dating back to the days when Dickens was a regular luncher, and Gladstone and Disraeli popped in for dinner. John Barclay looks on with admiration while Andrew Wingfield Digby, on my other side, takes a calmer approach than the rest of us.

thing slightly off about it because they had become used to the blandness. I wondered if they would care for the stronger taste. Fortunately, everyone was delighted with it.'

He went on, 'It is more expensive to do it that way because the carcass will lose between ten and twelve per cent in weight during hanging, but we feel it is worth it to provide the better quality. English food went through a period when it had such a lousy reputation, so we take pride in the fact that we have helped restore that reputation. It's good to take the time and trouble to look at the quality of what you're buying.'

Robin is saddened by the fact that so many butchers and fishmongers have disappeared from our towns and villages. 'People shop in supermarkets now, and I accept that it is convenient, but it's a shame that we're losing out on the small specialised businesses.'

He assumed that if people buy well, they are unlikely to muck things up in the cooking process – unless, of course, their name is H.D. Bird.

Robin told me that he very often takes youngsters who are thinking of going into the business to the meat fridge and asks them, 'When you go shopping with your mum and dad, what do they go for?' The answer, invariably, is the bright red meat because it looks fresh and really nice. Wrong. Said Robin, 'It's the worst possible meat. When our beef comes in, the ends are actually black, and we trim them off. Yet often in the supermarkets you will see a special reduced price on those bits of meat that have gone a bit dark coloured.'

Simpson's also serve delightful fish dishes and one of the greatest tragedies, said Robin, was that about 70 per cent of our fishing catch goes abroad. He remembers driving up to Scotland with his wife a few years ago and on the way calling in at a place near Morecambe where they were looking forward to enjoying the local speciality of Morecambe Bay potted shrimps. But there were none to be had. They were all for export.

The cover on Simpson's menu is in the form of a chess board, and a board is still available for anyone wishing to play. In the upstairs bar they have introduced a biannual tournament for the world's greatest players, the trophy for which is housed at Simpson's. The downstairs room remains very masculine, very imposing, and it has been written about by many people. In fact, there are those who believe that Sherlock Holmes was a real person. Robin gets Americans writing to him saying they have dined at Simpson's and would be thrilled to know more about Holmes and which table he sat at when he had a meal there.

Enjoying our lunch so much, cricketing chums John Barclay, Andrew Wingfield Digby and I could not help but reflect on our visits to India, where our staple diet had been so totally different from what was now in front of us. I used to take a caseful of gingerbread men and Cadbury's fruit and nut chocolate, and I used to eat plenty of bananas. I also poured into my tea a few drops of those bitters you put in pink gin. West Indian paceman Malcolm Marshall gave me that tip. He said I'd never have any problem with my stomach if I did that. John had scrambled eggs every single day. Most importantly, all three of us avoided the curries and we were never ill there.

One or two others fell into temptation and paid for it. John recalled Alf Gover running up to bowl in the first over after lunch, having had a curry, and continuing his run straight back to the pavilion where he remained in the smallest room for the rest of the afternoon session. And Andrew remembered seeing a colleague hitching a ride on a scooter and being transported flat out from third man to the same convenient venue because he could not hold out for another minute. Delhi belly had struck again.

But enough of lunches and dinners. What about tea?

Afternoon tea at The Ritz has been popular since the hotel opened in 1906 and, as well as members of the royal family, has been enjoyed by a very wide clientele, including Charlie Chaplin, Sir Winston Churchill, General de Gaulle, Noel Coward, Judy Garland, Evelyn

Afternoon tea at The Ritz with my book publicist Katie Luther. The Palm Court may be pricey, but it is definitely tea with style.

Waugh, Burt Lancaster, Adam Faith, Selina Scott, Hugh Grant and Elton John.

Princess Margaret had her birthday party there in 2000 at the same time as a group of eighteen-year-olds were celebrating theirs. It was a magical moment, so I am told, when Princess Margaret walked past, closely followed by the Queen. Everybody stood up, bowed and curtsied. Those teenagers would never forget that moment.

I was about to partake of afternoon tea in the Palm Court. It really does take your breath away. There was I, the son of a Yorkshire miner, having tea in such a place as this. Unbelievable. I looked round at impressive, widely spaced marble columns, framed by archways and deep steps. The central niche to the rear of the room contains a female figure in gilded lead, and on either side, mirrors from floor to ceiling enhance and enlarge the area. Above, light streams in through a central glazed roof. Additional artificial lighting boosts a dull day and ensures that bad light does not result in an early tea. Two shell windows flank the central roof light and a pair of hanging wrought-iron lamps, like fanciful birdcages, are twined with painted metal flowers, while the trellis adds a golden sheen throughout the room. It really is awesome.

The fine bone china has an exclusive Palm Court design, featuring gold, pale green and rose colours, which blend perfectly with the light and charm of the room. Tea is served in silver teapots with silver milk jugs and I was left staring questioningly at the deposit at the bottom of my cup before realising that this was no place for teabags. Habit had made me forget to use the silver tea strainer provided.

For many, tea at The Ritz is a lifetime ambition and a wonderful memory. I was told of one guest, having tea with an admirer, who was surprised when presented with a large cake on which the words 'Will you marry me?' were inscribed. It was the first she knew of his intentions but, realising how honourable they were, she delightedly accepted the proposal.

For those unfamiliar with what The Ritz has to offer, a quick

Tea at Betty's in Harrogate with my sister Marjorie. Like The Ritz it keeps up the highest standards.

run-down of the afternoon tea menu might be appropriate. Finger sandwiches, which include smoked salmon, cucumber, egg mayonnaise with mustard cress, poached salmon and watercress, roast beef with horseradish, cream cheese and chives, and ham with sun-dried tomato, are served on the base of a three-tiered stand. To complement these, there is a middle tier of freshly baked scones with jam and Cornish clotted cream, and a top tier selection of cakes and pastries. Then, of course, there are the selected teas or filter coffee and all this for a mere £27. Perhaps I should add that you can have as many sandwiches as you want. Otherwise, to the ordinary punter, it might seem a touch expensive. But what an experience.

The selected teas comprise Ritz traditional English ('a full-bodied tea which is a good example of a tea blended to give both colour and flavour'); China Oolong ('a smooth light tea with exquisite bouquet' – sounds more like a wine to me); Lapsang Souchong ('a smoky tea, much loved by connoisseurs throughout the world'); Earl Grey ('a delicately scented tea, famous for its exceptional lightness and fragrance'); Ceylon Orange Pekoe ('a flavoursome tea, with light golden orange liquor'); Darjeeling ('a subtle, distinctive tea of unusual character and light of colour, mild and mellow'); and Jasmine ('a fragrant tea, the classic Chinese green tea which is so soothing and calming').

What? No Yorkshire tea? Still, I must admit that I found the cup – or should I say cups – that I consumed most refreshing. So much so that I resisted the temptation to have a glass of champagne with my afternoon tea, particularly when I saw that it cost £11. For a glass! A half bottle was £21.50 and a full bottle £42. Mind you, it was Cuvee Privee N.V., whatever that means.

To avoid guests having the annoyance and inconvenience of a common queue, The Ritz takes bookings for three sittings – at 1.30, 3.30 and 5.30. Those who have tea at 5.30 are usually going on to the theatre in the evening, although it has been known for some to stay on for drinks, which are served until 11 p.m.

Being a big tea-drinker myself, I decided to take the opportunity of finding out from The Ritz experts their top tips for making a perfect cuppa, and they gave me a golden-rule list of fourteen as follows:

1   Use freshly drawn water.
2   Use a filter if you have hard water.
3   Boil the kettle and warm the pot.
4   Put one dessertspoonful of leaves per person, plus half a dessertspoonful for the pot (use a removable filter if possible).
5   Boil the kettle again and fill up the pot.
6   Steep for two to three minutes.
7   Use semi-skimmed or skimmed milk rather than full fat milk.

8   Pour the tea, filling up the pot with fresh boiling water.

9   When the tea has brewed sufficiently remove the filter so that the tea doesn't get stewed.

10 If using lemon instead of milk, put the lemon in before pouring the tea.

11 Rinse the pot out after use to prevent the build-up of tannin.

12 Always keep the tea leaves in a dark air-tight container, especially fragrant teas.

13 Experiment with your own blends.

14 Use a good-quality china cup, not some thumping great mug.

So that's where I've been going wrong – points 1 to 14. Mind you, I wonder what some of the truckers would say if Val served them up with some Earl Grey in a tiny china cup, plus silver tea-strainer, on a raw winter's afternoon over the Woodhead Pass on the Pennines.

You could not think of a greater contrast than between The Ritz and Val's, but I appreciate both. I don't want you to think that I eat out only at the big posh restaurants. I'm just as content to savour the delights of the smaller establishments – and they don't come any smaller than Val's Café. I say café, but in fact it is just a tiny trailer, towed to its regular spot every day to meet the needs of the truckers, the van drivers and motorists who frequent that busy and often inhospitable road, the Woodhead Pass. The truck drivers in particular know where the best

Val's bacon butties take some beating on the way to Old Trafford.

Louise Shillito tempts me with some of her speciality scones at Crickets in Barnsley.

grub is. They know where to get value for money. So if you see a lot of lorries parked up, you know you're on to a good thing.

I've always called in at Val's on my way to umpire at Old Trafford – or, in more recent years, when I've been a spectator – and I can honestly say that Val's bacon butties take some beating. Get one of those down you, with a cup of her freshly brewed tea, and it fair warms the cockles of your heart. And, boy, do you need something to warm you on that stretch of road. The Pennines can be breathtakingly beautiful, but they can also be treacherous when the weather turns nasty, as it can do without warning up there. I've set off from Barnsley in lovely warm sunshine and ended up wolfing down Val's bacon butty and tea in snow and sleet, and that's in July.

Whenever I make the much shorter and less fraught journey into Barnsley to do a bit of shopping, to get more blood pressure pills from my doctor, to have my teeth fixed or to check my bank account, I make a point of calling in at Crickets for a snack.

The owner, Louise Shillito, bakes what must be the best and biggest scones in the world. Just one of these monsters is a meal on its own and it sets me up for the rest of the day. If I fancy something hot, I'll have a bowl of homemade soup, some fish or gammon, beans on toast, or a roast pork sandwich.

Louise admits her scones are her speciality. She makes them on the premises. It is one of the first things she does when she arrives early in the morning. She cannot remember where she got the original recipe from and confided to me, 'I didn't set out to make them bigger than anywhere else. They just came out like that the first time I did them. They proved so popular that I decided to carry on baking them that way.' I'm glad she did.

Louise does all her own cooking and baking on the premises. She also serves, washes up and cleans up. She does the lot with five part-time staff to help. She opens every day except Sunday and, as well as the restaurant area which seats thirty, there are the sandwich take-away customers to keep happy.

A typical day means getting up at six, setting off from home at seven, fetching the milk, bread etc from the cash and carry, opening up, baking, getting ready for the dinner-time rush, which starts at twelve noon, finishing at three o'clock, and finally catching up with husband John – unless he's playing cricket or golf, which he often is.

I wondered why Louise had decided on the name 'Crickets' for the shop. She said she wanted to have a theme, to give people an interest when they went inside, and she chose cricket because she was keen on the sport.

'I just wanted to make it different from anywhere else in town, with pictures round the walls and everything. So I bought some from Jack Russell's studio in Chipping Sodbury, managed to get hold of some press pictures, and took some photographs myself. Now I have quite a collection and they are always a talking point.' Well, I have to confess it was the name that first attracted me to the Regent Street premises.

Louise may not be able to remember how she came across the original recipe for her scones, but it is a different story – and a very interesting one – at Lily's near the Sheffield Wednesday Football Club at Hillsborough.

The recipe for the bread baked there was found by Lily's husband, Raymond, forty years ago in an old book at the bottom of his grand-mother's cupboard. At the time, Lily's was a pork shop, so Raymond experimented by selling pork sandwiches, using the recipe to make the bread. Shortly afterwards, dripping butties were introduced and both have now become famous. The dripping butties are my favourites. I can't resist them.

Lily's pork is tremendous and the dripping is out of this world – all the juices from the pork, with those little brown bits, which are tastiest of all. Can't beat it. Makes me hungry just writing about it. And the fruit pies aren't bad, either.

To give you some idea of how this family firm has grown, they origi-nally made three dozen bread cakes per day. Now they make 500 dozen and they're all baked on the premises that same day. You can't get fresher.

All the Sheffield Wednesday players buy their sandwiches from Lily's. The German World Cup squad of 1966 were regulars. The snooker players taking part in the annual world championships at The Crucible theatre shop there, as does former world boxing champion Prince Naseem Hamed. Local cricketers, golfers and radio presenters also frequent the place.

A sight to make your mouth water – the dripping butty production line at Lily's of Sheffield.

Raymond's sister Margaret, who originally agreed to help out for a couple of hours a week and is still there forty years on, explained the reasons for Lily's popularity.

'This is the bread that grandma used to bake. We stick to the original recipe. We include no so-called improvers. That's what makes our product different from others. Nor do we sell bread that isn't made the same day. We used to be busy just for an hour or so at lunchtimes, but now it's almost non-stop from eleven in the morning to three in the afternoon. We are even busy early in the morning. We open at half past six in the week and six on Saturdays, and people come in for breakfast sarnies. We get taxi-men just starting out and night-clubbers on their way home.'

Since the Hillsborough tragedy, Lily's doesn't open on match days any more. I used to pop in when I'd been to one of Sheffield Wednesday's games although, as a Barnsley season-ticket holder, I ought not to confess to frequenting Hillsborough – I can hear the 'Owls of protest now – but it was mainly to savour the pork and dripping butties, or maybe a minced beef and onion pie.

Oh, dear me, that's the healthy diet gone for a burton, isn't it? Bacon butties, dripping butties, pies, massive scones – I shouldn't be eating all those, should I? I dread to think what my cholesterol level is. But I simply can't resist them. They are too finger-lickingly good. Is it any wonder I once overheard someone remark, 'Yon Birdy could eyt for England.'

Anyway, I'm still doing my exercises every morning – just.

The BAT & BALL
John Nyren of Hambledon
· 1764 · 1837 ·

THIS STONE MARKS THE SITE
OF THE GROUND
OF THE
HAMBLEDON CRICKET CLUB

HISTORY IN THE MAKING

Ashes to ashes. The most famous exhibit in the Lord's museum.

Left: Former landlord of The Bat and Ball Richard Nyren was the driving force behind all that happened on Broadhalfpenny Down. The stone opposite marks where the game was played from 1750–87.

CRICKET is an English game. We invented it. Let nobody kid you about that. Even if we do now get spots knocked off us by those pesky Aussies, it is our game and it was developed here.

If you want proof, just pay a visit to The Bat and Ball pub at Hambledon in Hampshire, where an inscription on the wall of one of the most famous hostelries in the country tells you that here lies 'the cradle of cricket and the first headquarters of English cricket'. In fact, the game had been played in the South Downs region for 200 years prior to that.

The modern game was formulated on the basis of rules drawn up by the Hambledon CC on Broadhalfpenny Down. This formidable club, led by Richard Nyren, the landlord of The Bat and Ball, played an England team on fifty-one occasions, winning no less than twenty-nine times, and while Hambledon may not be the birthplace of cricket, it is certainly where the game grew up. If it was not born there, that was where it reached maturity.

Cricket is the way it is now because of the way it was at Hambledon all those years ago, and it is something to be proud about. After all, we may be fitter, bigger, stronger and faster these days, but we are not inventing too many new sports, are we? Cricket and football both originated in this country and they are part of our heritage. I would go so far as to say that this is the greatest country for inventing games. The Americans have a go, but they are still no match for us in this respect.

In view of its importance, therefore, I found it strange that upon entering the village of Hambledon from the A32 via the B2150, there are no signs directing people to the ground – or the pub. Many bewildered visitors must scratch their heads in bemusement as they journey down the main street only to find themselves exiting at the other end still searching for the home of English cricket.

It is, in fact, three miles further down the road. You would have thought that such a significant part of our sporting heritage would be better publicised as a tourist attraction – especially when the current landlord, Dick Orders, is a cricket lover and a most hospitable man.

When you do eventually find the ground, now the home of Broadhalfpenny Brigands CC, you have to be impressed at the wonderful location and the lovely village atmosphere. Tall trees line one side of the ground, there is a small but handsome pavilion and just across the lane, The Bat and Ball. The rolling downs provide a delightful backdrop.

It was there that John Ford, who wrote the definitive book on the early days of English cricket, filled me in on the historic details. He explained to me that Hambledon was regarded as the home of cricket because the first professionally organised game there led to the development of specific laws, which had to be laid down as a result of the gambling that took place on the outcome of matches.

'There had been organised cricket before,' John went on, 'and there had been gambling, but it was the Hambledon Club that really kick-started the modern game. The principal patrons were the wealthy Sir Horace Mann, the Duke of Dorset and the Earl of Tankerville, who paid the players. So the Hambledon team was professional in that sense. These were not just country boys coming in for a game of village cricket. It was fairly serious stuff, and it was made more serious by the amount of money being wagered on matches.

The cradle of English cricket at Hambledon – and still rocking.

MCC Ladies v. the Sirens at Hambledon. What would the game's founding fathers, Richard Nyren and Lumpy Stevens, have made of them!

Cricket historian John Ford surveys the modern game from the Hambledon pavilion.

'It had all started with boys playing in graveyards, hitting an object with a stick, but when the game began to develop and attract gamblers, rules had to be drawn up, agreed by all parties. And that's what happened at Hambledon. What developed was not the archetypal village cricket. This was different. This was hardened, serious cricket. Players had to deliver and do their stuff because they were being paid by the wealthy patrons – and there was big money to be won or lost.'

In the second part of the eighteenth century, Hambledon became very much a Gentleman's Club, with a subscription in 1770 of three guineas, which is the best part of £250 in today's money. That sparked off the greatest period of the Hambledon Club, but by 1787 attention had begun to focus more on London, where Thomas Lord had acquired his first ground, and definitive laws of the game were drawn up at The Star and Garter Hotel.

When Hambledon had their meetings, it was very much the gentlemen coming together for a good night out, and a record of one of those meetings confides that 'on a wet day, only three members were present, but eight bottles of wine were consumed'. Nothing changes, does it?

As John explained, that was the era when the sociability of cricket and the association with pubs and inns developed, largely because of the fact that the game's headquarters at The Bat and Ball were directly opposite the ground. All publicans in those days liked to have some

At the bar of cricket history, the famous Bat and Ball pub, Hambledon.

kind of sport to attract the customers. Such things as skittles and pigeon shooting were already popular, and cricket was an ideal way to swell the coffers in the summer months.

Said John, 'Just imagine two thousand people round the boundary at Hambledon, with the publican right on the doorstep. What an opportunity for him. As well as his own bar, he could have a tent on the ground. So, naturally enough, he was all in favour of the development of cricket.'

That was how the association between pubs, booze and the thwack of willow on leather came about.

Richard Nyren, the landlord of The Bat and Ball, was the inspiration and driving force behind all that happened on Broadhalfpenny Down in the glory days between the late 1750s and 1791, and was therefore ultimately responsible for all that happens there to this day. A testimonial on the wall of the pub, which displays many other artefacts relating to the origin of cricket, reads as follows:

So long as cricket is played and cricketers use Broadhalfpenny Down, The Bat and Ball will remain a memorial to Richard Nyren, a man of integrity and enterprise, a man of stout build and great energy, who was called 'The General', which must have amused him.

An exceptional cricketer, with four skills in one, he was a good left-hand bowler, safe attacking batsman, born tactician and a natural leader of men. It was he who first experimented with length bowling. Previously they bowled all along the ground. It was a simple, yet revolutionary idea which he honed to perfection with a vigour which eventually turned a country pastime into a national sport. Richard Nyren was the true father of the modern game.

As a captain he excelled, he was an ideal man, and as a player fully worth his place in the side. He could outthink the opposition; a man who could earn and keep the devotion of his team; and a man with the ability to marshal their collective resources to relive victory time and again. Many is the side in the modern game which could wish for such a player.

He had an exceptional knowledge of the game, was one of the most influential contributors to any discussion of the laws, looked after the ground opposite, and even collected overdue subscriptions from members of the Hambledon Club. Truly the club's head and right arm.

His talents as an innkeeper were almost as legendary as his exploits on the cricket field. He was the life and soul of The Bat and Ball, turning it into a vibrant centre of local entertainment, regularly advertising great matches on Broadhalfpenny Down in the Hampshire Chronicle, and inviting crowds to watch little Hambledon take on All England yet again.

When Richard and his friends were not thrashing the hide off an England team they were out for all hours hunting, shooting and fishing; men who lived life to the full. Winter was never going to be dull, just different. After the sport it was back to the warmth of the pub for songs and fine ale.

Richard Nyren, a true sportsman, inspirational cricketer, and great character. Long may his memory live in this place and across the road.

He must have been some bloke. There were other terrific characters around as well, 'Lumpy' Stevens for instance, who invented the off break, much I am sure to the delight of the late great Jim Laker, who was one of the finest exponents of that type of bowling in the twentieth century.

In the early days, the ball was bowled along the ground, maybe just hopping a little bit as it went, but then came the introduction of length bowling and with it the off-break revolution. I suppose some-one had to come up with the idea, and that someone was Lumpy. Unfortunately, despite his ground-breaking discovery, Lumpy was not too bright. He couldn't figure it through. He kept pitching the ball on middle and leg and therefore found batsmen constantly hitting him to leg. It was left to his benefactor, Sir Horace Mann, to point out to Lumpy that he just might get better results if he pitched the ball a little bit wide of the off stump. Lumpy was one of Sir Horace's paid men in a wager sport, so the latter had good reason for wanting him to do well.

In those days they played with two stumps, between which there was quite a big gap, and it was a constant source of frustration to the bowlers when they beat a batsman all ends up only to see the ball pass straight through the middle without touching the stumps. It is recorded that on one such occasion Lumpy was heard to observe, 'My, but that was tedious close, sir.'

That has an echo in more recent times in the story told of Fiery Freddie Trueman, that great Yorkshire and England bowling legend. After two confident shouts for lbw had been turned down by the umpire in successive deliveries, Fiery charged in for the next ball and all three stumps went cartwheeling out of the ground. He turned to the umpire and snarled, 'By 'eck, but tha knows I very nearly 'ed 'im that time.' Or words to that effect.

Then there was Noah Mann, who was typical of the Hambledon lads. He used to ride twenty miles on horseback to practice sessions, and then ride home afterwards. Obviously he must have been a good horseman, but you're talking about an hour and a half's ride in each direction. That's a pretty fair gallop. I couldn't see Goughy doing that, could you? On match days, Noah would entertain the crowds at the conclusion of play by placing handkerchiefs round the boundary's edge. Then he would ride round on his horse, leaning from the saddle to snatch them up, like a circus performer. Needless to say, there were wagers on whether or not he would collect them all.

Sadly, poor old Noah came to an untimely end. One night, having consumed a large amount of ale and not wanting to be caught drunk in charge of a horse on his twenty-mile gallop home, he decided to stay overnight at The Bat and Ball. Unfortunately, he fell asleep in his chair, and when everyone else had retired to bed, he fell into the fire and was cremated on the spot.

David Harris was one of the quicker bowlers of his time, and there is a fine action picture of him in The Bat and Ball pub, looking very much like a baseball pitcher, with his foot raised and arm drawn back. He would probably have delivered the ball at a fair speed, and no doubt the wicket-keepers would be made to hop about a bit because they didn't wear pads in those days.

One of the biggest heroes was James Aylward, who made 167 when Hambledon scored their most comprehensive victory over All England by an innings and 168 runs over three days in June 1777. Remarkably, the scorecard for the game shows him batting at number ten, but in those class-conscious days the batsmen were listed according to their status, not where they actually batted. In other words, not so much a batting order as a social pecking order. Aylward was a lowly gardener, so his name was relegated to near the bottom of the scorecard, despite his match-winning innings. On the other hand, top of the order was

The exterior of the famous Bat and Ball Inn

Lord Tankerville, one of the patrons, who probably batted somewhere more befitting his score, which was 3.

Incidentally, it was shortly after Aylward's 167 that the middle stump was introduced. I wonder if this was because the England bowlers had kept finding the gap between the original two?

In the formative days it was all underarm bowling and because the ball rolled mainly along the ground the batting action, with a curved bat, was more of a sweep. Not the sweep we know today, going down on one knee and playing the ball backwards of square, but sweeping as with a brush. The playing surface was not anywhere like as good as today. The pitches were rolled with stone rollers but remained quite bumpy so, as you can imagine, there were quite a lot of extras and overthrows. Because of that, they always had a long-stop, like we used to do when we played as kids in the local field.

I learned that the umpire at the bowler's end did not stand behind the stumps, but halfway between the wickets and mid-on. Just as well there were no lbws. That rule was not introduced until the nineteenth century. But there must have been pressures on umpires even in those days, with fifty guineas – or about £5,000 in today's money – very often riding on the result.

It is remarkable how little the game has changed since those laws were first formulated at Broadhalfpenny Down. We keep thinking that we have moved on so much but in many ways cricket is very much the same as it was then. The one big change came as long ago as 1830 when they started bowling round arm. That altered the character of the game.

We also think that match-fixing, sledging and crowd invasions are curses of the modern game but, according to historians such as John Ford, matches were thrown, decisions disputed, and sledging was commonplace 250 years ago, while spectators regularly flooded on to the pitch. They used to have stewards on the Hambledon boundary to prevent people who had gambled on the outcome running on and interfering with play. It was quite common, for example, for a spectator who had wagered money on a batting-side victory to run and stop the ball just before the fielder reached it because the umpire would then have to award a four. So there was nothing new in the pitch invasions that blighted the game when England entertained Pakistan in 2001.

Women also used to play regularly in the early days. In 1745 there is a record of a game between Hambledon Maids and Bramley Maids – the forerunner of the MCC Ladies v. Sirens encounter. And the girls are still trying, after more than 250 years, to be taken seriously.

Women's cricket is often regarded, even now, as something of a joke by men whose opinions are based on the differences in sheer power and physique which makes it impossible for the two sexes to compete on anything like equal terms. I have always maintained that, in all things, one sex is no better than the other – just different. And I can say, with some authority from first-hand knowledge, that the fairer sex play a pretty mean game of cricket. While they lack the strength of their male counterparts and cannot achieve the same pace with their bowling, or power with their batting, those at the top have tremendous ability.

The first Women's World Cup was staged in England in 1973 and I was proud to be invited to umpire at the 1981 event in New Zealand. The match between England and Australia remains one of my fondest memories. Competing so seriously, women obviously need the same sort of body protection as men, plus a little bit extra. Denise Alderman, sister of the great Australian Test bowler Terry, was batting at the time, and the England bowler, wicket-keeper and close fielders all went up for a catch behind. I heard some contact, but was not certain that the ball had touched the bat. It did not give the right sound. So I said not out.

When Denise came down to my end a little later she looked at me and grinned. 'Great decision, Dickie,' she said. 'The ball hit my chest protector.' Well, you've got to keep abreast of the times.

Speaking of which reminds me of a conversation I had about the problems of modern umpiring with Graeme Wright, editor of *Wisden*. Despite what some people might think, Graeme did not feel that player behaviour is getting worse. In fact, since the introduction of the match referee, he thought it had improved. However, if they are not becoming more unruly, players certainly do not make the umpires' task any easier by making decisions for them. That was why it is becoming increasingly difficult to be an umpire.

When I was playing, I always knew if the ball had feathered my glove so, if I thought the catch had been taken cleanly, I walked. Brian Sellers, our captain at Yorkshire, was an old-fashioned amateur and he had standards. If you knew you were out, on your bike. He drilled that into us. And we did as we were told or ran the risk of never playing for the county again. In those days, if an umpire asked a batsman a question, he would tell the truth. Nowadays, while the players don't exactly lie, they say, 'I don't know. You're the umpire. You're paid to make those decisions.'

In the same way, umpires tend to hide behind the safety net of action replays. The third umpire has become more important than the officials out there in the middle. It is particularly blatant with run-outs. I used to train down at Barnsley Football Club doing fifteen-yard bursts so that I would be quick enough to get in position to judge a run-out. They don't bother now. They just stand behind the stumps, knowing that they can always call on the third umpire.

At the same time, I have to say that I have always thought that the

Wisden wisdom from the last three editors, Matthew Engel, John Woodcock and Graeme Wright.

close run-out is the most difficult decision an umpire has to make, and the cameras can be a big help. It is hard to judge in such instances because you have to be watching the sliding bat, the gloves of the wicket-keeper, the ball and the stumps at the same time. If it is really close, it is an almost impossible decision to give with the naked eye. In these circumstances, I'm not sure that even the batsman knows whether he is out or not. So, if the help is there, who can criticise the umpires for taking advantage of it? I still feel that they are calling for that help when it is not necessary, and I would like to see umpires having more confidence in their own judgement.

However, when it comes to the use of electronic and computer wizardry in decision-making, I have a particular bee in my bonnet. It's to do with Hawkeye, which is used by television 'experts' to assess lbws, and has been talked of as a possible official aid for umpires.

Let me say this – unless you are at eye level with what is happening twenty-two yards away, you do not have the best picture. The camera is elevated and is therefore looking down. The angle is wrong. That is one reason why Hawkeye cannot judge on lbw decisions. And there are many other things to be taken into consideration – where the bowler delivered the ball from; how much it swung in the air; how much it jagged off the seam; what it had done the previous five balls of the over.

Graeme took up the theme. 'Groundsmen tell you that by using different soils you get different bounces, even on the same twenty-two yards. You can get a pocket of air – a spot where the ball hardly bounces at all – and another where it might fly. You can't be sure that just because a ball lands six yards from the stumps it is going over the top. In theory it should; the mathematics may tell you it should; but it doesn't work like that. Every ball is different. The ball gets softer, for example, and Darren Gough bowls a terrific slower ball which is obviously not going to bounce the same as his quicker deliveries. You have big guys and shorter guys, and that, too, has to be taken into account.'

An umpire, you see, does take all these things into consideration before making his decision. Does Hawkeye? Does it heck.

As Graeme so eloquently put it, 'You have all the latest technology available, but don't forget that technology was being used in the Gulf War and they still didn't hit what they thought they were going to hit.'

With lbw decisions, the experience of the umpire should be the key factor. There are times when an umpire is not sure so he gives the batsman not out. That is how I operated. Always the batsman had the benefit of any doubt. That's how it should be. You have to be a hundred per cent certain in your mind.

I wouldn't want to face up to the quickies with this old bat.

Having said all this, we have to be aware that technology has brought a bigger audience to the game. People who don't understand it are being helped immensely by all the graphics and so on, but we have to be very careful with it.

I believe that the camera angle is still probably the most important aspect. Take that disputed catch by Mark Waugh in the Headingley Test of 2001. I have known Mark since he first came in to Test cricket, and he is as honest as the day is long. He always walks if he knows he's got a nick. So when he told me the following day that he had taken that catch fairly, I believed him – especially as I had just bought a new 38-inch television and, although my eyes are not what they used to be, I'd seen an action replay of the ball going into his hands as clean as a whistle. Yet unbelievably the third umpire gave the batsman not out. The only explanation I can offer is that the picture he saw came from a camera that was either not in the right place or not at the right angle.

Said Graeme, 'I always think that first impressions are usually right.

You get that instinctive reaction, that gut feeling. The more you look at replay after replay the harder it gets. The doubts grow.'

Despite his reservations, however, Graeme was of the opinion that the technological argument would eventually win the day, and that even lbw decisions would be decided in that fashion, not for cricketing reasons but because television goes everywhere and you can't stop people using technology.

'You can't have two games. You can't have one game on the ground and another that's going out to millions of people at home, who are going to look at decisions over and over again. It will devalue the game if people think that the umpire is getting it wrong more often than not, even though that may not be the case.'

With lbw decisions, Graeme believes they will allow the umpire in the middle to talk to the third umpire whenever there is an appeal. Hawkeye will do its thing, which takes under a minute, and the third umpire will report back, 'It pitched in line, height looks good, but you have the final decision.'

Arbitration will thus be left to the official out there, who will have the evidence provided by technology to add to the evidence of his own eyes and experience. Sounds reasonable but I'm still not convinced. I've watched Hawkeye, and most of the play-backs show the ball hitting the stumps. If we took notice of Hawkeye, Test matches would be over in a day and a half.

I remember one Benson & Hedges match being rained off, so we decided the issue with a bowling competition. The bowlers couldn't hit the stumps for love nor money and I thought to myself, 'How on earth could anyone give this lot lbw decisions? They can't even hit the stumps when there's no batsman.'

Graeme is a New Zealander very much involved with the game in this country, and I was interested to hear what he had to say about the state of English cricket. He told me, 'Coming from outside and not growing up in county cricket, I look at the situation from the view-point of someone who loves the game and likes to see good cricket played. And there is not enough of that at county level, which is the level before Test cricket.'

The answer, Graeme suggests, is to have fewer counties – maybe only twelve – and make the competition tougher, so that it brings through the cream of young players. He concedes that the decision to have two divisions has made the game more competitive, but that does not mean that standards have been raised.

For all Graeme's pessimism, there are some exciting prospects around, including Steve Kirby of Yorkshire. Here is a player full of the self-belief that Graeme feels so many Englishmen lack. With England trailing 2–0 in the Ashes series of 2001, he called me over during a Yorkshire practice session at Headingley. 'Mr Bird,' he said, 'you know the selectors, don't you?' I told him I did. 'Well, do you want to win this series?' That, I replied, went without saying. 'Right,' he proclaimed, 'tell them selectors to pick me and I'll win the series for you.'

What an attitude to find in a kid of only twenty-one. What confidence. Cocky, maybe, but isn't it wonderful to have that self-belief? It's the Australian way. When Yorkshire played Lancashire in a Roses match at Headingley, he knocked Michael Atherton's castle over twice. The second time, as Athers walked past him, Kirby grunted, 'I thought I read somewhere that you could bat.' This from a lad who had only just got into the Yorkshire team. No wonder they hauled him in front of the committee. But he is a really good prospect. If his aggression can be channelled in the right direction, he could be top-class.

Some of the best captains and batsmen have been amateurs, including Peter May.

Although Graeme admits that there is no way it can now be changed, he has never been keen on the game being fully professional, and I agree with him. The best captains I played under were all amateurs, and some of the best batsmen were also amateurs. Peter May, Colin Cowdrey and Ted Dexter are the prime examples.

Graeme also mentioned that youngsters are no longer inclined to listen to, and learn from, the more experienced players on the county circuit. Ray Illingworth, for example, learned the game by apprenticeship, and when he became captain of Yorkshire he could not understand why the young players did not want to talk about the game with him. After all, he had been a particularly good England captain with tremendous knowledge.

I learned by talking to people such as Illy, Len Hutton, Johnny Wardle, Brian Close, Maurice Leyland and Arthur Mitchell – people who knew the game. But that apprenticeship style has gone. Kids now think they know it all straightaway. They are unwilling to learn from the old hands, as we did in the past.

The Aussies, on the other hand, worship older players, wherever they come from. I remember Steve Waugh inviting Mike Brearley into the Australian dressing-room at Lord's to discuss the art of captaincy. He wanted to learn from a man who had done it successfully. It didn't matter one jot that he was English.

It was the same with me and my old mate Dennis Lillee. I was prepared to give him advice and he was prepared to listen. Take that time at Edgbaston in 1975, when Lillee played a big part in destroying England on a rain-affected pitch. Helped by the conditions on the second day, he took 3 for 13 from my end in an unbelievable spell as England slumped to 83 for 7. He had been bowling far too short in those conditions until I told him to pitch 'em up.

My words of wisdom did not exactly endear me to the England players, however. I wondered if they might have been responsible for demoting my bust at the Lord's museum.

Mike Brearley, master tactician, places his field. Steve Waugh once invited him into the Aussie dressing-room at Lord's to glean some tips on the art of captaincy.

So that's where it is! My bronze bust at Lord's, now safely under lock and key.

I am talking about a bronze bust, sculpted by the son of former Northamptonshire wicket-keeper Keith Andrew. I was determined to find out what had happened to it, so I paid Lord's a visit. I thought it best to find the curator Stephen Green – a starry-eyed youngster once addressed him as 'creator', which he felt was slightly over the top. He would know.

Sure enough, Stephen was able to lead me to where it had been switched from its prime site near the entrance. It had a new resting place in a cabinet along with all the rest of the umpires' and scorers' memorabilia.

'Thought you'd be safer in there,' he said. 'After all, you must be our second most famous exhibit after the Ashes urn. And we keep that under lock and key.'

People seeing the urn for the first time are apt to exclaim, 'Is that all there is to it?' It really is tiny. However, if there was a fire Stephen said it was the first thing he would grab, which, as he admitted, is a rather silly remark when you think about it – Ashes to ashes and all that.

Most cricket enthusiasts know how the Ashes originated, but I was still fascinated to hear Stephen's account of it. England had been beaten at home by Australia for the first time, losing at The Oval in 1882, and the Sporting Times put a mock obituary in its columns saying that English cricket had done so badly it must have died and the ashes been carted off to Australia.

Said Stephen, 'It was, oddly enough, just at the time that parliament had passed a Commission Act to legalise the cremation of human bodies, so it was a typically macabre Victorian joke.'

Consequently, when we sent a team out to Australia the following English winter, some ladies in Melbourne burnt a bail, put it in an urn and gave all the bits and pieces to the England captain, who later married one of those ladies and went on to become Lord Derby. When he died, his widow decided to donate the urn to Lord's, and there it has remained ever since.

'So you see,' said Stephen, 'it is not a trophy in the ordinary sense of the word. It doesn't normally change hands. But it does exist as the ashes of a bail and it is still our most famous exhibit.'

The urn was loaned to Australia in 1988 for their bicentenary – the MCC cadged a lift for it on the royal plane – and the Ashes have also been to the Victoria and Albert Museum. There has been pressure from the Australians for the Ashes to be held by the team winning the series of Tests between the two old rivals, but Stephen reflected, 'The urn is very fragile, so we don't really want to see it being moved around. In any case, a lot of Australians see it here. Whether or not it ever goes back to Australia is up to the committee. But this would seem to be the best – and safest – place for the Ashes.'

There is a wonderful photograph in the museum, taken on board ship, of the first England team to tour North America, and Stephen observed that if they had known what was ahead of them they probably would not have gone. Apparently, their ship struck an iceberg and at one point someone is reported to have remarked that 'the sea would benefit from a heavy roller'.

Also on display is the earliest version of the laws of cricket, which reminded me of my Hambledon trip, but what really caught my eye was a beautiful bowl, commissioned, so it is thought, by Sir Thomas Lord himself. Stephen told me there are two reasons for this. Firstly, under the Union flag is the word 'Thirkses', which does not appear to make any sense until you recall that Thomas Lord was born at Thirsk. The theory is that the Chinese potter spelled the word wrongly. Secondly, on the side of the bowl is a painting of a cricket match, and according to the British Museum, this is the only known piece of Chinese export pottery which features such a scene.

The Lord's museum houses a film theatre in memory of that fine cricket commentator Brian Johnston, and there is a plaque of him on the wall. It is a terrific likeness. I thought they had done his nose particularly well. I also liked the painting of Sir Colin Cowdrey. It captures his kindness but it has him looking slightly puzzled – as he always was. The painting of Graham Gooch is rather more controversial. That marvellous cricket writer and broadcaster E.W. Swanton was apoplectic when he saw it. He raged about Gooch not having had the decency to have a shave before the picture was painted.

Upstairs I found a painting that features many of the great English players. Stephen reflected, 'It's probably my favourite. Apart from anything else it was economical to bundle them all together in one painting, but still interesting to do what the Victorians would call a conversation piece. It also shows that we caught a number of people in the nick of time. Fifty per cent of those in the picture are now dead.'

I had no trouble in identifying them all. The four in the background are Bill Edrich, Ken Barrington, Len Hutton and Jim Laker. The others are Godfrey Evans, Trevor Bailey, Peter May, Brian Statham, Denis Compton, Alec Bedser, Colin Cowdrey, Fred Trueman, Ted Dexter and Tom Graveney. What a team you could have picked from that lot. Hutton and Edrich to open; a choice of May, Cowdrey, Compton, Graveney and Barrington for the rest of the upper and middle order;

Coming more up to date, the painting of Graham Gooch gave E.W. Swanton apoplexy.

Dexter or Bailey as the all-rounder; Evans as wicket-keeper; Laker providing the spin; Bedser the medium pace; and Trueman and Statham the opening strike force. Wow!

There is a more recent Long Room group, but the artist decided he needed a spectator to make it more authentic, and, for better or worse, he persuaded Stephen to pose. So there he is, surrounded by top cricketers of his time. I think he was chuffed to bits to be asked – and now he takes great pride in asking visitors if they can spot the odd one out.

Another painting of a group of players includes those three great Yorkshiremen, Geoff Boycott, Ray Illingworth and Brian Close. Rumour has it that Boycs sat at the back because he wouldn't be painted sitting at the front with Illy and Closey, but Stephen put me right. 'The trouble with Geoff was that he didn't come at all. The artist added him to the picture afterwards.'

Stephen moved on to an eye-catching painting of the England v. Australia match at Lord's in the 1880s. The old pavilion is visible in the background. W.G. Grace is batting and everybody who was anybody is in the picture – including the Prince and Princess of Wales. Stephen pointed out, quite mischievously I thought, that in the foreground you

Look carefully and you'll see you have three pictures in one. How many faces can you put a name to in the foreground grouping?

So colourful clothing wasn't a Packer invention, as these dapper lads of 1880 reveal, dominated as ever by a bearded W.G. Grace.

could see the Prince's lady friend, Lillie Langtry, tactfully turning away as he passes with his wife. Well, it simply wasn't cricket, was it?

I paused before a smaller version of a painting that hung in the Long Room and stretched out my arm towards it. Stephen nearly had a Dickie fit. He thought I was going to touch it and he had visions of all the alarms going off, bells ringing, police sirens wailing, and people frantically dashing about trying to prevent one of the most famous

The Prince and Princess of Wales at an England v. Australia match at Lord's. In the foreground, the Prince's mistress Lillie Langtry tactfully averts her gaze.

exhibits from being stolen. I was, I maintained, simply pointing out the lovely expression on the little boy's face in that picture of 'The Toss'. Had I reached a little further, I have a feeling that I would have been the one being tossed – right out of the building.

There is also a charming tableau showing a straw-boatered MCC member having a picnic and, of course, picnic parties have always been great occasions on match days at Lord's. On close inspection, however, this particular spectator, glasses slipping off his nose, had apparently dozed off in the warm afternoon sun. Either Boycott was batting, or the Pimms had taken effect.

An additional room is dedicated to the one hundred Lord's Test matches, and I was delighted to find a Dickie Bird toby jug in a display cabinet there. One of the best exhibitions held in that room, recalled with great affection by Stephen, was on the occasion of the 150th anniversary of W.G. Grace's birth, when all the surviving Graces were brought together. He recalled, 'They were so nice, really sweet. There was W.G.'s granddaughter, who was then the last living person to know him well. She was ninety-three at the time. I remember that she and Jim Swanton had a very enjoyable conversation. It was one of my happiest days here. It was a very curious mixture

Lord's today with its space-capsule media centre.

Lord's, my second home.

The Cricketers Almanack of 1864, the very first *Wisden*, in the Lord's library.

because it was held on the day of the charity match arranged as a tribute to Princess Diana, but it was certainly a great success all round.'

In the library, I was intrigued to find a full set of *Wisden*, including the original, the title page of which does not indicate any special emphasis on cricket, referring also to horse racing, bowls, quoits – even knur and spell, a game which is still played in some parts of the north, including Barnsley.

The stained-glass window just inside the entrance is another pride and joy of the museum. Stephen recalled that it was installed at a time when the IRA were very active and Lord's received an urgent message from Downing Street not to let people know when John Major, then the prime minister, was going to unveil it.

'There were two snags,' said Stephen. 'One was that Dennis Silk, the MCC president, had just given the date out at a club dinner attended by a hundred and fifty people. The other was that the bally window had the date of the opening inscribed on it. Thankfully, John Major is still alive and kicking.'

In all my years as a player and umpire I had never thought too much about the history of the game, but my visits to Hambledon and the Lord's museum, and my chat with Graeme Wright, reminded me of just how great a part cricket has played in the life of our nation throughout the last 350 years or so.

CHAPTER 6

SPREADING THE WORD

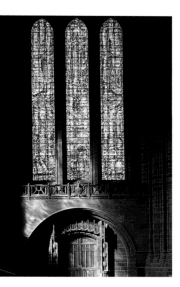

Left and above: David Sheppard's Anglican Cathedral in Liverpool.

Right: The pulpit area in the lovely new Methodist Church in Staincross where I worship today.

MY Christian faith has always played a big part in my life. I suppose it was the way I was brought up. My parents took my two sisters, Marjorie and Sylvia, and me to the Elim Pentecostal church in Barnsley every Sunday. Now I go to the Methodist church in Staincross. Two churches in the village joined together a few years ago and last year there was great excitement when a new church building was opened by the former president of the Methodist Conference, the Reverend Inderjit Bhogal. The members had performed miracles to raise £650,000 in five years and it was a great example of what faith – and prayer – can do.

During my travels around the world, I have always looked for a place to go to worship. I particularly remember a Methodist church in Barbados. It was jam-packed, with women in their Sunday finery and chaps in their best suits. I sat at the back. The preacher stood up and everyone waited expectantly for him to begin the service.

'Brothers and sisters,' he said. 'We have a great surprise for you today.'

A loud 'oooh' echoed round the church.

'Yes, brothers and sisters, we have in our midst Mr Dickie Bird, the Test umpire from England.'

At once the congregation stood up and clapped and cheered. I couldn't believe it. And after the service I couldn't get away. Everyone wanted to talk to me. It was a great feeling. There I was, thousands of miles away from home, yet among so many friends. That is what belonging to a church family means, and I believe my faith has helped me through many dark times.

It is not easy, being a Christian in sport, as the Reverend Andrew Wingfield Digby will tell you. He has found living his faith in cricket a constant struggle and challenge. It has been very hard for him. But he faced up to the challenge and is now a director of an organisation called Christians in Sport, which has links with 150 countries around the world. Andrew was brought up in church, his father being the vicar of Sherborne, in Dorset, but he did not become a Christian until he worked with the Reverend David Sheppard at a family centre in Canning Town in the period between leaving school and going to college. David Sheppard is the England cricketer who went on to become the Bishop of Liverpool, and with his help and under his guidance, Andrew was introduced to a new way of life.

I remember Andrew playing against Leicestershire in 1975, when he edged one to wicket-keeper Roger Tolchard, who took a good catch.

'Shit!' spluttered Andrew.

'I beg your pardon,' said Roger. 'It is true, isn't it, that you're going to be a vicar?'

Andrew Wingfield Digby, wicket-taking Rev. and tested Test chaplain.

'Yes,' replied Andrew.

'Well, then, you can't use language like that.'

'You should have heard what I used to say,' retorted Andrew.

During that same year, Andrew decided to go forward for ordination to the Church of England, and he went to see his sponsor, the Bishop of Salisbury, who was keen on cricket.

'I think it would be a good idea if you went and studied at Ridley Hall, Cambridge, where David Sheppard went,' the Bishop said.

Andrew recoiled. 'Ridley Hall?' he echoed. 'Fenner's? I'll never get a wicket at Fenner's. I'm going back to Oxford – it's an absolute minefield at The Parks.'

'My dear boy,' remonstrated the Bishop, 'that's no way to choose your theological college.'

But Andrew got his wish, and two years later found himself playing for Oxford University against Glamorgan at The Parks. At that time, Glamorgan had a wonderful bowler called Tony Cordle, who was the only West Indian I have ever met with a Welsh accent. It was the day before the Queen's Silver Jubilee and Oxford were 60 for 6 on a wet day. Andrew had just gone in at number eight. Tony ran past, bowled, and the player at the other end missed. As he walked back to his mark, Tony said to Andrew, 'I want to go to church tomorrow.' He ran in again, the batsman played and missed, and as he walked past Andrew this time, Tony remarked, 'You're going to be a vicar, aren't you? Then you should be able to tell me where to go to church tomorrow.' Before Andrew could reply Tony was on his way again.

Andrew thought he had better act quickly. If he didn't strike while the iron was hot Tony might change his mind. So after the next ball, Andrew walked back with him, explaining as he did so where they could meet next morning to go to church. Only then did he realise he was twenty-five yards behind the umpire at the start of the bowler's run-up. So he was forced to run with him.

'It was a very funny sight,' he chuckled. 'There was Tony tearing in to bowl, and there was I, charging in alongside him, separating only as we reached the crease. To cap it all, he still didn't turn up for church next morning.'

Christians in Sport came into being in the late seventies when Andrew and a number of other similarly minded people came to the conclusion that there was a gulf between the world of sport and the church. They argued that Christian faith and sport could go together, and there are some high-profile people who are proof of this – Jonathan Edwards and Kriss Akabusi in athletics, Bernhard Langer in golf, Chris Powell (Charlton Athletic) in football, Ian Bishop in cricket, and Stephanie Cook in the modern pentathlon.

Incidentally, Andrew told me that he was once very tempted to run an article on Ian Bishop in one of the Christians in Sport magazines with the headline, 'At last, a Bishop who believes in the Resurrection', but he chickened out, which may be just as well.

Christians in Sport remains a growing concern, with branches all over the country. It attracts a lot of young people for whom the organisation runs camps which fly in the face of current opinion.

Said Andrew, 'When I went to camp as a youngster, because I was reasonably good at cricket, I was made to bat right-handed instead of with my natural left, in order to give all the other lads a chance. The theory was that you had to be nice to people. Competition was bad – let the other chap win. But this concept of non-competitiveness has been disastrous. It has helped to kill sport in school. So now we have reversed the trend. We tell the young people that God has given them a talent, so they should use it. They should be as good as they possibly can be. People learn how to deal with life through success and failure. You have to learn to win, and how to win. And you have to learn to lose, and how to lose.'

Mind you, having played for Dorset and Oxford University, Andrew has had plenty of practice in learning how to lose. It has not been a problem for him. He recalled how, when he was first made captain of Dorset, they were faced with an opening fixture against Shropshire, and he sat in the dressing room telling his players, 'Right, lads. Let's get off to a good start. We can win this one.'

They all looked at him in amazement. Dorset? Winning? The two words simply did not go together. But they did go on to win the Minor Counties one-day knockout competition, the Holt Trophy, that year – 1988 – and it was the high point of Andrew's career.

'There may have been only three men and a dog watching the final at Weymouth, but we actually won something, and it was a great feeling.'

Andrew has been involved with the England cricket team, to varying degrees, since 1991. Ted Dexter, who had been in charge of the tour of Australia which had resulted in another decisive 4–1 Ashes defeat, met a Baptist minister there who said he was the chaplain for the Australian team. That set Ted thinking. Maybe what England needed was not a complete new set of players, but a chaplain. So he rang Andrew, who told me, 'Ted is an extraordinary chap with a very active mind. He can have twenty-five ideas before breakfast, most of which are completely useless. But he does occasionally hit the jackpot.'

What Ted envisaged was a spiritual adviser who would have the same impact on the team as David Sheppard had as a player in the 1950s. Andrew pitched up at Lord's for the first match of the summer series against the West Indies in a terribly nervous state, wondering how to justify his existence. He knocked on the door of the England dressing-room and a voice shouted, 'Come in.' He entered to find Ian Botham lying on a couch, surrounded by the rest of the players. On seeing Andrew, Both propped himself up and exclaimed, 'Ah, Wingers, great to see you. Lamby and I will both sing in the choir.' And that broke the ice.

When Raymond Illingworth took over as team manager, Andrew had to explain once again exactly what his role was. They met at Trent Bridge on the first day of a Test and had a friendly chat. The next day Andrew had another engagement, and on the Saturday he was playing at Fenner's. He was on his way back from that game when a Daily Mail reporter rang him on his mobile and asked if he had anything to say about being sacked as England chaplain. Andrew told him he did not know what he was talking about.

On the Monday morning, Garry Richardson rang from Radio Four. 'Could you give us a comment on why you've been sacked by Ray Illingworth?' Obviously he could do no such thing because he still had no idea what was going on.

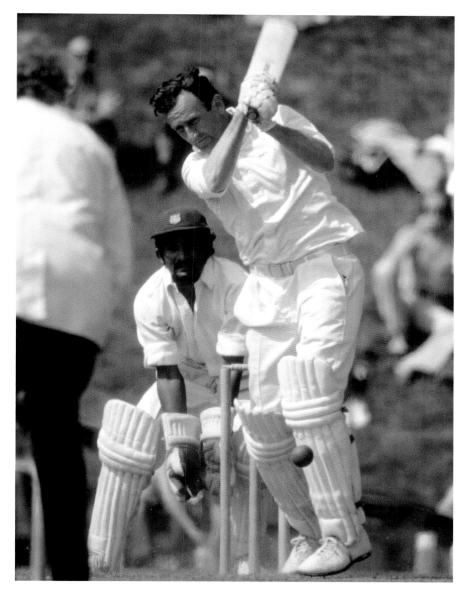

Ted Dexter, who often had twenty-five ideas before breakfast, decided English cricket needed a spiritual adviser.

On the way to his office he was caught up in a traffic jam and a chap stranded in an adjacent car wound down his window and asked, 'Hey, are you Andrew Wingfield Digby?'

Andrew preened himself. How marvellous, he thought, to be recognised by this complete stranger. Fame at last. But when Andrew admitted to his identity the guy exclaimed, 'I thought it was. Your picture's in the *Sun*. It says "Knickers to the Vicar".'

It turned out that on the Friday, a journalist had remarked mischievously to Illingworth, 'No sign of Wingers today then?' And Raymond, being the blunt Yorkshireman that he is, replied, 'No, we tough chaps don't need a shoulder to cry on.' End of conversation.

But the journalist went back to the press room and said, 'Hey, great story, lads. You know Raymond's banned mobile phones and dark glasses? Well, now he's banned the vicar as well.'

When they tackled Raymond about it at the press conference later that day, he said he did not think there was much need for a chaplain. So, as there had been no official appointment in the first place – it was completely voluntary – Andrew ended up being sacked from a job he didn't have.

TCCB chief Alan Smith rang him immediately to apologise for 'a little bit of an administrative cock-up', and, stubborn though he might be, Raymond also contacted Andrew soon afterwards to pour oil on troubled waters. 'Sorry, Rev., to have landed you in it. Didn't mean to. As far as I'm concerned the door is still open to you. Come and go exactly as you want.'

When they next met, Illy asked, 'What exactly are you trying to do, Andrew? Is it your intention to be a crutch for weak people?'

Andrew assured him that was the last thing he wanted. He told Illy that the hardest thing in the world was to follow Jesus. Jesus was tough, being a Christian was tough, and he wanted the players to be tough through finding God, to become the people that God wanted them to be.

Said Illy, 'So you want them to become Christians?'

'I do.'

'Well, you can take it from me that I'm not that bothered myself.' There was a pause. 'But I don't mind if they do.'

Once he understood Andrew's motives he was fine about the situation, but as it turned out it didn't really matter anyway. Shortly afterwards, Illy was relieved of his position as chairman of selectors.

There were no problems when David Lloyd was appointed manager because Andrew was already a great friend of his, and, with Michael Atherton as captain, the door was always open. It has, he admits, not been quite as easy with the combination of Duncan Fletcher and Nasser Hussain.

It was in the aftermath of Atherton's marathon match-saving ten and a half hour knock in Johannesburg on the 1995-96 tour of South Africa – one of the greatest backs-to-the-wall innings of all time – that the skipper was invited by Andrew to join him and John Barclay for a day's fishing. Being absolutely exhausted he agreed. He thought it might be an ideal way to relax.

'He had never been fishing in his life,' recalled Andrew, 'and how he didn't drown I'll never know because he was constantly falling into the water. But in that fantastic setting, in the middle of nowhere, Mike caught the bug – as well as a few fish. Now he's become a fanatical angler.'

Athers was later thrilled to catch his first salmon when the three of them went fishing in Scotland. He was so excited and so proud. He put his fish on the river bank and went to fetch Andrew and John, who were fishing further upstream. 'I've got one, I've got one,' he shouted. But when they returned to view the trophy, they were met with a very sorry sight. All that remained of the fish were the bones. Beside it stood Andrew's dog, looking very sheepish.

'Thankfully, it has not put Mike off,' said Andrew. 'He still loves the sport. So he's a convert to angling, at least.'

Andrew had earlier spoken in glowing terms of the Right Reverend David Sheppard, who played for his country twenty-two times between 1950 and 1963 and was the Bishop of Liverpool for twenty-two years between 1975 and 1997. I remember my first meeting with him when I was an up-and-coming youngster on the Yorkshire staff and he was an up-and-coming curate, playing just bits and pieces of cricket. I was thrilled in later years when he agreed to appear on the 'Songs of Praise' programme on BBC Television which revolved around my life and faith, and it remains one of my warmest memories to have chatted

Equally highly respected as an England opener and a radical bishop, the Right Reverend David Sheppard.

to him in his garden on that day, just before his retirement. It was a wonderful privilege.

As an umpire I had lots of difficult decisions to make, but David was faced with a massive one when it became a choice between cricket and the church. However, he told me, 'By the time it came to making that decision, going into the church was the thing I most wanted to do in the whole world.'

Even so, when he went away to be ordained he could hardly have dreamed that he would continue playing cricket for England. He chuckled, 'They kept having disasters and calling me up for the last two games of a series.'

Freddie Trueman was not too impressed with David's slip-catching prowess, and after seeing yet another chance put down he strolled over and muttered, 'I did think, Reverend, that when you, of all people, put yer 'ands together, you'd mek it stick.'

I asked David if there was anything he had been able to take from cricket into the church that had helped him, and he replied, 'Two things. Firstly, you need great powers of concentration in order to build up an innings and make a lot of runs. You have to shut everything else out. And I believe that ability to concentrate has helped me in my church work. Secondly, cricket is very much a team game, and I have found that experience very valuable, as I have had to enter into a lot of partnerships in my work and life as a bishop.'

Taking important stands had been quite a test for him. One example is the public declaration he made about playing cricket against South Africa when the apartheid issue was a hot topic of the day. He told me, 'I had always thought of Christian faith as something personal and private, so it was a very big step for me to go public on such matters. It was exactly the opposite of how we had been brought up as sportsmen – no religion, no politics, just get on with the game.'

People often think of Christians as boring, with no fun at all in their lives. Well, you certainly cannot say that about either Andrew Wingfield Digby or David Sheppard – or me, for that matter. I have had a lot of laughs meeting and talking with other Christians of all denominations.

Elsewhere in this book you will come across a vicar in Wales who was anything but boring, and one of the Methodist ministers in the Barnsley circuit, the cricket-loving Derek Hinchliffe, had me in stitches with the following story.

It was a dark and foggy night at sea. A ship was sailing along when the helmsman saw a bright light ahead. Immediately he realised that the ship was heading for a collision, so he radioed to the source of the approaching light, 'Get out of my way. Alter course two degrees sou'-by-sou'-west.'

Back came the reply, 'No, you get out of my way. Alter course two degrees nor'-by-nor'-east.'

The ship's helmsman was angry and repeated his order. 'Alter course two degrees sou'-by-sou'-west.'

He received the same reply. 'If you know what's good for you, alter course two degrees nor'-by-nor'-east.'

The helmsman summoned the captain, who spoke indignantly over the radio. 'Get out of my way. Alter course two degrees sou'-by-sou'-west.'

The lights were coming closer together and the captain yelled down the radio, 'For the last time, I'm ordering you to alter your course. This is the captain speaking, and this is a very large ocean-going liner.'

Back came the response, 'That may well be. But I still think it would be better if you altered course. I'm the lighthouse keeper.'

The beautiful entrance to Westminster Abbey. I was deeply moved when I went to the memorial service at the Abbey for my old friend Colin Cowdrey.

CHAPTER 7

MY WHITE ROSE WORLD

Sunrise on the River Ure at Middleham, North Yorkshire

Right: Proud as punch outside Barnsley Town Hall with the scroll that gives me the freedom of the borough.

Left: A thriving modern city. I still feel as if I am stepping back in time when I visit York Minster.

SOME people find it strange that I have never felt the urge to live anywhere other than Barnsley. I suppose many of them think of Barnsley as a typical mining town – dirty, dreary, dowdy, surrounded by slag heaps and populated by families with umpteen kids and pet whippets. Maybe in my young days that was not too far from the truth. But the people were the salt of the earth, honest and straight as a die. They would never say anything behind your back. If they had any criticism it was to your face, and if you were in trouble there was always a helping hand. The pits may have gone, and there is no doubt that the running down of the mining industry caused severe problems in the area, but the people have not changed. They are still as warm-hearted as ever. I have a lot of time for them. You would be hard pushed to find a friendlier bunch anywhere in the world.

That is why I am immensely proud to have been given the freedom of the Borough of Barnsley. It is an honour that means more to me than people realise.

Now the slag heaps have been covered with grass and trees, and more places with a countryside feel have been added to the beautiful areas already surrounding the town. Within easy reach there is some of the loveliest scenery you could wish for. I can look out of my cottage window in the village of Staincross, three miles from Barnsley, and I can see the start of the Pennine chain. You could hardly ask for a better view.

But then, you can travel the length and breadth of the broad acres and you will be stirred to echo those sentiments. For example, the North Yorkshire moors are an absolute delight. As for the Dales, I read recently of an Australian who described his best day out as being his first visit to that part of the world where he had been bowled over by his mini tour of James Herriot country, which he had previously only read about. He said he found himself spellbound by one particular view from Grinton. He had never seen anything like it, and he felt on top of the world as he looked down from Sutton Bank later in the day. I know how he felt. The Dales with their rivers, patchwork fields, dry-stone walls, picturesque villages, friendly pubs, market towns and the contrasting moorland have a magic of their own. I'll never tire of it. In addition, places such as York and Whitby provide a sense of history. If you could guarantee the weather, such is the beauty of Yorkshire's east-coast resorts that I doubt half as many people would be tripping off to the Med for their holidays in the sun.

So many wonderful memories are here, at Headingley, shared on this occasion with Yorkshire CC chairman, Keith Moss.

As a youngster, it was a great thrill to be in the same nets as the likes of Ray Illingworth (*left*) and Brian Close.

I was born in Barnsley, I was brought up in Barnsley and I have everything I need here. Why should I look elsewhere? I have travelled all round the world, but I have always looked forward to coming back. It has always felt marvellous to walk up my pathway, unlock the door, throw my gear into the kitchen, put the kettle on and slump into my favourite armchair. I think, there, I'm back home. It has always been my home and it will remain so until the day I die because, for me, it is the best little town in the world.

I go into the village, or nip into town, and people will greet me with 'Good old Dickie' or 'Look out, here's Dickie with his bags of shopping' or 'Ey up, Dickie, how's things?' It's simply great to be among friends like that, to feel wanted and at home. I can honestly say that nowhere along the way have I felt an urge to pack up and leave.

I have a similar feeling for Yorkshire. There is no better county as far as I am concerned and I am proud to be a Yorkshireman – some may say a typical Yorkshireman. I'm sometimes too blunt for my own good and I'm not easily parted with my brass, but I have always worked hard and done my best. I have a good sense of humour and I like to think that once I have made a friend he or she is a friend for life. We Yorkshiremen are very loyal.

Yorkshire County Cricket Club has played a big part in my life. It is now fifty-one years since I first walked through the gates at Headingley for my first practices. It was a great thrill for me, just a kid, to be in the same nets as such wonderful players as Len Hutton, Fred Trueman, Bob Appleyard, Johnny Wardle, Brian Close, Ray Illingworth and Norman Yardley.

Do you know, I was so proud and happy to become part of that Yorkshire squad that I would have played for nothing. I think of that side and I honestly believe it would have beaten a lot of today's Test teams. But we'll never know. You can't really compare different generations. We have moved on since then. Times have changed, and dramatically so.

Since those early days, I have built up a store of wonderful memories of Headingley. Like Lord's, it is the home of legends, steeped in history. I played county cricket there, I umpired my first Test there – England v. New Zealand – and I stood at my last county championship match there – Yorkshire v. Warwickshire. Lord's asked me where I would like to finish and I said, if at all possible, Yorkshire at Headingley. I therefore completed the full circle, and those fifty-one years have simply flown by. I look back and wonder where they all went.

However, I treasure the memories and the fact that Yorkshire have made me an honorary life member. That is a tremendous honour for me. Then there are the flags. They fly above the West Stand, bearing the names of thirty-two people who have achieved outstanding success in cricket. There are thirty-one great cricketers up there and one umpire – me. The flag carries my name and my record – 66 Tests, 93 one-day internationals, 4 World Cup finals.

I'm so proud that this fine new clock at Headingley was dedicated to me in April 2002.

There is also a box named after me, and a clock – no ordinary clock, either. It measures six feet by five feet and cost £40,000. It is there for all to see on the new West Stand. This will be the clock by which the two umpires will go at all matches for the start and close of play, lunch and tea. It has been sponsored by Phillip Stoner Jewellery (Shipley) in recognition of my 'outstanding services to cricket' and it gave me a great thrill to unveil it officially when Yorkshire played Surrey on ladies' day in 2002. I take a lot of pleasure and pride from the fact that now, in one sense, it will always be my time at Headingley, even after I'm dead and gone.

I was, of course, elated by Yorkshire's county championship success in 2001, but I was saddened by the furore surrounding the opening of the new gates at Headingley. John Major was invited to perform the opening ceremony, but Geoff Boycott, Freddie Trueman, Brian Close and Raymond Illingworth voiced their opposition in no uncertain terms and threatened to boycott the event. Maybe the former prime minister's Surrey connection was too hard to take. There has never been any love lost between the two counties. Anyway, the upshot of it

The great Len Hutton Gates controversy was resolved when his widow was chosen to open them and his son Richard (pictured) spoke at the opening ceremony.

all was that the committee decided to back down and Lady Hutton, widow of Sir Leonard, was invited instead. I thought the ideal person would have been the Duchess of Kent, who is a lovely lady. Her father, Sir William Worsley, was a former captain and president – he was there when I was a player. Sadly, however, she was not well, which was a great shame. I think everyone would have gone along with her as the opener. But Lady Hutton was also a popular choice.

As a postscript to that little episode, I was having a cup of tea with Lady Hutton in the banqueting suite afterwards and she said to me, 'Do you know, if it had been my choice, with all this hassle, and everybody arguing, I'd have let Dickie Bird open the gates.' Now wasn't that nice of her?

Headingley is also now the headquarters of the Leeds Rhinos Rugby League Club, whose chief executive, Gary Hetherington, is quite a remarkable man. It was Gary's Uncle Tom who introduced him to the delights of rugby league, taking him as a lad to Wheldon Lane to watch Castleford – Classy Cas – on the back of his scooter in return for a couple of hours gardening. What Gary did not realise until years later was that Uncle Tom did not take him until half-time. Then, you see, they could get in for free. Chuckled Gary, 'Uncle Tom was a typical Yorkshireman. If he could get owt for nowt he would. It was a long time before I realised there were two halves to a rugby game, although I did start to wonder why the players came out all dirty at what I thought was the start. Couldn't they afford to get anyone to wash the kit, I wondered.'

But half a match was enough to get Gary hooked and at eighteen he signed for Wakefield Trinity, making his debut against Doncaster in 1973 as A.N. Other to cover up the fact he was still at school and schoolboys were not eligible to play in the first team. Through a playing career of 300 first-team matches with Trinity, York, Leeds and Huddersfield, Gary was always concerned for the wider needs of the game, such as proper coaching and players' insurance payments, and he set about seeing to these things when he became player/manager/coach to Sheffield Eagles.

By now he was married to Kath who had been brought up supporting Castleford's arch-rivals Featherstone Rovers. It was her Auntie May who used to take her to games. Said Gary, 'I never knew her, but Kath tells me she was the quietest, most inoffensive person you could ever wish to meet – until she got to Post Office Road. Then she used to hang her handbag on the railings and from first whistle to last she never stopped verbally abusing the referee.'

Sheffield Eagles was the club the Hetheringtons built up between them, in the early days going out to sell double-glazing in the evening to make ends meet. Kath became the first woman on the Council of the Rugby League Executive and in 1995, as the game celebrated its centenary, she became the first female president of the Rugby Football League. Incidentally, Gary told me that the people at Featherstone always said that Kath was a better player than her four brothers.

Meanwhile, Gary had decided to take on a fresh challenge at Leeds. When he and Paul Caddick talked about going to Headingley they were advised not to do it, and no wonder. The club was £5 million in debt; the likelihood at the time was that Yorkshire County Cricket Club would be leaving to go to a new ground at Durkar; and the team had only just avoided relegation the previous season.

'They were at their lowest point,' recalled Gary. 'They could not see how to operate the following year without losing another half a million quid. So it was a pretty traumatic time. It seemed the only way to pay off the debts would be for the cricket to move to Durkar and the rugby club to Elland Road, where they would link up with Leeds United, with Headingley being sold to developers. It was a horrendous prospect really.'

But Gary and Paul took on the tremendous challenge. The first thing they did was persuade Yorkshire CCC that their future was at

Headingley and that they wanted to work with them in developing the stadium, giving them greater ownership.

So 1997 was a fairly eventful year. The team's name was changed to Leeds Rhinos, they introduced a mascot, Ronnie Rhino, and performances and crowds began to improve. In 1999, the Rhinos won the Rugby League Challenge Cup – their first major trophy for twenty-one years.

Gary enthused, 'We now have a terrific youth system, with lads in Leeds eager to play for their home-town club. We run trials, and in the last few years we have taken ownership of the Leeds Tykes, which means that we are now the only club in the world to run both rugby league and rugby union teams.

'We've got one training base for all the players at Kirkstall and both teams play matches here at Headingley, which is a unique partnership in itself. We have top-class rugby union in the winter with the Tykes and top-class rugby league in the summer with the Rhinos. And then, of course, we have county and international cricket. So we have a terrific venue here at Headingley, full of tradition and history.

'We feel Headingley belongs to the people of Yorkshire. When we came here, the only way you could come in was to pay to watch a sporting event. We have changed that philosophy. Now we open up Headingley to the community. We have a classroom here and school-children come in every day. We have tours and we are hoping to provide a museum and an archive. We should have these things because we are a county of great tradition and history. We also go out into the community. All the Rhinos players go into schools coaching. We like to think that the whole operation at Headingley is very much part of Leeds and very much part of Yorkshire.'

Leeds Rhinos Rugby League Club chief executive Gary Hetherington and his wife Kath on the very spot at Headingley where they first met.

Gary is chief executive of both the Rhinos and the Tykes and obviously he wants both to be successful. He sees part of his job as integrating the two and he told me, 'From a business point of view it makes so much sense. We have one marketing team, one for commercial sales, one telephone receptionist, even one physio and one medical department, so we can reduce the costs of the whole operation.'

Gary went on, 'There are people now who actually think that the games will draw so close together that they will become one again. I hope that doesn't happen. The two games have their own distinctive style and tradition. They are different. Rugby league is so ingrained into the hearts and minds of people, particularly in the north, that they would be devastated if there was a merger with union. A third of the population of Castleford goes to watch their team at home. It's the same at Featherstone, Dewsbury, Oldham and other such towns. Take away rugby league and you take away what that town stands for.

'I feel it is so important that we maintain and develop rugby league. It is such a great game to build character among youngsters. That's why we place so much emphasis on coaching in schools.'

Gary has gone through a lot to get where he is today and when we got to talking about the pressures of the job he retorted, 'Compared with my early days at the Eagles there is no pressure. That was pressure, when I had no money and we didn't know if we could survive from one day to the next.'

He told me of the time he was really keen to sign a lad, but it would cost £1,000, which he had not got. So he decided to look for sponsors, and one of the supporters suggested that he had a word with the woman in the pub where they used to go after games.

Gary went on, 'I thought I'd give it a go. The woman in question, Ruth Roper-Tye, had rather a large chest, which was a big attraction for the players, and she played up to them. There was always a terrific atmosphere in the pub on match days.'

Gary asked her about sponsoring the new player and she advised him to see Jimmy Mullins, who owned a car dealership. He agreed to put up £500. Back Gary went and told Ruth that Jimmy had agreed to go half but he still needed another £500. She looked at him studiously for a minute or so and then asked, 'What does this young lad you're trying to sign look like?'

Fortunately, Gary had a photograph of the lad in his pocket, and he showed it to her. Ruth's eyes lit up. There was only the slightest pause before she declared, 'Oh, all right, then. I'll chip in with the other five hundred.' Then she added, still with that gleam in her eye, 'But I want the bottom half.'

Gary recalled that the first job every week on a Sunday morning

A Pakistani line-up of cricket-loving taxi drivers who regularly ferry me home from Wakefield Westgate station after my trips to London.

involved a bucket and spade. You see, the Eagles played at Owlerton Stadium in those days, and Saturday night was greyhound night.

'All their mess had to be cleared up before we could start to prepare for the game, and there was no one else to do it, except me. It usually took me a good half an hour. Then I'd put all the barriers out, set up the bar, and at midday I'd change into my suit to meet the sponsors. After that I'd change back into my kit, go out and play, then get showered and changed to meet up with the sponsors again. Once everyone had gone, we'd go on to Ruth's pub until midnight.

'It was a hectic day, and I'd get a few belts round the head to boot. But there was such terrific commitment at the club in those days and there was always this dream that we were working towards playing in the top flight. That's the great thing in any sport, to have ambition, to have a dream, to have a goal and to achieve it one day. It was the same with Barnsley Football Club and their rise from the Fourth Division to the Premiership. The Challenge Cup triumph was, for me, the culmination of all the hard work, determination, commitment and dedication that had gone in to getting the Eagles off the ground, working seven days a week. I packed a lifetime's experience into those twelve years.'

Gary was born into a mining background. He has grafted for success, eventually achieving it, not as a player, but as an official. Throughout all the highs and lows of his career, he has remained true to his roots, and proud to be a Yorkshireman – a bit like me really.

CHAPTER 8

A HIGHLAND FLING

Competitor in the Solo Piping Class.

Left: Fancy footwork is not confined to the strong men. Highland dancing has always been as fiercely contested.

I WILL never forget my last match in Scotland. I had just completed a long spell of umpiring – nearly four and a half weeks all over the place without a break – and I simply could not face the 360 mile drive up to Forfar, where I was to stand at the Benson & Hedges game between Scotland and Derbyshire. So I decided to go by train. On arriving in Edinburgh, I was told that I should take a train to Dundee. 'But I don't want to go to Dundee,' I argued. 'I want to go to Forfar.'

'That,' came the reply, 'might be a problem. You see, Forfar doesn't have a station.'

Dundee, it turned out, was the nearest point by rail, and that was still a fair way from my destination. When I got there, it turned out that the only option was to take a taxi. While I was looking for one, I was spotted by a chap who recognised me and, hearing my plight, offered me a lift to Forfar. Great, I thought, problem solved, and I looked round for his car. But the only vehicle in sight was a cattle truck. That turned out to be my last-leg transport. By this time I was too tired to care. All the same, I was thankful that he allowed me to sit in the front with him rather than share the back with the sheep.

Despite this escapade, I have always enjoyed going to Scotland – beautiful scenery, Highland games, whisky, haggis and wonderful people. I was always determined to return when I retired and so I did one autumn weekend for a typical sample of this marvellous country.

There was a first taste for me of that most famous of all Scottish delicacies. I had been told that the Rogano, in Glasgow was the best place to go for haggis. So that's precisely where I went, in the company of Scottish journalist Jack Webster, a former Daily Express features writer.

Rather than take the complete main course plunge, I played safe and ordered the dish as a starter, just as a taster, served with mashed potato and turnip. I was left wishing I had gone the whole hog because it really was quite delicious. When I was told afterwards that it was made from sheep's heart, lungs and liver, chopped with oatmeal, suet and onion and boiled in the stomach bag, I have to admit I felt a bit queasy. But I'll certainly have it again. To my surprise, I really enjoyed it.

There are some people, Jack told me, who said you should pour a touch of whisky on the haggis, but he was not too keen on the idea. He believed you should just enjoy the haggis as it was. There is a lot of good in it, lots of protein, and it is first-class food. He added that it is always eaten at traditional Burns suppers every year. There is even an address to the haggis that begins, 'Great Chieftain of the puddin' race'.

Jack proved to be a very interesting and entertaining dinner companion. A journalist for fifty-four years, twenty of them on the Express, he had also been the ghost writer for Muhammad Ali the year after Ali caused such a sensation by beating Sonny Liston in 1964, and for the great Pele when he came here in 1966. He spent a whole week with Ali and took him up to Scotland where they visited Burns' cottage, and the American legend sat in Burns' chair. Jack told me he wished he had been able to put Ali's thoughts on tape because he was treated to a selection of some of the first of the famous doggerels – 'Float like a butterfly, sting like a bee' and all that.

Jack was obviously very impressed with Ali and, as far as boxing is concerned, I have no doubt that the former Cassius Clay was indeed the Greatest, as he so often boasted. My old mate Michael Parkinson reckons he was the greatest sportsman ever, despite the fact that Ali lost his temper and threatened Parky when he went on his television show. Parky's dad was in the audience that night, and after the show he went into the dressing-room to remonstrate with his lad.

'What did you think you were playing at, son,' he stormed. 'I wouldn't have put up with that.'

Parky asked, 'But what could I do, Dad?'

Replied Parkinson senior, 'Do? I'll tell you what I'd have done if he'd talked to me like that. I'd have dropped him one straight on his bloody chin.' And, believe me, he would have done.

Ali was a magnificent sportsman, no doubt about that. But there is one other I would put above him and I challenged Jack to name him. His guesses included Sir Donald Bradman, Sir Stanley Matthews, Jesse Owens, Michael Johnson, Juan Fangio and C.B. Fry, before a hint or two led him to Sir Garfield Sobers. In my mind there is no doubt that he was the best. He had all-round brilliance in every department of the game. His record speaks for itself. He was the first Test cricketer to hit more than 8,000 runs, that total including 365 not out for the West Indies against Pakistan at Kingston in 1957-58, thus creating a new record at the time for the highest individual innings in Test cricket. He is one of the few bowlers to capture more than 200 Test wickets; he took 109 catches; and he captained the West Indies in 39 Tests, which was, at the time, another record.

Jack Webster gave me a fascinating description of sporting life in Scotland. Columnist of the Year in 1996, Jack was also Speaker of the Year during the same period. A most impressive man.

Born in Glasgow, Sir Alex Ferguson took Aberdeen to victory in the 1983 European Cup Winners' Cup before moving on to Manchester United.

But enough of cricket. What of Scotland? What, indeed, of Glasgow? Jack explained the city is a great conglomeration of smaller districts – such as Govan, Partick and Springburn – which have all grown together yet still retain their separate identities. Govan is the ship-building area where Sir Alex Ferguson grew up and went to work as an apprentice in one of the yards. Football was always in his blood, and he was signed by Rangers after emerging through the junior ranks in local football. However, from the moment he married a Catholic his days at Rangers were numbered. It was, of course, as manager of Manchester United that Sir Alex enjoyed his greatest triumphs, eclipsing even such a legendary predecessor as that other great Scot, Sir Matt Busby.

Jack knew Sir Matt well and escorted his mother to the European Cup final at Wembley in 1968. Sir Matt was fifty-nine at the time and his mother was only seventeen years older, having been a young bride in the few years before Sir Matt's father met his death in the First World War.

Recalled Jack, 'After the game, which United won by beating Benfica, the wee lady said she'd like to see Matt, so I managed to bluff my way through to the dressing-room by telling everybody this was Matt Busby's mum. And that was a tremendous moment. Here was this wee wifie from Lanarkshire hugging her son in his moment of greatest triumph. It was very emotional. I knew they were both thinking about the man who had been husband and father; the man Matt barely remembered. If only he could have been there for that magical moment.

'Then we went to the Russell Hotel. Joe Loss and his orchestra were playing in the big ballroom, but Matt had this wee private room and I was invited in there with a small gathering, including his mother, away from all the noise, the bustle, and the cheering crowds. Matt said how pleased he was to be surrounded by friends and family. And that was one of the greatest moments of my life. Ten years earlier Matt had been at death's door. Now here he was, at the pinnacle of his career, enjoying a lovely peaceful ending to a marvellous night of celebration. And I was part of it. I'll treasure that night as long as I live.'

Ten years earlier, Sir Matt had survived the Munich air crash that wiped out so many of his young team.

Sir Matt, Jack told me, was 'a lovely man'. He had a 'gentlemanly way about him', a different style from Fergie, although the latter had expanded as a person as the years went by. Jock Stein, another famous Scottish manager, was 'an extraordinary human being'. He had come from a coalmining background, as had Busby and Bill Shankly, and it was this, Jack argued, that gave him such tremendous character.

Football was an escape from the pits, or in Fergie's case from the factory.

I fully appreciated what he was saying because, had it not been for sport, I would have ended up working down the pit. However, I had to disagree with Jack on one thing. He said Fergie was the best manager. I believe there was one better – Bob Paisley, of Liverpool. You have only to look at his record. But Jack insisted on having the last word. He argued that Fergie had done everything in Scotland, with a team that was neither Rangers nor Celtic, having won a European trophy with Aberdeen – a great feat in itself. Then he had gone south of the border to conquer Europe with Manchester United. Paisley, Jack pointed out, had enjoyed success only in England. We agreed to differ on that one.

One of Jack's greatest joys in being a features writer was that he could fulfil many of his own personal ambitions, and he eventually caught up with his footballing hero, Sir Stanley Matthews, when the wizard of dribble had reached the grand old age of sixty-four. Stan was still playing for a Post Office team in Malta, and Jack asked him if he had retained the skill of his heyday, when he had an aura about him that made him so special.

'Oh, yes,' Stan replied, 'I have the skill. I can still do what I want with the ball. But my balance is not what it was. That's the problem.' He was dead right. Balance is essential for any sportsman. Lose that, and you lose everything.

Stan and I became very close friends. When we were both in South Africa, we used to go to Soweto with a police escort to coach the village lads in football and cricket. At the time they were much more interested in football, which presented a bit of a problem for me. I well remember a young lad, bizarrely wearing a bowler hat and carrying a brolly but with nothing on his feet, asking me, 'Are you Mr Dickie Bird, Professor of Cricket?'

I nodded, modestly, and he said, 'Good. Then we are your pupils. We are here for the coaching.'

Looking round, I saw that there were quite a lot of them, mostly raggy-arsed, most without shoes or sandals, and none dressed for cricket; nor did they have any gear and I didn't have enough equipment to go round. So I split them into small groups, each with bat and ball. They had no idea at first. I went to each group trying to explain the rudiments of the game, but as soon as my back was turned they started playing football. It was unbelievable. There they were, bare-footed, kicking a cricket ball around, flicking it up in the air, controlling it on their thighs and instep as it came down. Just so long as they don't start heading it, I thought.

Much as I admired Stan, I still think that Tommy Finney was a better player. But Jack insisted, 'I've always said that Stan Matthews was the Fred Astaire of football. The movement, the style, the twinkling feet – both still had it in their seventies.'

Having travelled extensively by road, rail, plane – and very occasionally boat – I was drawn to the new Museum of Transport overlooking the River Kelvin, and I was not disappointed. It uses traditional and modern methods of display and what makes it so interesting is that you can actually walk among the exhibits. It is quite an eerie experience to stroll down a simulated Glasgow street of 1938, for example, with its period shop fronts and window displays, its street lamps and signs, and to see private and commercial vehicles of the day parked on the cobbled roadway. It is so real that I was tempted to pop into the picture house to see what film was showing.

The old electric trams used to hurtle along at 18 mph with a safety device under the platform to save passengers who fell out from a slow death under the wheels.

I hitch a sit in a 10.9 hp Galloway in Glasgow's Museum of Transport. It's a bit different from my Jag!

Another innovation is the display of mass-produced motor cars in an authentic showroom setting, so that it is possible to get the flavour of that bygone age. I was allowed to sit in a 10.9 horsepower Galloway from around 1924. It was a bit different from my Jag, I have to say. The controls were much simpler for a start. When I first took delivery of my XJ8, it took me ages to work out what all the buttons and switches were for. In fact, I drove all the way down to Torquay on a very warm September day with the heater on full blast. I didn't have the foggiest idea how to turn the damn thing off. I felt like a roasted pig when I arrived. They could have served me up for the evening meal with an apple stuffed in my mouth.

I also liked the old electric trams with safety features that included lifeguard apparatus under the platform to prevent anyone who fell out of the vehicle being run over by the wheels. I don't know if that was a common occurrence but they were obviously taking nothing for granted. The trams used to trundle along at no more than eighteen miles an hour, but by 1904 they could take you eight miles from Glasgow and were therefore promoted as being a means of escaping into the countryside from the grime of the city. Travel eight miles from the centre today and you'd probably still be in Glasgow, especially if you get caught up in the one-way systems.

My original intention on re-visiting Scotland was to take in the famous Braemar Games, but when this became impossible I switched my attention to the Pitlochry Gathering. The strongman competition is the highlight of any such event, and two of the most successful exponents have been English – both former shot-putt champions. Geoff Capes is the most recent, but the man who first dared to take on the Scots at their own Games was Arthur Rowe, who comes from my neck of the woods in Barnsley.

He was a giant of a man, weighing almost eighteen stone. It was said he had to turn sideways to ease his enormous shoulders through the doors of his semi, and shaking his hand was like grappling with a Barnsley chop. Arthur used to keep his muscles in shape by chucking an eighteen-foot telegraph pole around a field. Those fearsome training sessions led to his becoming 'the 'ammer of the Scots'.

The Scots, who take their traditional pleasures so seriously, were forced to acknowledge an English giant in a borrowed kilt as champion of their own Highland Games. The former colliery blacksmith beat Scotland's finest and strongest so often that he eventually travelled around the world giving exhibitions of tossing the caber, sponsored by a firm of Scotch whisky distillers.

However, Arthur, already world famous for his amateur shot-putting exploits – he also played rugby league – was hardly an overnight sensation when he first went over the border.

'I was useless at first,' he admitted. 'It was a good two years before I mastered the different techniques and began winning anything.'

There is a special art to caber-tossing. It is no easy thing to hoist a 200-pound caber on to your shoulder and send it spinning. The first time Arthur tried it, it took him an hour just to get it up to his shoulder.

At one Games he nearly made *The Guinness Book of Records* as 'the man who killed the most spectators with one caber'. He had the caber on his shoulder when the wind caught it and sent him backwards. At the edge of the field the caber went over his shoulder and into the crowd, which parted as dramatically as the Red Sea on the command of Moses. The caber missed everyone. And that, Arthur always said, was another miracle.

The Highland Games can be like that, teetering between high drama and slapstick comedy. Once, a worm-eaten caber snapped in two as Arthur ran with it, the top half toppling over and nearly decapitating him. Apparently, it is also liable to bounce and deliver a hefty thump on the sporran. Now that really does make your eyes water.

Another time, Arthur forgot the shorts he wore under his kilt and, he recalled, 'I decided to compete without them. It wasn't too bad until I came to the hammer, when I had to spin round. You can imagine how the kilt flares up. So I just had to make sure I didn't spin round as fast as I usually did.'

Arthur eventually mastered all the events to such a degree that he went on to throw the Scottish hammer further than anyone else,

become the world professional shot-putt champion, win the world title in the unique Games event of heaving a weight over a bar, and clinch the world caber-tossing championship at Aberdeen in 1969. For the latter triumph he received a hundred guineas, a trophy – and a gallon of whisky.

When he returned home to Barnsley he always used to hide his kilt away. 'You won't catch me wearing it round here,' he used to say, reddening at the thought of what his hard-bitten mining mates might say if they saw him 'in a skirt'. 'It's bad enough if you're caught wearing a suit,' he laughed.

He was once walking with a Scot in London's Oxford Street when a couple of giggling women demanded to know, 'Is anything worn under the kilt?'

Arthur was tongue-tied but his Scottish companion politely replied, 'No, madam, everything is in perfect working order.'

Pitlochry has some of the most beautiful scenery in Europe. It is surrounded by dramatic countryside, mountains and lochs, tumbling burns and woodland trails. The Games are staged at the end of the season in September, so there is sometimes a problem with the weather, but it was a glorious afternoon when I paid a visit.

I was thrilled to see the massed pipe bands as they marched through the streets and into the arena that afternoon – although a bit taken

Pitlochry can boast some of the finest scenery in Europe. It's a great setting for the Games.

aback when I was asked to judge which of them was best. Thankfully, my choice coincided with the experts' opinion, and at least it was better than being asked to toss the caber.

The heavy events remain the biggest attraction, and traditionally putting the stone is the first on the programme. Originally, so I was told, they used a smooth stone from the river bed, sometimes shaped by the local mason. The stones used to vary greatly in shape and weight, particularly those used for tests of strength, where stones of up to 265 pounds presented a formidable challenge. Now the stone is either sixteen or twenty-two pounds and has to be put with one hand from in front of the shoulders with a run-up not exceeding seven foot six inches. It's all there in the rules.

Throwing the hammer represents an old contest where young locals would compete to see who could throw the blacksmith's heavy sledge-hammer the furthest. The sphere of the hammer now weighs either sixteen or twenty-two pounds, and, unlike the hammer used in the Olympic Games, the Scottish hammer has a wooden shaft measuring four foot six inches long. No turning is allowed. The thrower stands with his back to what they call the trig and takes a good grip, with the aid of six-inch spikes that protrude from the front of his boots. The hammer is swung round the head to gather momentum, and then

Putting the stone is traditionally first on the heavy events programme.

released. It should fly off straight behind the thrower – but it requires great strength and good timing.

I suppose the most graceful of the heavy events is throwing the weight for distance, which combines rhythm with power. The weight in this case is an iron sphere of twenty-eight pounds on a chain, with a handle at the end, measuring eighteen inches overall. It is delivered from behind the trig, with a run-up not exceeding nine feet. The thrower swings the weight to the side, then round behind him, letting the weight drag as far as he can. He then waltzes round once, twice, and on the third turn he heaves the weight round and throws it. The main problem here for the thrower, having gathered up so much speed in turning, is to stop at the trig. Step over and the throw doesn't count.

Tossing the weight over the bar requires great strength, although it seemed to me that competitors adopt a nonchalant attitude to this event. The weight is fifty-six pounds, with a ring attached. Like in the high jump, each competitor has three attempts at each height. Thrown correctly, the weight narrowly misses the competitor on the way back down. If it is thrown incorrectly, the poor chap has to look lively to avoid being hit and put out for the count – if not permanently. The weight is equivalent to half a bag of coal, yet the Pitlochry ground record stands at nineteen feet nine inches, and that, believe it or not, is like throwing a seven-year-old over a double-decker bus.

Heave! Heave! I lend a voice if not a hand to one of the tug o' war teams.

There is a definite
technique to tossing
the caber.
I didn't try this either!

Most spectacular of the heavy events is tossing the caber. The competitor lifts the caber by placing his interlocked hands under the narrower end, resting its length against his shoulder. He then runs as fast as he can, stops dead and tosses the end he is holding up in the air so that the heavy end lands on the ground and the light end passes over it, pointing away from him on landing. I thought that the winner would be the competitor who tossed the caber furthest, but not so. The winner is the one who tosses it straightest. The competition is judged with the aid of an imaginary clock face. Think about a competitor delivering his throw at six o'clock, aiming to land

the caber in the centre of the dial. A perfect throw is one that goes straight over, with the light end landing at twelve o'clock precisely. Nowt to it, really.

14,000 casks on site already and obviously many more to come!

The Games were co-sponsored by the local Blair Athol distillery, where David Hardy is the manager, and that was another port of call I was determined not to miss.

There is one industry in Britain that remains an undisputed world leader – and that is Scotch whisky. It is sold in more than 200 countries and around a billion bottles are shifted each year. David told me that its origins date back to the ancient Celts, who practised the art of distilling to produce a fiery liquid known as *uisge beatha* – 'the water of life'.

The Blair Athol distillery is one of the oldest, dating back to 1798. It was established on the site of a farm and the original farmhouse still exists. It was named after the burn that runs through it – the burn of the otter – and the otter remains the mascot. David told me they still get one or two coming up the stream, which supplies water for the distillation.

As he took me on a tour of the premises, I was struck by the aroma. I swear you could get drunk just by breathing it in. I came out feeling quite boozed up and it needed the welcome rush of fresh air to clear my head. As I said to David, 'That's reight whisky, that is.'

I wondered about the bottles I had back home. Would the whisky go off if I left it too long? After all, I opened a bottle only when I had special visitors. David reassured me. 'If you don't open the bottle and keep it out of the light and reasonably cool it will last for fifty years. Whisky in a bottle is more than forty per cent alcohol, so not much can live in it. It is obviously affected while it remains in the cask. If you don't keep it long enough it will have too much of the immaturity of the original spirit; keep it too long and it will have too much of the character of the cask itself.'

At the time of my visit Blair Athol had 14,000 casks on site, some as old as 1968, and David remarked, 'It will be interesting to sample the older whisky and compare it to the twelve year old. It will be special, no doubt; it will be different; it will be a one-off. You don't get much whisky matured for this long and we certainly won't keep it much longer. It would be nice to produce a special cask-strength bottling'.

The water used in the distillation comes from two or three miles away, from two lochs in the surrounding hills. The distillers

David Hardy takes me on a tour of one of Scotland's oldest distilleries at Blair Athol.

Blair Castle is the seat of the Dukes of Atholl who by ancient statute are entitled to maintain a private army. I won't tell the Scottish Assembly if you won't.

The smallest distillery in Scotland, Edradour, near Pitlochry, is the last to produce a rare handcrafted single malt.

don't filter the water, or boil it, or purify it. They just let it run through a gauze and mesh, which takes out the leaves, sticks, and the fish, including the famous salmon. The problem that David occasionally has with the water flow, maybe once a year, is flash flooding.

'It is important that we keep the burn flowing into the river rather than into the distillery,' he joked. 'Stands to reason, you can't have all that water spilling into a distillery. It does rather spoil the strength and taste of the whisky.'

David is rightly proud of his product. 'It is a winning formula, so why change it? I do tweak things occasionally to make sure that we get the best out of it, but that's all. At the end of the day you can go only so far before you start affecting the product. So, if people continue to like it and buy it, then it will stay as it is. If it's not broke, don't mend it, as they say.'

There is a large visitor centre at Blair Athol, which caters for about 40,000 people a year. It is open seven days a week, and there are guides who like to spend as much time as possible with the visitors as they take them on a tour – and for a welcoming taster.

Coincidentally, just three miles up the road from one of the biggest distilleries in Scotland lies the smallest – Edradour – which was established in 1825. Nestling in the hills east of Pitlochry, this most picturesque of distilleries stands alone as Scotland's last to produce a handcrafted malt in limited quantity and of unique quality.

The neat cluster of whitewashed buildings, which have remained virtually unchanged for the last 150 years, house equipment only just capable of producing commercial quantities. Indeed, I discovered that just twelve casks a week are produced, making Edradour single malt whisky a rare treat, as anyone enjoying a wee dram there will agree.

CHAPTER 9

CRICKET FOR CHARITY AND FUN

The umpire's bonus, finding a guardian angel looking down from the roof beams of St Peter and St Paul's church, Alconbury.

Left: Everything about Alconbury speaks to me of what is good about this country.

IT never ceases to amaze me how much time top sports people and other celebrities are prepared to give to help various charitable causes. This has been brought home forcibly to me in recent years when I have travelled down to umpire the annual charity match at Alconbury Recreation Field.

The game, which usually features John Major's XI versus the Bunburys, is played in aid of the Royal Society for Mentally Handicapped Children and Adults, or Mencap for short. John Major is president of Surrey County Cricket Club, and Norma Major is the chairman of Mencap's Huntingdon branch.

Bunbury Cricket Club was formed sixteen years ago and has raised close on £8 million for charity and schools cricket throughout the world – a remarkable achievement. Much of the credit for the success of the Bunburys must go to founder David English, who is chairman of ChildLine, a vice-president of the English Schools' Cricket Association, and has been Ian Botham's right-hand man for the last twenty years, accompanying him on his marathon charity walks. This qualifies him perfectly to captain an eleven whose performances on and off the field can be described, in his own words, as 'unruly and occasionally psychopathic'.

David is also former president of the world famous RSO Records (Eric Clapton and the Bee Gees are two of the label's best-known acts), author of the best-selling Bunbury Tails, and a legend in his own lunchtime when it comes to the big screen. He will always be remembered for his touching role in 'A Bridge Too Far'. He had two lines – one to Robert Redford, the other to Sean Connery – before spending the rest of the film as a dead German.

The Bunburys will play anywhere for a deserving cause, whether on a village green like Alconbury, The Foster's Oval, Windsor Castle, or the schoolyard. In millennium year they staged the greatest charity cricket game ever played in memory of that great West Indian cricketer, Malcolm Marshall. Incredibly, forty-eight Test stars, including eighteen captains, took part in the encounter at the Honourable Artillery Company ground in London, raising £50,000 on the day for Malcolm's son, Mali.

As for Alconbury, it remains one of the annual highlights on the Bunburys' calendar, as David explained to me. 'There is a magic about Alconbury. Timeless trips up the A1, past the perennial roadworks and the welcome sign of the church spire peeking over the hill, and then the sign "To the Alconburys". You drive through the village – there's never a soul in sight – and then hear the sound of the Tannoy crackling in the distance . . . "One, two, three, testing. Welcome to Mrs Major's cricket match here at Alconbury."'

He fondly recalled some of the highlights, like the time the legendary South African batsman Barry Richards flew in from Queensland specially to play. On arrival he had no gear, just a well-worn pair of golf shoes. But, using borrowed equipment and a bat so old it had cobwebs all over the handle, he scored, as David put it, 'a peerless fifty-two from memory'.

He went on, 'I've seen Mohammad Azharuddin hit Imran Khan off the back foot over the Mr Whippy ice-cream van at the far end – a carry of ninety-five yards. I've stood next to Bill Wyman in the gully when he caught Brian Close left-handed off the bowling of Ian Wright, while clutching his favourite Benson & Hedges in his right hand. And I've seen Aussie Ryan Campbell hit ninety before retiring – despite the fact that the Bunburys had twenty-three fielders on the pitch.'

Three years ago the great Wasim Akram opened the bowling for the Bunburys, and David gave him his orders from mid-off. 'Go on, give him your inswinger,' or 'Try the outswinger.' It must have been top-class advice because Wasim, bowling from the bouncy castle end, swung the ball left and right, had the poor batsmen jumping about as though firecrackers had been thrown at their feet, and bowled 9 overs at a cost of a mere 4 runs. It was a miracle that he failed to take a wicket.

Then David took over – and what a transformation. One of the batsmen who had been in so much trouble promptly hit the first three balls over the church steeple. As David conceded, 'Same game, same batsman, different bowler, different class.'

I also recall one game that included Gavin Hastings, Freddie Trueman, Richie Benaud, Brian Johnston, Bill Clinton, Henry Blofeld, Geoff Boycott, Bob Willis, Princess Di, John Major, Neil Kinnock and George Bush. Don't believe me? Ask Rory Bremner.

The Alconbury fixture began in 1990 on the off chance that the Member of Parliament for Huntingdon, the cricket-loving Mr Major, might just be willing to play in a charity game in his constituency. As it turned out, he was unable to do so, but offered his services as an umpire, and the first match duly took place on Friday the thirteenth. Far from being unlucky, it sowed the seeds for a hugely popular annual occasion. That inaugural fixture was between John Major's XI and

Teams, umpires and officials line up with Norma Major at Alconbury before the annual charity match in aid of Mencap.

Brian Close's XI, which was extremely appropriate as the vicar of the church that overlooks the ground just happened to be the Reverend Brian Close, who had conceived the idea of a charity match to assist in raising funds for repairs to the church steeple.

Closey, incidentally, played – when I umpired – at the age of seventy-two. He remains as enthusiastic, gutsy and bloody-minded as ever. No way will he give his wicket away cheaply, not even in a charity match. It is simply not in his nature. There was one year – he was sixty-nine at the time (in years not runs) – when he scored 8 in 39 overs while Alvin Kallicharran rattled up 68 in less than half the time at the other end. Having done what he believed to be his duty Closey retired because he was 'dying for a fag'.

In the year following that first fixture, John Major became prime minister, and so, although he retained a keen interest in the event, his active involvement had to come to an end. The representative side became Mrs Norma Major's XI, with the Bunburys lined up as the regular opposition.

All those who have taken part have thoroughly enjoyed the day. Take Gary Lineker, for example. The former England international footballer is an outstanding all-round cricketer, not to mention crisp walker. (Pause for ad break.) He opens for the Bunburys, bowls medium pace, fields like a demon, and doesn't like missing a match.

One time when he was due to play at Finchley CC, he rang to say he shouldn't really be playing cricket that day as he was due to turn out for Spurs in the London derby at West Ham that evening. But he still took his place at the crease to score 102 not out before nipping over to Upton Park, where he notched a hat-trick.

When the Bunburys played their Victory match in millennium year, he finished 'Football Focus' at one o'clock, then leapt into a car that took him from the BBC to The Oval. He changed in the back seat, walked out to the middle amid tumultuous applause, stroked four classy boundaries before giving away his wicket, then returned to the BBC via the waiting car to monitor the games to be shown on 'Match of the Day' that evening. If the BBC production team, in the dark about all this, had switched to Sky Sports, they would have seen their star presenter batting live.

Gary played at Alconbury when I made my first appearance there in 1999 along with several other debutants, including former Northants and England batsman David Steele, former BBC racing commentator Julian Wilson, ex-West Indies wicket-keeper Deryck Murray, and television presenter Jamie Theakston. I was delighted to find that, despite my retirement, the fans had not forgotten me. In fact, when I took up my duties in my familiar white cap there were cheers all round the ground and I was for ever signing autographs before the game started, during tea and at the close of play.

Like Brian Close, David Steele is deadly serious. He plays as if it is a Test match, and in the 2001 encounter he got a really rough decision. My colleague – no names, no pack drill – gave him out lbw, despite the fact that the ball obviously hit him in the stomach. Just the teeniest bit high, I thought to myself from square leg. I wouldn't have given it in a month of Sundays. Steeley didn't like it one bit. He spent the rest of the day whingeing about it.

He's a great chap, though, even if he is a bit on the mean side. Split a currant in two would Steeley. Rumour has it that he still has the first halfpenny his grandmother gave him.

Another of the Bunbury characters who has become something of an institution at Alconbury and elsewhere is Joe 'The Hat' Cuby, a millionaire publisher who has a unique style, in both the batting and bowling departments. His spiralling deliveries – which even donkey-droppers would disown – must come close to penetrating the ozone layer. I remember one ball going up and up and up and then coming down and hitting him on the top of his head. I thought I saw dandruff spray the wicket-keeper and close fielders. It turned out to be snow.

His batting, however, has improved beyond recognition, and I like to think I can take some credit for that, as the cautionary tale of the seven little ducks illustrates. During the millennium match, he mentioned to me that in seven years at Alconbury he had failed to score a single run.

'Don't worry about that, Joe,' I said. 'I'm umpiring today. I'll make sure you don't get another duck. But for goodness sake don't tell the ICC.'

The first ball hit his pad and I shouted for him to run – and run he did, as only Joe can. Instead of signalling to the scorebox for a leg bye, I indicated that Joe had laid bat on ball to score his first run in eight attempts. He hugged me for all he was worth, and he didn't seem to mind when he was bowled middle stump off the next delivery he had to face.

The following year I again took him under my wing. I got him standing sideways on when batting instead of facing the bowlers square, as he had been doing. To his surprise – as well as mine – it worked. He made the highest score of his career. He boasted afterwards to anyone who cared to listen that he had made double figures. The scorecard showed he had not quite reached those dizzy heights – it was 8, not 10 – but what's a couple of runs between friends. He was so chuffed he sent me a bottle of champagne.

Another memorable 'Mighty Hat' occasion featured two England players, Mark Ramprakash and Gus Fraser. They formed a late-wicket pair smashing sixes into the car park and looking set to seal victory. Joe had other ideas. He demonstrated that cricket is also about cunning and artful tactics. His solution was simple. He put eighteen fielders in the car park. And it paid off – although it still needed England rugby union international Mike Catt to show all his turn of pace to race from the car park to an adjacent field to hold a stunning match-clinching catch.

Joe will play for charity anywhere and any time, combining his love for cricket with his love for a good cause. He is typical of all those who turn out in such matches the length and breadth of Britain. The ebullient Barry Fry, former Barnet, Southend and Birmingham City FC manager, now with Peterborough United, is another Alconbury regular, and he provided a delightful moment, which reminded me of that famous Test match episode involving Ian Botham, Allan Lamb, me and a mobile phone. Coming out to bat, Lamby explained that he had inadvertently kept his mobile in his pocket and asked me to look after it. Imagine my horror when, standing at square leg, I heard the phone ring. I took it out, held it up to my ear, and said, 'Dickie Bird here, who's speaking please?' A voice boomed, 'This is Ian Botham. Tell that Lamby to get a move on or he's in big trouble.'

When Barry's phone rang while he was fielding in the deep, he must have felt similar embarrassment – especially when the call turned out to be for his wife, who was watching from the sidelines.

I always feel comfortable when close to a weather-forecaster, in this case John Kettley.

Barry will be the first to admit that he is not the most athletic of fielders, but he always has a good excuse whenever he makes a mess of things. A dropped catch on this occasion brought the explanation, relayed to the crowd by the Bunburys' resident commentator, Huw Williams, 'I couldn't see a thing. The sun was in my eyes.' The sun, as one of his colleagues wryly observed, was behind him at the time.

Another commentator, Charles Colvile, who is also a big supporter of the Bunburys, told me of an egg-on-face time when he announced to the startled nation in a lunchtime news bulletin that 'A Russian submarine has been stranded on rocks six miles south of Swindon.' There was an embarrassed pause, after which Charles added, 'I'm sorry, that should have read Sweden.'

He also admits that he had never heard of the medical condition 'shin splints' until Andy Caddick suffered from it in the West Indies in 1994, and he has never been allowed to forget that he naïvely asked the question, 'So how long has he been wearing them?'

Everything about Alconbury speaks to me of much that is good about this country. In addition to such self-deprecating humour, there is camaraderie, fun and entertainment, all gift-wrapped in a typically English village cricket club setting, with gala day additions of bouncy castles, adventure playground, ice-cream vans, assorted stalls, marquees, barbecue, deckchairs, travel rugs, picnic tables and thermos flasks. The parish church, with its imposing spire rising majestically from the surrounding trees, seems to look on kindly as personalities from the sporting and entertainment worlds combine to raise money for a worthy cause. What more could you want?

Former England captain Colin Cowdrey married a member of the Norfolk family and always took great pains to support charity cricket.

Another charity match, at Arundel, has a special place in my affections because it was there that I was honoured to umpire the memorial match for that great Surrey and England captain, Peter May. It also happens to be one of the most unusual, as well as picturesque, grounds in Britain. It is sited in the grounds of an imposing castle, the home of the Norfolk family.

As well as the whole setting being as pretty as a picture, the square and outfield are the equal of many in first-class cricket.

The Norfolk family and cricket are bound together by tradition, the ground having been laid out by the Duke of Norfolk and opened by the then secretary of the MCC, Billy Griffith, in 1936. The current wooden pavilion – a splendid sight in itself – was opened in 1966, and inside there are some top-notch cricket paintings and photographs, many of them autographed.

It has always been the custom of the Duke of Norfolk's XI to play a curtain-raising one-day game with the season's tourists, and that

Arundel, a fairytale castle that is also a family home.

provides a great opportunity for people to get a glimpse of the latest demon paceman, hurricane hitter or spin sensation. It has always been a very popular event – especially when Australia or the West Indies have been the visitors. When the sixteenth Duke died, his widow Lavinia continued the tradition, and now that Lord Edward, Earl of Arundel, and his family have made the castle their home, the team is known as the Lord Arundel XI.

I was invited as a guest for a charity fixture with an Old England XI, but it teemed with rain on the journey south, with flash floods on some roads, and I knew that we would not be seeing any play that day. So it proved, but it did give me the opportunity to pay a first visit to the castle. When you look at it from below, it is like something out of a fairytale, with only the TV aerials on top of one of the Victorian west-wing towers giving the game away.

I have never delved much into history, but I have always been fascinated by places like this, so I was determined to find out more. My charming guide, Lizzie Gilks, could not have been more helpful. Lizzie told me that the castle originated in 1067, when William the Conqueror rewarded his friend and ally Roger de Montgomery by making him Earl of Arundel. In the castle's magnificent vaulted dining room, originally built by Henry II, there is a display of Mary Queen of Scots' priceless relics, including the beautiful rosary beads of gold and enamel that she carried to her execution at Fotheringay Castle. Lizzie showed them to me – and then went into the gory details of Mary's death. Did you know that it took the executioner three attempts before he eventually managed to decapitate her? Talk about being stiff-necked.

The so-called Barons' Hall – built on the site of the original hall – is

The Barons' Hall is big enough to play cricket in, and the boundary rope is already in place.

So that's what it's like at the sharp end! I made a point of visiting the Armoury.

When rain stopped play, my charming guide Lizzie Gilks took me on a tour of the castle.

so huge you could just about play a cricket match in it. It has been known for between five and six hundred people to sit down to dine there. It was so named to commemorate the signing of the Magna Carta in 1215 and the part the barons played in that historic event. It is so richly furnished and decorated it made me gasp.

As for the Armoury, well, what can I say? It was just like the set from one of those old Hammer Horror movies. Remember them? Or maybe one of those Ealing comedies I remember as a lad where you are supposed to believe there is a ghost in an old country house and someone hides in a suit of armour. Get the picture?

It was in the Armoury that Lizzie told me that Arundel has not one ghost, but four. Suddenly the suits of armour seemed to take on a life of their own. I kept nervously glancing over my shoulder, expecting at any minute to see an apparition of some sort gliding up behind me. Roger de Montgomery, they say, haunts the Norman keep. A young woman in white wanders around a tower from which she flung herself to her death after a tragic love affair. The Blue Man searches restlessly through the books in the Library – obviously looking for a copy of my auto-biography – and when a white owl flutters from one of the castle win-dows, it is said to foretell the death of someone connected to the castle.

As you will gather, a visit to Arundel Castle is an extraordinary experience. All that history is made more real by knowing that the place has been passed down through ten centuries. Lizzie confided that the youngest lords and ladies of the family can these days be seen skateboarding down the endless corridors, whizzing past picture galleries of a whole string of Dukes and Duchesses of Norfolk and Earls of Arundel, all arranged in order of descent. What a way to get to know your family history. Get your skates on and . . . whoosh.

Left: Arundel's Library has the warm glow of polished wood containing so much history.

Below: Sitting pretty in the drawing room.

I did wonder if any of the Queen's grandchildren had ever skateboarded down the galleries and corridors of Windsor Castle. I can't really imagine it, can you?

It just goes to emphasise that Arundel Castle is very much a family home, not quite like yours and mine, I have to admit, but, after all, the Duke of Norfolk is the premier duke of the land and head of the nation's leading Catholic family.

As I walked back to the cricket ground I noticed that, despite the gloomy weather, spectators were beginning to gather near the pavilion, complete with blankets, folding chairs, picnic baskets, hats and sunglasses, and the inevitable anoraks. They were obviously prepared for any eventuality. However, I feared that play was not going to be one of them.

It was a great shame and I shared the frustration of the optimistic fans. The ground has a natural grass banking where people can sit, and it opens out to beautiful views. Now they could only stand and stare balefully at the sad sight of covers on the pitch. I just hoped they wouldn't blame me for the weather. Cricket crowds usually did.

However, there were a good number of people who had booked lunch with the players, so they would still be able to mingle with their past heroes and enjoy the camaraderie and goodwill which is characteristic of the Old England games.

A holiday crowd seek the shade on a better day than I had at Arundel to watch Lord Arundel's XI v. Old England.

Old England started life in 1969 as the Whitbread Wanderers and was the brainchild of that great Test batsman Tom Graveney and Whitbread Brewery's Frank Twiselton. Since then, about 200 matches, featuring nearly a hundred Test and county players, have raised more than quarter of a million pounds for a variety of good causes.

There were quite a few Sussex players around, as you would expect – Jim Parks, the former England wicket-keeper/batsman, who became Old England's manager in 1980, John Snow, and another who could well figure in a cricket quiz. Let me test you out. Name the bowler who was playing club cricket when he was summoned to play his one and only game for England.

Give in?

Then I'll put you out of your misery. It is Tony Pigott, a fast medium bowler who was playing club cricket in New Zealand during an England tour when he was called up to the Test team because late injuries meant that replacements could not be flown out in time. Tony didn't let his country down. He took a few wickets to help them win the match, but he never played another Test.

He had the cheek to remind me of a cricket dinner he had attended when I was a guest speaker.

'Do you remember,' he chuckled, 'you started off at half past eleven and you were still going strong at a quarter to one. Every time we thought you'd finished you said, "Just one more story."'

No doubt Tony was relieved to find that all I was called on to do at Arundel was draw the raffle after an excellent lunch. The latter was served in the annexe at the rear of the pavilion, which is usually occupied by the practice nets. It is here that my old friend John Barclay struts his stuff as a coach for kids from all over the country. He does a great job, which is no surprise to anyone who has known him. He has always been an excellent leader of men and could have captained England. He showed his mettle by facing up to and making many difficult decisions as captain of Sussex. There was the time, for example, when, in order to try to force a victory, he announced a declaration with Gehan Mendis on 97 not out and chasing his fifth century in six innings. John's observation was typical Old Etonian – 'Oh, dear, I do hope Gehan doesn't think me a swine and a cad.'

John was, and still is, a bit of a character, as Imran Khan will affirm. The two of them had to share a room one night in a boring hotel in the back of beyond, and Imran was surprised to find John tucked up in bed very early in the evening.

'What's the matter, John?' he queried. 'Are you sick or something?'

'Good heavens, no,' John replied. 'I just want to get a good night's sleep. Remember, I've got to face Clive Rice and Richard Hadlee in the morning.'

I meet up at Arundel with former England and Sussex fast bowler John Snow.

Imran promised to keep the volume on the telly turned down, but John couldn't get to sleep. After tossing and turning for a long time, he ended up watching the late-night film and then complained it had given him a headache. And so it went on. Imran finally nodded off, only to be woken, in what seemed to be no time at all, by the sound of the radio and the kettle being filled. He leaped out of bed, thinking he must have overslept, but when he drew back the curtains he was amazed to find it was still quite dark. He looked at his watch. It was 5 a.m.

After giving Imran a ticking off for making him watch the film and thus bringing on his headache, John headed for the door saying he needed a walk along the river to restore his peace of mind. And he left poor Imran unable to get another wink of sleep and feeling distinctly out of sorts. No wonder Imran regarded his colleague as the archetypal English eccentric – little wonder, too, that they never shared a room again.

In my experience, cricket followers are always generous in their support of charities, and so it proved at Arundel. The items auctioned included a signed picture of the Red Devils, a set of reservations for rides on the London Eye, the usual array of autographed bats, and many other bits and pieces. So despite the lack of cricket, it was still a successful fund-raising event. And I played my part. I autographed a copy of my book, *White Cap and Bails*, and it fetched £100 in the auction. That absolutely made my day.

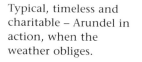

Typical, timeless and charitable – Arundel in action, when the weather obliges.

CHAPTER 10

BATTY ABOUT BATS

THE making of cricket bats has been the lifetime's work of Eric Loxton. Many of the top Test players from all over the world have good reason to be grateful for his skills. Just take a look at this list of star names. They have all used bats that Eric has made at the Slazenger factories in Barnsley and Horbury: Viv Richards, Des Haynes, Carl Hooper, Richie Richardson, Sachin Tendulkar, Mohammad Azharuddin, Geoff Boycott, Graham Gooch, Alec Stewart, Allan Lamb, Chris Adams, Mark Ramprakash, Alistair Brown, Robert Croft, Andrew Flintoff, Mark Butcher, Adam Hollioake, Neil Fairbrother, John Crawley, Dermot Reeves, Robin Bailey, Aravinda de Silva, Jacques Kallis, Shaun Pollock, Peter Willey, Mark Taylor, Mark Waugh, Kim Hughes, Matthew Maynard, the Flower brothers . . . it is almost endless.

Eric proudly told me, 'There aren't many top players whom I haven't supplied with a bat at some time or another, and there are those who have been with me since they were lads, including Stewart, Brown and Butcher.'

What makes the work so interesting for Eric is that all the bats differ in shape, size and weight. The thinnest he has ever made was for Azharuddin and the heaviest – a mighty three pounds one ounce – for Gooch. Willey used to have four or five grips on his for some reason.

When players are going through a lean time, they sometimes come to Eric and ask him to make a bat with a slightly different shape or weight. They'll try anything to get out of the rut they are in.

'When that happens, I can see that things are getting on top of them,' said Eric, 'so I do all I can to help, even though it may be merely psychological. I remember Neil Fairbrother having a really bad time in his younger days. He had just got back into the first XI at Lancashire and suddenly found that the runs had dried up. He was here every other week. Finally, after lots of discussion, he decided to try a bat that was as light as possible. He'd been using one about two pounds eight ounces. I made him one that was about two pounds three ounces. You couldn't have stirred a curry with it. Yet next day he went out and got a hundred. There was no stopping him after that.'

Left: When players are out of form they sometimes come to Eric in the hope that a new bat will work like a magic wand.

Batsmen have their own little idiosyncrasies when it comes to bat design, but Eric has been dealing with some players for so long he could probably produce a bat blindfold that met all their requirements. He knows all their little quirks and fads. For example, Carl Hooper wanted a handle that was square at the bottom; Geoff Boycott insisted that his handle was a little bit square at the bottom but round and thin at the top; Paul Nixon's is oval, like an egg; Alec Stewart's is semi-oval at the bottom, going round and not too thick; Mark Butcher prefers it very thin at the bottom.

'They all vary in some way,' said Eric. 'They come to see me, explain what they want, and every bat is tailor-made for each person.' All the bats Eric makes for individual players carry an E stamped on the shoulder. It is the mark of a master craftsman.

Allan Lamb's bats had to be two pounds eleven or twelve ounces, with two grips, and the ball had to really bounce off them. Other than that, he could hardly care less. The wood could have been black, green or yellow. It would not have bothered him.

Eric was once in the process of discarding a bat he was making for someone else when Lamby, who was watching, intervened. 'Hold on a minute, Eric, let me have a feel. It looks all right to me.'

Lamby took the bat and tried it out with a ball. It really pinged off the blade and Eric could see that the Northants and England batsman quite liked it.

'If you're thinking what I think you're thinking,' he said, 'can I just say that, as a Test player, you will be expected to have a better-looking bat than that. If my bosses or other companies saw you using it for England, it would not reflect too well on me or the firm.'

But Lamby snorted, 'I don't care what the **** it looks like, it feels fine to me.'

So he took the bat, and whacked a hundred with it at Headingley.

Eric was just an apprentice with the firm when Garry Sobers first started getting his bats from Slazenger, and he recalled, 'He would come in, pick up half a dozen or so bats that we had set aside for him, and try them out. If he liked the pick-up of a bat he would have it. If not, he'd reject it. Appearance didn't matter. It was how it felt that was important.'

One year when the West Indies were on tour, Viv Richards, Andy Roberts and a couple of other players visited the Horbury factory and Eric was designated to look after them. Because they were also making a video at the time, the quartet needed to be around longer than usual so somewhere had to be found for them to eat. Eric's instructions were to take them to a 'posh pub' for lunch. Eric explained to them what the plan was.

A bat's appearance never mattered to Garry Sobers. It was how it felt in the hand that was important.

'It's a top quality pub. Nothing tacky. I'm sure you'll like it,' he said.

The West Indians looked at each other, and spokesman Viv replied, 'That's as may be, Eric, but isn't there a fish and chip shop around here?'

So it was fish and chips five times, eaten in the traditional manner out of the newspaper – and they loved it.

A lifetime's knowledge and craft go into every one of the bats that Eric Loxton creates at the Slazenger factory in Barnsley.

Often when the overseas lads used to pop into the Horbury shop, Eric and his mates would roll up a rubber grip, fasten it with tape, and have the tourists bowl it at them down the yellow lines in the middle of the factory floor. Can you imagine Wes Hall or Charlie Griffith tearing in? Of course, the rubber with the tape round it didn't bounce very high so the taunt was, 'Go on, sling 'em down, you don't scare us.'

They always had a lot of fun, but what with all the scoffing and mucking about it's a wonder they ever got round to making bats.

The worst people to satisfy are the second XI players who have stars in their eyes after being given a couple of games in the first team. Said Eric, 'They swagger in, thinking they're superstars already.'

There was one young lad from Somerset who complained that his bat was turning on the ground as he took his guard.

'Hold it a bit tighter, then,' Eric suggested, helpfully.

'Oh no, that's not the problem,' came the reply. 'It's the bat. You see here, right at the bottom. If you make the bat heavier on one side, I'm sure that'll do the trick.'

The poor misguided soul returned a few weeks later still complaining that the bat was not right. Eric looked at the bat, noted all the worn edges, and asked, 'How do you know the bat's not right? You haven't managed to hit anything in the middle yet.'

Then there are the mothers who buy bats for their sons. Now they really do drive Eric batty, or at least, some of them do. One complained, 'Look here, my man, I paid well over a hundred pounds for this bat, and it's hardly been used, but just look at the state of it. There are red marks all over.'

'The best cure for that, Madam,' Eric retorted, 'is to tell your lad to stop hitting the ball.'

Slazenger bats are made from cane handles and willow blades. The new nine-piece handles are hand-made in Barnsley by Eric, using the finest Manou cane, and they provide the perfect combination of stiffness and flexibility for top performance. The wooden blades are made from either English or Kashmir willow.

You may ask why other wood is not used, but willow is the only one that stands up to the hammering given to it by a cricket ball. When compressed, willow keeps its density and it is also light and durable. None of the other hard woods give the right sound, the ball doesn't bounce off, and you can't press them.

Said Eric, 'We've tried other woods, but they just don't work. The nearest was poplar, but that wasn't durable enough.'

So willow it has to be. Anyway, 'the sound of leather on poplar' would not have quite the same ring to it.

The highest quality bats are made from English willow, which is

The tools of Eric's trade, and the ball with which he tests the bats to see if they have the right rebound properties.

found mainly in Essex, Norfolk, Suffolk and East Anglia, where, because of the combination of climate and soil, it tends to grow better. Slazenger did try some from up north but it was slower growing and therefore not economical. The willow grows best on soggy, non-arable areas, or on river banks, mainly on big estates where there is land that is really wet and unworkable. It is there that you get the willow plantations. English willow combines lightness with good rebound properties and bats made from this wood therefore give the best performance, although they are more expensive and need proper care. Kashmir willow is more economical, but is heavier and has less rebound.

The pressing of the bat ensures maximum rebound of the ball off the blade. English willow, in its natural state, is soft and fibrous, so it has to be seasoned before the shaping and pressing process. The bat has to be hard enough to withstand most impacts by a ball and yet soft enough to give good rebound off the blade. The softer the blade, the better the performance in terms of rebound, but the blade is more prone to dent. The harder the blade the worse the performance, but the blade will be more durable. Even the medium-pressed blade can be damaged if the batsman digs out a yorker or edges the ball.

It seems that nobody has yet found a wood that gives good rebound performance without indenting if the ball is edged. Toe and edge damage to the bat is still, therefore, an inevitable part of cricket. However, such damage can usually be repaired. And it certainly does not mean that the blade is faulty.

Eric takes great pride in seeing players achieve success using a bat he has made – like the one with which Mark Butcher scored that brilliant century in the only victory of the series against the Aussies at Headingley in 2001. It had been specially made by Eric just two days before the match.

'Mark had not been having a very good spell for about eighteen months and was really down in the dumps, despite his recall to the Test side, which had come about only because of injuries. So he came to see me and we discussed how we could modify his bat here and there. Eventually, at his request, I made him one with a bit more wood at the bottom, thinned out the handle all the way up, and opened it out a bit near the shoulders. That seemed to suit him and it worked a treat. It is so important for a player to have confidence in the bat he is using.

'These people know if there is the slightest difference. It may be a better bat than the one they previously had but the quality has nothing to do with it. In their mind, it is not quite right. It doesn't feel right. So they reject it.'

Willow pattern Barnsley-style – some of the wood being seasoned in the factory.

At one time Geoff Boycott used a heavier bat to start his innings, when he was fresh. If he was still there later in the day, he would switch to a lighter bat as he tired. We're talking ounces here, but Boycs believed that it made a big difference and was a tremendous help to him. That's typical of the attention to detail that helped to make him such a great player.

Most cricketers are very good to Eric. They make sure he has the best seats when he goes to matches, with lunch, tea, drinks and all that thrown in. There was an unfortunate incident when he went to watch Surrey play Yorkshire at Scarborough in a one-dayer. The visitors hit a record-breaking 300 and odd, whacking the White Rose bowling all over the place. For Eric, however, there was the consolation that Alec Stewart, Mark Butcher, Alistair Brown and Adam Hollioake were all using his bats.

There had already been two centuries when Hollioake went in and hit a thumping great six. The ball soared straight towards Eric, who instinctively stuck up his hand and brought off a brilliant catch. Then he felt an excruciating pain and was devastated to discover that he had broken his finger. He winced at the memory. 'Imagine that,' he said. 'From a hit off a bat I'd made.'

To make matters worse, Hollioake went round after the game, not realising what had happened, and asked Eric, 'Can you repair this bat and send it back down to me?'

Eric retorted, 'Get stuffed, you cheeky sod. Can you repair this finger so that I can go back to work in the morning?'

CHAPTER 11

RACING CERTS

Newmarket's famous clock tower at the top of the High Street.

Left: Foreign Affairs storms home to win the forty-second running of the John Smith's Magnet Cup at York.

I ONCE read in a cricket brochure that two great men had attended Harrow School, men of charisma, both born leaders. One was Winston Churchill, the other Julian Wilson. Well, we all know about Churchill's achievements. But what of the retired horse-racing commentator? What has he done to be elevated to such a pinnacle? And in what cricketing context? It just so happens that Julian is the inspirational captain of the Newmarket Racing XI, as well as being a slow left-arm bowler with what he claims is a 'dignified, elegant style of delivery'.

He once offered his perfect scenario for a game of cricket as follows:

1   Arrive punctually, just in time for a pint of best bitter before an athlete's lunch of pasta, washed down with high-quality wine.
2   Win toss and bat. Top-order batsmen entertain large crowd with sparkling strokeplay while number 11 (J.D.B. Wilson) monitors the afternoon's racing on mobile phone/ceefax.
3   Number 11 not required to bat.
4   Tea.
5   After pace bowlers have struggled against the top order, number 11 comes on to bowl left-arm, baffling world-class players with his unplayable chinamen, and demolishing the star-studded opposition single-handed.
6   Carried shoulder high from the square by an army of Charlie's Angels and Baywatch Babes, who join the heroic leg-spinner in a foaming tub.

I have to say that while numbers 1–4 are fairly realistic expectations, numbers 5 and 6 remain unfulfilled fantasy for the poor chap.

The Newmarket Trainers – now renamed the Newmarket Racing XI – came into existence thirty years ago and Julian has been involved for the last twenty after moving to Burrough Green, where the cricket field backs on to his cottage. In 1981, Lester Piggott put up a trophy to be competed for between Julian's team and the village team on the first Sunday of September, and that match has been played ever since. In alternating years, money is raised for Motor Neurone Disease and

Left: Julian Wilson, tea interval auctioneer, during the annual charity match at Burrough Green.

Below left: Julian reveals an unexpected talent with the bat for the Newmarket Racing XI. Michael Holding is the umpire, without benefit of Hawkeye.

Michael Bell supervising the start of training in the early hours after suffering a dodgy lbw decision the previous day.

the Macmillan Cancer Fund. Said Julian proudly, 'It's only a small village, but we always raise more than a thousand pounds through this event.'

On the cold blustery September day when I saw him in action, he revealed an unexpected talent with the bat, making 27, including two fives, accumulated via two half-hearted prods for singles followed by a couple of fours from overthrows. It was his highest knock of the summer. Michael Bell, one of the trainers, got out when he thought he was miles down the pitch, with the ball possibly going down the leg side to boot, when he was the victim of a dubious decision by my old mate Michael Holding, that great West Indian pace bowler, who was one of the umpires.

'I thought it was a bit dodgy,' said the batsman. 'I'm sure Hawkeye would have shown it was not out. But unfortunately we don't have that facility at Burrough Green. Still, I have to admit that he had been quite kind to me with an earlier decision, so I can't really complain.'

I had not expected to see Holding at the game although, knowing his fondness for the racing world, maybe I should have. In any case, it was lovely to meet up with him again. I included him in my world squad in my autobiography, and he was truly one of the greats of my time as an umpire.

His nickname was Whispering Death because when he ran up on his approach, there was scarcely a sound. With other fast bowlers I was always aware of them pounding up behind me, getting closer and closer, until they exploded into action. With Holding it was different. It was so quiet, just like the calm before a storm. He would glide smoothly and effortlessly over the ground and then 'whoosh', he would rocket past me at the point of delivery, the ball arrowing its way through the air at a frightening pace.

He was a marvellous bowler but, having seen the lbw decision that tolled the Bell for the Newmarket trainer, I can't say the same about his umpiring.

One of the greatest weeks that the Newmarket Racing team has experienced came in 1987, when they went on tour to Barbados. They had three fixtures, one of which was at the Kensington Oval where Sir Garfield Sobers, Wes Hall, Charlie Griffith and Seymour Nurse all played. That was the occasion when Sobers walked down the steps of the pavilion that had been named after him for the first time.

It is, of course, as a racing commentator that Julian has made a name for himself since starting out when television was still showing black and white pictures. He has commentated on twenty-four Grand Nationals, the two most emotional being Red Rum's first and third victories.

'In a way,' he recalled, 'the first was the more memorable for me because I covered the section from the third fence to Valentines – the

Safely over Becher's, but you have to do it twice.

A morning canter to sort out future Classic winners.

Becher's area – for all those years, and I will never forget the sight of Crisp coming through the second time round. He was about a fence clear before Becher's, and I remember saying I had never seen a horse so far clear at that stage of the National. He went away from me still well clear and it looked as though there was no way he could be beaten. But, as everyone knows, Red Rum caught and passed him so dramatically in the last few strides.'

It was heartbreaking in a way, but the irony of it was that 'Grandstand' had asked Julian to do a feature called 'Follow the Favourite' in the six weeks leading up to the National, and he had chosen to follow Red Rum because there was a good story behind him. His trainer, Ginger McCain, of whom no one had heard at the time, was a taxi driver, and he galloped his horse on the beach.

Said Julian, 'It was a miracle that Red Rum should win the National at twenty to one. And all those wonderful pictures you will have seen a hundred times of the horse going down to the beach are images that will live forever. It's like a small broadcasting memorial to the Red Rum story.'

Another of Julian's most precious memories is of trainer Josh Gifford, one of his oldest pals, winning the National with Aldaniti, ridden by Bob Champion, who had fought cancer to fulfil his dream – and at 33–1 too.

Julian's final meeting before his retirement was at Chepstow for the Welsh Grand National in 1997. The programme prepared a 'This is Your Racing Life' tribute to Julian, with which Graham Cowdrey was very much involved, and that was 'great fun, as well as being very emotional'. Julian spoke his pay-off line in the unsaddling enclosure, something like, 'It's au revoir from them and goodbye from me.'

'I have always been very lucky for people,' he told me. 'Earth Summit won the Welsh Grand National that day, and I told the owners that I hoped he would go on and win the big one. And he did. So it was a great way for me to go.'

Julian was also an owner, and in 1977 one of his horses, Tumbledownwind, won the Gimcrack Stakes at York's Ebor meeting.

'In racing terms,' he reflected, 'that was probably the most important day of my life. Not only did I do the commentary for BBC radio, which was very nerve-racking, but in winning the race, Tumbledownwind became a very valuable horse.

It all came as a wonderful surprise because Tumbledownwind was much better on firm ground and when Julian woke up at four in the morning and heard the pitter-patter of the rain, he feared the worst. When it continued non-stop until race time twelve hours later, he thought the horse had no chance.

'But, glory be,' chuckled Julian, 'he ploughed his way through the mud to win, and that will always be a very special day in Yorkshire.'

Studying form before the off in the York sunshine.

*

There are fifty-nine racecourses in the UK, some catering for National Hunt – over the sticks – and others for flat racing. York comes into the latter category, staging fifteen days' racing a year, which doesn't seem much on the face of it and, like many other people not directly associated with the sport, I have often wondered what happens at these courses for the remaining 350 days of the year.

John Smith, manager/secretary and clerk of the course for sixteen years, told me it was a question he was asked all the time.

'After one meeting, my wife had a call at home asking if I was there. When she said I was at the office, the chap replied, "Oh, really?" in the kind of tone that suggested he could not believe there was anything for me to do there now that the racing had finished.'

But John assured me that they really do need the time between meetings to get things prepared and, with all the other functions that are held at the course – conferences, wedding receptions, banquets, exhibitions, and the like – there is always so much going on.

When I visited, a very big project was on the go – the building of a new £20 million stand. John told me, 'We have to provide the facilities that people expect to see at a major sporting event these days. We have all been to football and cricket grounds where you had to sit on hard benches. Expectations are so much greater now. People want comfort.'

York has 1,800 members, with a waiting list of 500. The main advantage of being a member is the discount on admission charges.

John Smith, manager/ secretary and clerk of the course at York, mislaid a blacksmith at his first meeting and kept the Queen's horse waiting.

The only other perk is a small bar accommodating less than a hundred people, with no viewing facility. So one of the main objectives of the new stand is to provide bars, plus viewing, for more members.

Said John, 'Some people have got the idea that it is going to be another of those corporate hospitality stands, but it isn't. We are trying to give our members a little bit more for their support.'

There has been racing on the site since 1731, and consequently there is a real feeling of history about the place. There used to be public hangings on the far side of the course, which is where the notorious highwayman Dick Turpin met his untimely end.

When John first arrived he could have been forgiven for thinking that they had named the first meeting in his honour, but it referred to the sponsors, the local brewery, and it turned out to be a real nerve-racking affair. About ten minutes before the start of the first race there was an announcement over the p.a. system asking for the blacksmith to go to the unsaddling enclosure as the Queen's horse needed re-plating. Now, the blacksmith in those days was a bit of a character. Rusty, it has to be said, liked a pint or three of the sponsor's brew, so when he could not be found, the other John Smith feared the worst.

He was responsible to the stewards for making sure that the meeting ran smoothly and, while earlier in the parade ring it was a case of 'Hello, John, nice to see you, you're doing a great job,' it was now 'Ah, there you are, Smith. What the hell's going on? Better get it sorted out pdq.'

By five to two there were 30,000 baying customers impatiently waiting for the off, jockeys and horses hanging about not quite knowing what was going on – and still no sign of Rusty.

Eventually he was tracked down, stone cold sober, to the stables right across the other side of the course, doing some work for a trainer. He finally saw to the Queen's horse, but the race started ten minutes late and that had a concertina effect on the whole afternoon's programme. They tried in vain to play catch-up.

'I can laugh about it now,' chuckled John, 'but it certainly wasn't funny at the time. Now when they refer to that particular John Smith's meeting, it has very much my name on it rather than the sponsor's. It was the day Rusty almost got me the sack.'

John also inherited a ruling that declared ties and jackets have to be worn in the county stand where the members congregate. No mention of trousers, you'll note. Anyway, this particular chap turned up, trousered, but otherwise improperly dressed.

'Sorry, Sir,' said John, 'you can't come in here without a jacket and tie.'

'Fair enough,' came the reply, 'but in that case I'm not going to allow my horse to run.' And he was as good as his word.

A packed Knavesmire for the John Smith's Magnet Cup.

Later, John had a letter from the owner, apologising. He admitted he was in the wrong. To make amends, he wanted to sponsor a race at the next meeting, and he wanted to call it The Collar and Tie Handicap. As for the trophy, John suggested it might be an idea to get one costing about £50 for a token presentation in the unsaddling enclosure.

Come the day of the race, the guy turned up with a huge box out of which he took a gigantic solid silver trophy in the form of a collar and tie. It had cost 750 quid.

'He was another great character,' John recalled. 'Lovely man. And it all came about because we wouldn't let him in the county stand without a collar and tie.'

I've heard of people losing their shirts at race meetings, but that takes the biscuit.

CHAPTER 12

LAND OF MY FATHERS

Blaengwinfi, near the Rhondda. Typical Welsh valleys landscape.

Left: The biggest of all the Welsh waterfalls at Llanrhaeadr-ym-Mochnant.

WHEN I think about Wales, my thoughts automatically turn to rugby, mining, choirs and chapel, and therefore Cliff Morgan. For Cliff, brought up in a mining family and a member of the local chapel choir, went on to become the most creative stand-off of his generation, capped by Cardiff, Wales, the Barbarians and the British Lions.

I had the great privilege of spending a couple of hours in his company over lunch and I was intrigued, amused and deeply moved in turn – as well as being thoroughly entertained – as this born storyteller spoke so passionately about the country of his birth. Wales reminds me so much of my native Yorkshire with its valleys, peaks, winding rivers, waterfalls, estuaries, historic buildings and people so fiercely proud of their background and traditions.

His father, he told me, had been a coalminer. So had mine. If it had not been for cricket, my life could have been spent down the pit so I knew what he was talking about when he went on to describe living conditions that were similar to the ones in which I had been brought up.

'My father,' he recalled, 'brought home three pounds a week if he was lucky. But we always had plenty to eat. My mother had learned from her mother how to make wonderful meals that cost very little. For example, she bought cheap cuts of neck of lamb for a broth, which would last two days. She also made beautiful apple tart, using apples from an orchard across the road. Then there were gooseberries and rhubarb from our own garden. And as children we gathered wimberries, to which mother would add a few blackcurrants to sharpen the taste.'

I licked my lips as Cliff went through a typical week's menu in the Morgan household and was left marvelling yet again at the resourcefulness and imagination of those mining families, both in Wales and Yorkshire. I smiled when he said that you could tell the day of the week from the food his mother put on the table. It was just like being back home in Barnsley in the thirties and forties.

Monday was always cold meat left from Sunday lunch, sometimes made into rissoles. The meat was cooked on the Saturday night – nothing interfered with attendance at chapel on Sunday morning. On

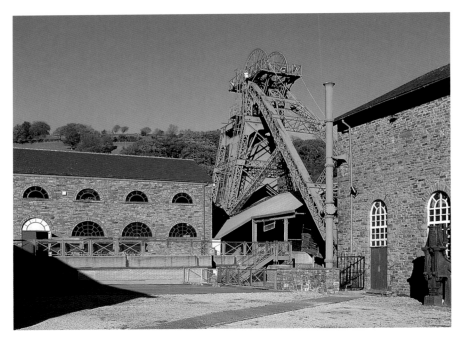

An example of the sort of pit on which a whole village would have depended. This one has become a mining museum.

Tuesdays a chap with a horse and cart sold fish door to door, so there was hake and chips that night. Wednesday and Thursday it was the lamb broth, and so it went on. There were never any surprises.

Cliff speaks of his mother with great fondness, and he has so much admiration for the way she lived out her faith.

'Although she never had very much money to spend, she always managed to put some in the envelope at the chapel. It was the first thing she put to one side when my father brought home his pay and gave it to her.'

It was not until after his mother died that Cliff found out that, for seventeen years while he was living in London, she had put half-a-crown into an envelope every week in his name, as a member of the chapel.

'She never told me,' said Cliff. 'But, you see, she didn't want my name to come off the chapel register. She was a remarkable woman. As kids we were greatly influenced by our parents, the chapel, and the village as a whole. We could trust the schoolteacher, the headmaster, the doctor, the village bobby. You would touch your cap to them as a mark of respect. Life centred round the chapel. You went three times on a Sunday – morning service, Sunday School in the afternoon, and then evening service, and straight after that you went to choir practice.'

Cliff remembers like it was yesterday being carried on his father's back to choir practice. He told me, 'By the time I was twelve, I knew all the parts – soprano, alto, tenor and bass – of all the great works, including Elijah, Twelfth Mass, Messiah. What a bloody din I could make.'

It must have been a tuneful din, though, if that is not a contradiction in terms, because he later sang with his mother and father in the 116-strong Porth and District Mixed Choir.

'You can't buy memories such as these,' he sighed. 'They were wonderful days.'

Cliff looked at me wistfully. 'That's all gone, hasn't it? Along with the freedom and the innocence. Who, today, would let a five-year-old walk a mile and a half out in the country to school and then back again? Nobody imagined any harm coming to us, and it never did. The streets were safer and we played a lot of games on the pavement. It was our playground. Ropes were hung from lampposts so we could swing round them, and the girls played hopscotch.'

They were also allowed to play in the fields, the most important of which was the Relay Field behind Cliff's house in Trebanog. It was so called because it had the Relay Shed in it, and that was the centre of broadcasting around the Rhondda Valley. In Trebanog, this relay

The view of Pen-y-Graig that Cliff Morgan would have had from his own village of Trebanog.

system meant they could listen to the BBC's Welsh Home Service and the Light Programme. One particular memory Cliff has of the Relay Shed is one summer night, 30 August 1937, when practically the entire village gathered in the field. The Shed had been specially opened up for the broadcast from America of the world heavyweight title fight between Tommy Farr, a Rhondda man from Tonypandy, and the great Joe Louis at the Yankee Stadium, New York.

He recalled, 'The fight commentary wasn't on the other stations we got at home. They had already closed down for the night. So hundreds of people went up to the Relay where the transmitter could pick up the American broadcast. I was seven at the time and was taken there by my father and mother. As kids we were running about playing while it went on, but I heard enough of Tommy Farr's defeat never to forget it.'

You can tell from all this that people were far more trusting in those days. Cliff's front door was never locked. His mother would leave the insurance book, and the money, under the cloth on the living-room table. The insurance man would walk into the empty house, enter the amount, take the money and leave the book. Nothing was ever stolen.

Like most mothers in Wales – and Yorkshire, too – Mrs Morgan shopped for almost everything at the Co-op. The system was that every so often you bought a certain number of Co-op cheques, say a pound's

In Cliff's childhood, life revolved around the chapel.

worth, and then used them to pay your bills for as long as they lasted. The cheques, therefore, were precious. Cliff's mother would leave them on the front doorstep with the empty bottles to pay for the milk without a second thought.

It's different now. My cottage is all alarmed, there are guards on the windows, and shutters on the doors. And I still don't feel safe leaving it for any length of time.

Musing on all this, Cliff observed, 'The essential difference from our days as kids and today is that the chapels were full. The influence of the chapels was enormous. Although it may have been suffocating for some in many ways, there was always that basic feeling of love and celebration. There were sermons that took you to heaven, if only for five minutes, there was marvellous singing, and a wonderful togetherness. Now who goes to chapel three times on a Sunday? Or even once?'

When his mother died, Cliff took his father a great big television set and, as it was the only one in the village, all his pals used to go round and watch the programmes with him, so it helped his loneliness. Visiting him some time later, Cliff asked, 'Tell me, what kind of programmes do you like watching?'

'Oh, you know,' came the reply, '"Panorama" and suchlike.'

'He was a liar,' said Cliff, affectionately. 'He used to watch "Steptoe and Son" and "The Two Ronnies". He loved all that – and, of course, the rugby and cricket.'

It was while watching his beloved Wales play New Zealand on the telly that Cliff's father finally lost his battle against the miners' disease, silicosis, and died. The last thing he was aware of was the sound of Cliff's voice on the commentary describing a try for the New Zealanders, scored by Murdoch in the right-hand corner of Cardiff Arms Park.

At his funeral the following week, 480 people, including Richard Burton, his brothers, and all the rugby boys, signed the register in the chapel. Cliff was there to greet them all. One of his dad's best pals, the local innkeeper, who had also worked with him at the pit, came up to shake hands.

'Cliff, bach,' he said, 'sad I am that you've lost your father. But sadder still for me. I've lost my best friend.' He turned away, but glanced over his shoulder as he added the punchline: 'But, Cliff bach, who could blame your father for having a heart attack in that second half?'

Cliff told that story at a dinner in London. There was a stony silence. He told it when speaking to the Wombwell Cricket Lovers' Society, near Barnsley, and it brought the house down. That, he said, emphasised the special empathy between mining communities. In life and in death, they were very much on the same wavelength. They understood each other.

That philosophical regard for funerals, so beloved by the Welsh, was also typified in an incident at Twickenham when Cliff was one of half-a-dozen people who had gathered to scatter the ashes of former England captain Eric Evans, 'a noisy, loveable Lancastrian' whose spirit Cliff admired.

That small group, including Eric's wheelchair-bound wife and his daughter, went to the halfway line, but Cliff remarked half-jokingly to the Lancashire secretary, 'I don't think this is the place to do it. You'd never find Eric on the halfway line. He was always on the twenty-five, waiting for kick-off.'

So they moved to the twenty-five, but as the secretary took a handful of the ashes and began to cast them over the ground, the wind blew them back, and the next thing they knew they were all covered in ash. There was an awkward, embarrassed silence before Cliff remarked, 'Eric never did like playing against the wind, did he?'

Immediately he thought what a stupid tactless thing to say. But, to his relief, it brought nothing but laughter. It was typically Eric. They all knew he would be having a good laugh as well.

Cliff will never forget his first invitation to play for Wales. It came from another Eric Evans. This one was secretary of the Welsh Rugby Union. Cliff recalled, 'People imagine that it comes on a beautifully embossed card of some kind, but it was on the kind of paper you would rip off a lavatory roll.'

What made matters worse was that, after all the details of arrangements for the day of the match in question – it was against Ireland at the Arms Park in 1951 – there was a postscript which said, 'You are to wear the white-topped stockings you wore against Scotland.' As far as Cliff was concerned, that was extremely difficult. He had not played against Scotland. But the message stressed, 'Don't forget to bring them, as stockings have become very scarce.'

Underneath there was the question, 'Are you going to wear your own shorts, or do you wish to borrow a pair of the Union's?'

Said Cliff, 'It was quite bizarre. The high point of your rugby career – your first cap – and you get a lunatic message like that.'

Cliff also noticed how everything was timed to make certain that the players did not have to stay overnight in a hotel at the Union's expense. They were instructed to go home after practice on the Friday night and return next morning on the bus. After the game, the dinner was laid on at six in order that it would finish by eight, enabling everybody to get home by train that same night. In the eight years that Cliff played for Wales, he never stayed in a hotel before or after a home match.

An hour after the game against Ireland ended in a draw, denying the Irish the Triple Crown, Cliff went to Evans for the travelling expenses he had incurred.

Born storyteller, instinctive rugby player, Cliff Morgan speaks passionately of the land of his fathers.

'Name?' queried Evans. Cliff thought it was a strange question in view of the fact that he'd been out there busting a gut for his country all afternoon. Still, best humour the fellow.

'Morgan, Sir,' he replied.

'Expenses?'

'Yes please.'

'I mean,' said Evans, though gritted teeth, 'how much?'

'Five shillings, Sir.'

Evans flicked through the pages of the school exercise book he had in front of him, then suddenly slammed it shut and banged on the table.

'You're a liar and a cheat, Morgan. It's two shillings and fourpence return from Trebanog to Cardiff. That's four shillings and eight pence in total.'

With that he gave Cliff half a crown, a two shilling piece and two pennies in an envelope. Cliff's father stuck it in his scrap book and there it stayed.

But Mrs Morgan gave her son a right ticking off. She told him, 'Mr Evans was quite right. It wasn't five shillings, was it? It was four and eightpence. You were cheating. You shouldn't do that. It's not worth it.'

Another lesson learned.

Incidentally, on the day of the match he boarded the bus as usual and heard two men talking about the impending international. One of them said, 'How the 'ell will he cope with their big fellows? He's only a titch. Too bloody small. I know. I see 'im regular. Bet you he's no more than ten stone wet through.'

His companion replied, 'Don't talk daft. He's more than that, mun. Saw 'im at a do last week. Got great big shoulders he has. I reckon he's eleven stone if he's an ounce.'

And so it went on until one of them turned to Cliff for a third opinion. 'You're standing there saying nothing. What do you think Morgan weighs?'

'Twelve stone,' he replied decisively.

'Bloody rubbish.'

'I tell you he is,' maintained Cliff.

The guy turned to the other folk on the bus. 'Would you credit it,' he barked. 'It's always the same. Them who knows bugger-all about it always argue the toss.'

It was at Twickenham the following July that Cliff felt, for the first time, what it was like to be on a winning Welsh side as they beat England in front of a crowd of 73,000, with many more thousands in the street. Naturally, after the game the Welsh were full of it. Having eventually reached the dressing-room, they started singing away, and Cliff was whisked off to the big bar by the Treorchy Male Voice Choir.

He smiled at the recollection. 'I stood on the counter conducting the singing, and got so caught up in my role that I missed the team bus back to town for the celebration dinner.' Luckily he got a lift from a policeman.

Welsh male voice choirs such as the Treorchy have a worldwide reputation, so I was a little surprised by what Cliff had to say about them.

'All the Welsh,' he confided, 'reckon they can sing. And that they can sing better than anybody else. But when you listen to the Huddersfield Choral Society doing 'Messiah' at Christmas, the intonation is perfect, the tempo, the pitch and everything else is exactly right. When you go to Wales and listen to the male voice choirs, the tempo isn't quite what it should be, and the intonation suffers, and they may sometimes wander ever so slightly off key, but there is great heart in the singing. And that is another curious thing that links the mining communities of Wales and Yorkshire. The heart. This thing from within you. And if you sing from the heart, it touches the hearts of those who are listening.'

After beating England, Wales went on to win the Triple Crown that year, the clincher coming with victory over Ireland at Lansdowne Road. Cliff broke his leg in that game, but did not realise it until after it was over, despite being in such pain that he had to be carried to the top of the stand to do an interview with Eamonn Andrews.

The latter asked what Cliff would remember most about the famous victory and was astounded to be told, 'My father lost his teeth.'

It was true. Cliff's dad had been sitting right up in the corner of the stand, and when Ken Jones went over for a try just below him, he jumped up and shouted so hard that he spat his top set of teeth fifteen rows in front of him. He never did get them back.

Cliff recalled with great pride the day in 1953 when his Cardiff team became the only club side to inflict a defeat on the All Black tourists that year. 'Every year since then,' he told me, 'on the Friday night before the anniversary of that win, we all meet up again at Cardiff. There were fifteen of us originally, then fourteen, thirteen, twelve, eleven, ten, nine, eight, seven. Now there are only six of us left. But we still meet.'

Harlech Castle looking magnificent.

He also well remembers playing for Wales against South Africa three days before Christmas in 1951. 'We lost to the buggers – but only just. Six-three it was. I had a bad game and I'm always reminded of it. I had lumps kicked out of me.'

He waited five years to gain his revenge, playing for the British Lions in a Test match in Johannesburg. The score was even closer, 23–22, and Cliff scored a vital try. 'I had to run and stretch to claim the ball, and as I did so I swung my body so that my great adversary, Basie Van Wyk, just missed my backside. Then I went in and beat Jack Van Der Schyff to score under the posts.'

As he lay there clutching the ball in triumph, Basie Van Wyk went up to him and muttered, 'You little bastard, Morgan.'

However, Cliff and his team-mates were still exchanging Christmas cards with all the members of that South African side and their wives – at least those who were still left – forty-seven years later, and he reflected, 'I doubt that people in international rugby now will even remember, ten years on, the players they played against, never mind send them greetings cards.'

There is no doubt in Cliff's mind that, on the whole, the game is better now than it was when he was playing. Players are faster, fitter and bigger. They also understand rugby better than Cliff and his colleagues ever did because in those far-off days they played off the cuff. A coach was a posh bus. Today's players, he admits, also know the rules, while few of those in Cliff's day ever read them. He therefore respects the modern player for giving up so much time and making so many sacrifices for rugby.

But he says, 'I find it sad that because of the level of professionalism now required, there will be no more doctors, lawyers, vets, accountants etc playing at the top. It makes life immeasurably duller. I also worry that with so much year-round rugby – like cricket and almost every other sport – players will not last so long.

'I don't think I could have given my life to a game where success was so important. I was too interested in the village, the chapel, the school orchestra, the singing. I could never have turned up for rugby training on a Wednesday evening. That was choir practice night. I'm grateful to have played rugby at a time when it was played for fun and friendship, when it demanded less and offered so much more.'

He illustrated his point by citing an incident in that Johannesburg Test against the South Africans when Tony O'Reilly crashed over the line, taking three Springboks with him. The referee awarded a try before noticing that the touch judge had his flag up. According to him, O'Reilly had put his foot in touch, and the try was disallowed.

Said Cliff, 'I don't think Tony was in touch, and nowadays I suppose there would have been hell to pay, with people arguing with the referee and the touch judge. But Tony just walked away. As we all did. Maybe that was the difference between the rugby that became professional and the rugby we played on tour. We wanted to play hard, we wanted to win, but our attitude was basically carefree. Maybe we had scored a try, maybe not. It didn't matter. It wasn't worth an argument.'

I was interested to hear that Cliff thought Gareth Edwards was the greatest of all the Welsh stars. 'He was better than Phil Bennett, better than Barry John, better than JPR Williams, better than Gerald Davies – and certainly better than me. He was built like a middleweight boxer – a strong pair of shoulders and a strong neck – and he was a great gymnast and athlete. He was head and shoulders above the rest.'

Gareth Edwards was the complete rugby player, head and shoulders above the rest, according to Cliff Morgan.

Wilf Wooller played rugby for Wales and captained Glamorgan at cricket.
He was a tremendous competitor for whom I had a lot of respect.

But what of more recent stars, such as Jonathan Davies and Neil Jenkins? Davies, said Cliff, did not have to think too much about what he was going to do next. It was instinctive with him. Any great fly-half had to have that moment of inspiration when, whatever the book said he should be doing, he offered something of his own, providing both mastery and mystery. As for Jenkins, while he had become the record cap-winner and points-scorer, Cliff always thought he would be better at full-back than fly-half, where he was drafted to do a job in a difficult period for Wales. But neither could hold a candle to Edwards.

Cliff has also maintained an interest in cricket and, of the Glamorgan players, he has particularly fond memories of Alan Watkins, Wilf Wooller, Emrys Davis, Don Shepherd, Jim McConnon and Gilbert Parkhouse. Cliff had terrific respect for the latter, who took a job serving petrol at a garage to make ends meet when he was still playing cricket.

Wooller, who also played rugby for Wales, was a tremendous competitor. I had a lot of admiration and respect for him and we became very friendly. He was the kind of guy who, if you were straight with him, would be straight with you. But he was not one for half measures. Once, when Brian Close was captaining Somerset and refusing to declare to make a game of it, Wilf went on the public address and told the spectators that if they wished to ask for their money back he was prepared to consider their applications. Closey batted on into the second day, forcing Glamorgan to follow on, and he smiled when he heard Wilf's announcement. Somerset won by an innings and some.

Then there was the time when, fielding at wide mid-off, Wilf questioned a decision by umpire Frank Lee in a championship match. Lee turned down a big lbw shout and Wilf had a right go at him. Frank took it in his stride, but when Wilf went in to bat later in the day and asked for guard, Frank walked slowly and deliberately to wide mid-off.

'I'll give you your guard from here, Wilf,' he said, 'in view of the fact that you obviously feel this is a much better position than behind the wicket to see if anything is in line with the stumps.'

Don Shepherd was the backbone of the Glamorgan bowling for twenty years and remains the only man from the county to have taken more than 2,000 first-class wickets.

I have always had a soft spot for Glamorgan ever since that day in May 1959 when I made my highest score in county cricket against them – 181 not out at Bradford Park Avenue. I could not help but retell the story to Cliff of how I had been recalled to the side because Ken Taylor was on England duty, and on a turning pitch against one of the best spin attacks in the championship – Shepherd, McConnon, Peter Walker and Jimmy Pressdee – I helped Yorkshire to an innings victory.

Cliff smiled. 'Very good, Dickie. But didn't I read somewhere that you were dropped for the next match?'

When his rugby career ended, Cliff turned to broadcasting, first on radio and later television. His most emotional moments on television came in the aftermath of the 1966 Aberfan disaster. He had already talked about doing a programme for 'This Week' about Wales when news came in that nearly a hundred children had lost their lives after incessant rain had washed a slag heap on to the village school, burying pupils and teachers. 'This Week' was due to be broadcast on the Thursday – the day they were burying the children in a communal grave.

Cliff told me, 'I had no idea how we were going to tackle that awful event. Clearly ITV's main current affairs programme would have to reflect the tragedy. But how?'

Within six hours they had got Stanley Baker, Sian Phillips, Huw Griffith, Donald Houston, Anita Williams and the Pendyrus Male Voice Choir to take part. All that was said as they went on air on the night was, 'Good evening. This is a programme about Wales, its music, its prose, its poetry. Here's Huw Griffith.'

Said Cliff, 'I can see him now, standing in front of the lectern, with his half-glasses and those big eyes of his. He looked into the camera and recited Dylan Thomas. Under Griffith's voice, as he finished the poem, came the choir singing 'I feel thy presence every passing night'. It was so moving, so emotional,' Cliff recalled.

Next on was Stanley Baker, reading Gwyn Thomas's 'Trip to the Sea', which was a reminder to Cliff of his own youth and the kids he knew.

'It was,' said Cliff, 'the most memorable night. We went through it without once mentioning Aberfan or the word disaster, and yet I'd like to think that we said everything important about it that was to be said.'

Today, Cliff watches the terrestrial channels when he feels like it. He doesn't watch Sky simply because he 'hasn't got the bloody thing'. It doesn't worry him and he doesn't miss it. He reads and listens to music. Cliff believes that television has ruined our standard of behaviour.

'Consider this,' he said, warming to his theme. 'If Mr Murdoch were to go to the England, Scotland, Ireland and Wales Rugby Unions when their television contracts were up and tell them he would pay them a hundred million pounds each for the next eight years' broadcasting rights, the English, Irish and Welsh Rugby Unions would say they'd take it and Scotland would say they'd bloody well take it. Then Ireland and Wales would be told their match would kick off at half past ten in the morning, while on the same day France would play England in Paris at nine o'clock in the evening. It would all be covered in the small print of clause nine on page twenty-six. And, by the way, they should note the fact that, in future, games would be of four quarters rather than two halves. See clause eleven. I know. I've dealt with the man.'

Cliff's right in a lot of what he says. It is the same with Sunday cricket. It is supposed to start at two o'clock, but you have to wait

The memorial garden at Aberfan on the site of the school where nearly a hundred children were killed by the collapse of a slag heap.

another five minutes until the television ads have finished. I got hauled over the coals several times when I was umpiring because when it got to two o'clock I used to shout 'Play' and we'd get on with the game, never mind the ads. What about the people who have actually paid through the turnstiles to watch the game at the ground? If nobody actually turned up at matches there would be no interest for television either. But at the moment, Sky rules – and it's not okay.

As it came to time to go, Cliff summed up his philosophy for me.

'You have to have faith. And you have to have a feeling for life and sport. I go back to all those singers who may not be technically perfect, but they can make the hairs on the back of your neck stand up because of the sheer emotional effect of the music that comes from the heart.'

Two of the things Cliff most despises in life are greed and jealousy.

'Cross my heart, I am not jealous of those rugby players today who can earn two hundred and fifty thousand pounds a year playing for Cardiff and Wales. I don't care what they earn because I believe I got much more than two hundred and fifty thousand pounds a year in the friendships I forged, in the memories I have, in the simple things. I feel rich in them.'

He pushed his plate to one side, and with the perfect timing he so admires in top entertainers such as Bob Hope, Sophie Tucker, Frank Sinatra, and all the great sports stars, he concluded, 'I've very much enjoyed my piece of liver, Dickie, but how much better to have peace of mind.'

CHAPTER 13

WALES REVISITED

Pride of place in Llanelli's club museum is this account of the Scarlets most famous victory, when they beat the All Blacks 9–3 at Stradey Park in 1972.

Left: The new face of Welsh rugby, the Millennium Stadium remains in the heart of Cardiff.

MY CHAT with Cliff Morgan left me with a great nostalgia for the Wales of his day. But what of now? What of the rugby, the mining, the choirs and the chapels in the early days of the twenty-first century? I decided to find out for myself. So I made for Llanelli, typical of the smaller Welsh towns, and met up with a man who has successfully bridged the gap between past and present – that great rugby international and British Lions hero, Phil Bennett.

He was an integral part of the Welsh team in the glory years of the seventies, and is still very much involved in rugby, writing for several newspapers, doing radio and television work, and speaking regularly on the after-dinner circuit.

When I greeted him at the Stradey Park Hotel, I could hardly believe how little he had changed – although I have a sneaking suspicion that his hair is not as naturally black as it appeared. It was still the same Phil Bennett with whom I had enjoyed many an after-play drink in the cricket clubhouse at Swansea, looking down on that great view over the bay.

Despite his extensive travels, like me he has always kept to his roots, and still lives only half a mile away from where he was born on the outskirts of Llanelli. He told me, 'I wouldn't live anywhere else. I have been to many countries, but it has always been nice to come home.'

So how have things changed in Welsh rugby?

Said Phil, 'We are still coming to terms with professionalism. We had been amateur for a hundred and twenty-five years and it is not an easy or comfortable change to make after all that time. Big fees are being paid, professional leagues have sprung up and, of course, the mines and most of the steelworks have disappeared, so the natural breeding grounds for Welsh stars are no longer there.'

I knew what he was getting at. In the old days in South Yorkshire, when the collieries were thriving, it was said that you had only to shout down the pit shaft and up would come the next international footballer.

But Phil remained as upbeat as ever. He admitted that Welsh rugby was struggling, largely because the national team had not been doing

A reunion with my old British Lion pal Phil Bennett, still struggling to sound neutral when commentating on a Llanelli game!

too well, and they were the shop window. It is the same in any sport. There is always a lift when the national team is successful. But while Wales were down and depressed just then, he was sure they would bounce back. It was just a matter of getting the balance right.

Having played with Llanelli for sixteen years, training three times a week, Phil found it very difficult commentating on their matches. Instead of saying that Llanelli were on the attack, Llanelli had scored a try or Llanelli were playing rugby to dream about, he kept saying 'we'. The producer was for ever berating him, 'What's this "we" business? You're supposed to be neutral.'

People often ask Phil if he would like to be playing in the professional game, when there is so much more money to be earned than in his day.

He replies, 'I am one of those people who never look back, only forward. Of course, it was a great experience to play for my country at Cardiff Arms Park with seventy thousand of my countrymen singing their hearts out. I'm just so proud to have been there at that time. It was a privilege. It was the greatest era in Welsh rugby, a magic time, and I enjoyed it immensely.'

We had to cut our chat short because Phil was dashing off to a speaking engagement in Kent, but before he went he told me about a Northern Sportsman of the Year charity dinner in Leeds. On each of the tables there was a top personality from the Yorkshire sports scene, and the MC introduced them one by one. Geoff Boycott was on one table, Billy Bremner on another. Then they came to table twenty-three. 'And here,' said the MC, 'we have the gentle giant, John Charles.' Everybody in the hall rose as one and there was thunderous applause. The introductions continued until they reached table forty-one. 'Will you welcome the golden boy of rugby league, Lewis Jones.' For the second time the entire audience rose to their feet. Phil observed, 'Two standing ovations at a Yorkshire dinner – and both for Welshmen. I was so proud.'

I wonder if any two Yorkshiremen have ever had a standing ovation at a Welsh dinner? I somehow doubt it.

I have always admired Phil. There was something special about him that used to excite me, and it was so good to meet up with him again.

Next stop was Stradey Park, home of the Llanelli Rugby Club, and the fact that it was pouring with rain on my arrival brought back memories of my last visit to the cricket ground at the rear of the stadium. I had travelled through the valleys to umpire a Sunday League match between Glamorgan and Leicestershire, and when I arrived the ground was waterlogged. David Gower, captain of the Leicestershire side, said to me, 'Right, Dickie, it's down to you, but you can call it off now. There's no chance we'll play on that.'

Quick on the uptake as I am, I immediately deduced that David was not too keen on turning out and, to be fair, I could hardly blame him. Conditions were pretty awful. However, it had stopped raining by this time, and the groundsmen were doing a magnificent job mopping up, so we eventually agreed to play thirteen overs a side.

Conditions still left a great deal to be desired – the mud was ankle-deep in parts – but we got through it, and David was happy enough in the end when his side knocked off the runs to win in 12.1 overs. But then, Golden Boy never was a stick-in-the-mud.

One of the first people to greet me as I walked into the Llanelli lounge was Stuart Gallacher, who had played for Llanelli, captained them, coached them, served as chairman, and had become the first chief executive of the now professional club. The son of Scottish parents – his father played professional soccer with Swansea City – Stu captained the side at a very young age and went on to win one cap against France before switching to rugby league. He played for Bradford Northern for several years before eventually returning to open a business in Llanelli. A giant of a man, with hands like buckets, he must have been a fine sight in his pomp as a second-row forward.

Taking pride of place on the honours boards that line the lounge walls are the names of the Llanelli players who became British Lions. It was quite remarkable, considering the size of the town – population 45,000 give or take the odd hundred or two – to see that long list all from the same club, plus one of the greatest Lions' coaches, Carwyn James. The best of them, in Stu's eyes, was my old mate, Phil Bennett.

Llanelli are not finding it easy now that professionalism has come into the game. When Stu played for the club, all fifteen members of the first team were from the town. Now, a squad of thirty-two includes two Americans, a Tongan, two Irishmen and two Englishmen – yes, they've even let the English in, and I dread to think what Phil feels about that. Just six of the boys in the squad I watched training were Llanelli born and bred.

Sighed Stu, 'We are still trying to develop our own players, but it's getting more and more difficult. Professional rugby means that you have to import the best in order to compete with the other clubs.'

But local pride in the club lives on with Stu and others like him, and the faithful fans. They still have people turning up for matches who were members before the war and remain season-ticket holders.

Said Stu, 'This is a club of the people. One-eyed, mind. They see only red. And there is no love lost for referees down here, either.'

Llanelli have a remarkable record against international opposition. Of the major touring teams, the only one they have failed to beat is South Africa, although they ran them very close one year when they were pipped by just one point. One of the most remarkable victories was by 9–3 against New Zealand at Stradey Park on 31 October 1972, and there is a display in the club's museum commemorating that truly astonishing triumph. The photograph of the conquering heroes includes coach Carwyn James, who appears to be asleep. It seemed to suggest that beating the All Blacks was something he could do with his eyes shut.

The next big name to emerge from Llanelli could be Mark Jones, with whom I had an enjoyable natter after training. He had already

To cap it all, Llanelli has this impressive display of international honours.

Reverend Eldon Phillips and I chat to Mark Jones, Llanelli's rising young star, hoping one day to see his name added to the honours board behind us.

played a few times for Wales, and was on the comeback trail after injuries to both knees. He is quick, has good hands, and seemed to be a very level-headed young man. Maybe, just maybe, here is another name destined for the honours board.

By this time I was also in the delightful company of the Reverend Eldon Phillips, who just happens to be the Llanelli club's chaplain and match-day announcer. His chaplaincy is unique. He is the only person in Wales to hold such a position officially. I wondered how the strapping rugby players had reacted to this small balding bespectacled man of the cloth invading their territory.

Said Eldon, 'They have accepted me; even, dare I say, welcomed me. And it is a very interesting, though demanding role, with a great deal of variety. For example, I've baptised children of players, visited players in hospital, and made sure that those out with long-term injuries are not forgotten or ignored. I have also conducted the funeral service of a relative of a player who did not know who to ask.' He broke off, looked at me, smiled disarmingly, and added, 'Of course, it does help that we also have an undertaker connected with the club, so between us we have all that sort of thing tied up. The Bishop of St David's is a rugby man and values this part of my work. He sees it as an extension of my duty of ministry. As a Llanelli boy, it means so much to me that I can serve the community in this way. Stradey Park is really the mission centre of Llanelli as far as I am concerned.'

Eldon and I left Stradey Park to travel together to the Gower peninsula. Sadly, what should have been a wonderful scenic drive was marred by poor visibility and continuing rain, but it was fine, though

An impromptu cricket coaching session for pupils of Llanrhidian Primary School, Gower.

cold, by the time we arrived at our next port of call, Llanrhidian Primary School, where Eldon is a governor. I was delighted to hear the pupils greet him excitedly, yet ever so politely, with a chorus of 'Good afternoon, Mr Phillips.'

My brief stay convinced me that the good manners and respect of Cliff Morgan's schoolboy days lives on – in Llanrhidian at least.

We paused at The North Gower hotel for soup and rolls before visiting the two oldest of Eldon's three churches, in which he takes justifiable pride.

The one at Llanmadoc – the smallest church on Gower – is thirteenth-century, built on the site of an earlier church, possibly sixth-century. Cheriton Church, just down the road, is also from the thirteenth century and was built to replace one that had been washed away by the sea into the marsh below. In the churchyard grounds Eldon pointed out the grave of Ernest Jones, who was Sigmund Freud's biographer as well as disciple. Jones rescued Freud from Nazi-occupied Austria in 1937 and brought him back to this country. Freud died in 1939, so he might have spent his last summer in Llanmadoc. Now, not a lot of people know that.

Eldon takes services at these two churches on alternate Sundays at 11 a.m., plus a service every Sunday at the largest of his churches in Llanrhidian. 'From here I can spit across the estuary to where I was born,' he said. 'In fact, I told my Bishop I wouldn't accept the living unless I could see the goalposts at the Stradey Park stadium. And you

Tiny Llanmadoc Church, one of Eldon's three ancient and picturesque north Gower parishes.

Rugby chaplain and cricket umpire (retd.) in Cheriton Church, known as the cathedral of Gower for its high ceiling.

can.' He pointed across the estuary. There was a pause. 'Well, you can on a clear day,' he smiled.

He told me, 'Originally the language on the north side of Gower was Welsh, and the two churches we visited are named after famous Welsh saints, so I am delighted to have been able to start a Welsh language communion service at Llanmadoc once a month. It's the only church on Gower that does it.'

Eldon does rugby and cricket commentaries for the local radio station and is press officer for the diocese of Swansea and Brecon. What I liked about him, apart from his obvious zest for life, was his humour – a fun vicar, if ever there was one. He's also prepared to laugh at himself. He told me, for example, that he was once rambling on in one of his sermons, oblivious to the passing of time, when he heard a little lad on the front row turn to his mother and say, 'Mam, is it still Sunday?'

Before I left Gower, we popped down the road to share a drink with the lads in Eldon's local, The Greyhound Inn. A real live greyhound was fast asleep on a bench it had commandeered for itself. Apparently, it snoozes the hours away there, day after day. I wasn't all that sure about a vicar in a pub, but it was just another example of Eldon's determination to take the church to the people if the people won't come to church, and he spends at last an hour there every week. Now that is a bit different from Cliff Morgan's time.

Time for a drink and a chat in The Greyhound at Old Walls, Llanrhidian, with landlord Paul Stevens (*left*).

Practice night with the Llanelli Male Voice Choir in Zion Chapel.

Incidentally, a few weeks later I was told that the outgoing Archbishop of Canterbury, with retirement on his mind, had bought a bungalow on the Gower peninsula – in one of Eldon's parishes. I'm sure the local vicar will be equal to the challenge, maybe even persuade Dr Carey along to Stradey Park one Saturday afternoon.

My day ended with a visit to the Zion Chapel in Llanelli to hear the Llanelli Male Voice Choir in their final rehearsal for their annual concert that weekend. What a moving experience that was. When these lads – all 102 of them – let rip it is a wonderful sound.

Founded in the village of Bynea in 1964, the choir has grown in stature and strength to become one of the leading male voice choirs in Wales, along with Treorchy and the Morriston Orpheus. They have been successful at all the major Welsh competitions, including winning five National Eisteddfod first prizes. They have graced the Royal Albert Hall and Westminster Abbey and travelled worldwide, including visits to America, Australia and New Zealand.

Now here I was, privileged to be given a free show. I was thrilled afterwards when they not only presented me with one of their CDs as a memento, but also sang that well-known Welsh hymn 'Llanfair', under the baton of their musical director Eifion Thomas – a Llanelli headmaster – in my honour.

Here is one Welsh choir, at least, still in good heart, and certainly in good voice.

*

Having said my farewells to Eldon and thanked him for a memorable day, it was time to head for Cardiff, where I was due to pay my first visit to the Millennium Stadium the following morning.

There I was taken on a tour by the Millennium Stadium Public Relations Officer, Rob Cole, and to say I was impressed would be an understatement. Right at the start, the dressing-rooms were a real eye-opener. I had been in the Manchester United dressing-rooms at Old Trafford but they were only half as big as these. Rob pointed out that in rugby you had to accommodate twenty-two players in the one room, but you've still got big squads in football, especially at Manchester United. The only dressing-rooms to compare in size are those at the Headingley County Cricket ground.

There was all the space you needed, individual baths and numerous showers. My mind boggled as I thought of the contrast with Wembley, where I had umpired a World XI v Rest of the World XI. The dressing-room facilities at England's national soccer arena had nothing on the Millennium Stadium.

At Cardiff they gave me the bird – in the nicest possible way. There I was, strolling round the ground, taking it all in, when this great big bird swooped down and gave me a bit of a fright. No flight of fancy this, just another important detail in the well-oiled Millennium machine. It was, I was informed, a Harris hawk, used for the control of pigeons and seagulls.

Explained Rob, 'You can't ask people to pay fifty quid for a seat which has a load of bird muck all over it. So we use the natural method. Scares the you-know-what out of them but they don't do it here. They won't come within squawking distance if they know there's a hawk flying around.'

Then he added impishly, 'Mind you, it's great for the firm that provides the hawks. They chase all the other birds away from here, then the firm sells its services to the next place where the birds end up, and so it goes on – a real domino effect. Talk about repeat business.'

The retractable roof is an awesome feature, and to give you some idea of the task that faced the contractors, there are close to 8,000 tonnes of steel in the roof, that weight being supported by four masts, which reach ninety-three metres in height and are the tallest points in Cardiff. It takes the roof twenty minutes to open – less than half the time of the Sky Dome roof in Toronto – and uses £4 of electricity.

I have umpired a cricket match in the Sky Dome with the roof closed, and that was a fantastic experience. There were more than 80,000 people inside for a World XI v Rest of the World match. I was interested to learn that it was planned to stage a cricket match between the West Indies and a British XI at the Millennium Stadium in October 2002.

Birds of a feather – I meet up with the Harris hawk that scares away the pigeons and seagulls and so prevents them doing what comes naturally on the Millennium Stadium seats.

When they staged the Rugby World Cup it was the kind of weather that Noah dreamed about and people said they should close the roof, but at the time regulations did not allow it. Today, as long as both teams agree, there is no problem. If it is raining heavily they close it, making it better for both players and spectators.

Said Rob, 'The stadium is an eternal credit to our chairman, Glanmor Griffiths, who wanted to keep it as intimate as possible. This was the place – right in the middle of the city – where they had to build, despite the limitations, because it was so steeped in history.'

While I was at the Millennium Stadium I watched the latest big hope, Iestyn Harris, training with the rest of the Welsh squad. He had been selected to play against Argentina the following day with only 120 minutes experience under his belt after switching from rugby league with Leeds Rhinos.

Glanmor Griffiths, the man with the vision for Cardiff's magnificent Millennium Stadium.

This is what Glanmor Griffiths had to say about him: 'He is a special talent. And we have no doubt that he will make as big an impact on the union game as he did in rugby league.'

Iestyn, who became the seventy-fifth player to don the famous number 10 shirt, confided, 'I didn't expect to get the call so quickly. These are early days. It could take me as long as six months to become used to playing the game. I came down here to learn and I don't dare to dream too much. I know that I still have a long way to go.'

Legendary Welsh fly-half Barry John said there was no doubt in his mind that Iestyn could be the single most important figure they have had in Welsh rugby since Jonathan Davies.

Iestyn did not have a very auspicious debut. Wales, once the best in the world, were crushed by an emerging Argentinian side, but time will tell. Despite the sport being in the doldrums, the Welsh remain passionate about their rugby. It is in the blood of not only every Welsh man, but every Welsh woman as well. 'Old Stager' summed it up in the *South Wales Argus* newspaper in 1930 when he wrote: 'A rugby international penetrates and permeates Welsh life to an extent that nothing else is capable of doing. Welsh life in all its many facets is never so truly expressed at any national event as at a rugby international in Wales. Creeds, political opinions and social distinctions are all forgotten.'

In many ways, Wales is not so very different now from when Cliff Morgan was knee-high to a grasshopper. There is still a good deal of which to be proud, especially the truly magical Millennium Stadium.

The Welsh team training at the Millennium Stadium.

CHAPTER 14

BRITISH INSTITUTIONS

High-tech with a view on the Weather Centre roof.

Left: HRH The Queen, a regular visitor to Lord's, receives a standing ovation from MCC members in the pavilion.

'SHALL I go, or shall I stay?' Don Masson tells me those words have become legendary at The Gallery.

It all came about during a match I was umpiring at Trent Bridge. This particular day it rained, and the forecast was for more rain. Play had been abandoned and the odds were against any resumption the following morning. I went back to Don's bed and breakfast place, undecided what to do. Half of me said get off home – after all, I could come back next morning, it was only an hour's drive – but the other half thought it would be better to stay put, so I would be on the spot straight away next day.

I decided to get a second, third and even fourth and fifth opinion. I asked Don, his wife Brenda, and their two helpers, Margaret and Nancy, 'What shall I do? Shall I go or shall I stay?' I kept repeating the question until Don eventually decided for me.

'Look, Dickie,' he said, 'you're booked in for tonight so you're going to have to pay for the room if I can't re-let it, which is highly unlikely at such short notice and with the match probably washed out.'

'Right,' I said, 'that settles it. I'll stay.'

Ever since then, so Don tells me, whenever Margaret and Nancy hear that I'm to be a guest, they chorus, 'Oh, dear me, shall I go or shall I stay?'

Although matches did not start until eleven o'clock, I used to go over to the nearby Trent Bridge ground at nine, and Don would say, 'It's only just up the road, for goodness sake. Why on earth do you need to be there two hours before play is due to start?' But I wanted to check things over, make sure everything was just as it should be. I wanted to leave nothing to chance.

There was one time, however, when I ended up in a bit of a flap. When I arrived at the ground, I couldn't open my locker in the umpire's room. The damn key wouldn't turn. I was furious. The air was blue. I called that key some names I can tell you, but it turned out there was nothing wrong with the key, or the lock. I had left my locker key at Don's and taken my bedroom key to Trent Bridge.

On one of my visits I was lucky enough to have a chauffeur-driven car, which was due to take me from Nottingham to London. Shortly after one o'clock, just before our scheduled departure time, I realised I was feeling a bit peckish. It seemed such a long time since breakfast and I didn't fancy having to wait until we got to London for a bite to eat, so I nipped down the road for some fish and chips. The chauffeur was none too pleased when he came out of Don's to find me in the front seat of his posh car tucking into my cod and a penn'orth out of some very greasy paper. He very nearly threw a wobbly. For a moment I thought I'd had my chips.

Bed and breakfast establishments are as British as fish and chips and from all my travels I reckon to be able to tell a good one when I find it. Most of the other umpires now stay with Don, including George Sharp. The two of them once got into conversation about the difficulty of keeping concentration, especially in county matches, where there might be only a couple of hundred people in the ground and with little at stake for the teams.

Bed and breakfast establishments like this one in Nottingham are as British as fish and chips.

Don Masson and his wife Brenda run The Gallery Hotel where I always stay when visiting Trent Bridge.

George admitted, 'In such circumstances thoughts do wander. You lose focus, concentration goes, and suddenly you hear this terrific shout of how's that, and automatically the finger will go up.' He hastened to add that it did not happen in Tests or in county championship or one-day matches of importance. But on a balmy Tuesday, with two teams simply going through the motions, then, by George, it was all too easy not to be quite as Sharp as usual.

Don used to be a professional footballer and during his spells with Notts County he helped them win promotion right through the divisions – from the fourth to the first – which had never been done before. There is a photograph on the wall of his bar at The Gallery which shows him with the other three people who were involved in all those promotions – chairman Jack Dunnett, manager Jimmy Sirrell and trainer Jack Wheeler. Not surprisingly, a suite in the new stand at Meadow Lane has been named after Don although he was so embarrassed about it he didn't tell his son. So when the latter turned up for the opening of the new stand, he was stunned to see 'Don Masson Suite' written across the ticket he was given for the ceremony. Unfortunately, in his unprepared state he was not allowed in because he was wearing jeans.

Many's the time I've sat in The Gallery with Don discussing the weather – it seems to be a topic that is bound to be brought into the conversation whenever two Britons get together. Now, with global warming and all that, it is becoming an even more controversial subject. So when I called in at the London Weather Centre, I decided to ask Alex Hill for his expert opinion. I was expecting him to explain it away in terms of a recurring weather pattern, and I was quite surprised when he said he found it difficult to suggest that these changes were natural.

Alex confessed, 'I have seen a photograph of a glacier in the Alps which, a hundred years ago, was all snow and ice. Now there's nothing but forests. That kind of thing suggests to me that there is something going wrong, and most scientists admit to that.'

Alex said he had seen predictions that the whole of East Anglia would disappear into the North Sea eventually. Now that's frightening. You do wonder what effect it will have on the lives of our grandchildren and great-grandchildren.

It is difficult, Alex admitted, to put a time scale on such dramatic climatic changes, but when it came to forecasting the immediate weather he was far more precise. He and his colleagues generally look five days ahead in reasonable detail. After that, it becomes more generalised. On a day-to-day basis, he maintained they could forecast rain, for example, to within ten or fifteen minutes.

My ears pricked up at that. As an umpire, I would have loved to know with some accuracy when rain was about to fall. But I was somewhat surprised to discover that the cricket authorities had never consulted the Weather Centre.

Above: Weather for ducks! Alex Hill of the London Weather Centre can't understand why the cricket authorities don't make use of localised forecasting services – nor can I.

Left: Formula 1 uses weather forecasting to help decide the kind of tyres for the next grand prix.

Said Alex, 'To be honest, I find that bizarre. It still astounds me that cricket does not make use of localised forecasts. I'm not sure why that is. We're not cheap, to be perfectly frank, but if you want experts these days you have to pay for them. Maybe they think it isn't necessary to put their hands in their pockets to that extent. I don't know. But you can end up with happy amateurs.'

The Weather Centre has done work for Wimbledon, even if they haven't always got the covers on quickly enough as a result. Motor sport uses the forecasts and such information can be crucial in, say, Ferrari making a decision on what kind of tyres to put on a car. Alex admitted that he did not know a lot about cricket, but he suggested that if selectors had reliable weather information it could help them in team selections, whether to play a spinner or a fast bowler, for example. In the days of uncovered pitches, I think that would have been a big advantage, but not now, not with covered pitches. However, it might help groundsmen in their preparations.

Alex and his lads would have come in very handy when England met Australia at Edgbaston in 1975. In those days, once the game had started, the pitch was left to the mercy of the elements during the day – they were covered overnight – so there was always the possibility that you could get caught on 'a sticky wicket'.

When England captain Mike Denness won the toss, he surprised everyone by putting the Aussies in to bat. There was a theory that the ball would swing under cloud cover on that first morning. Whatever the reasoning behind the decision was, it backfired big time. The Aussies scored well over 300 and, with their last pair at the wicket just

On the famous London Weather Centre roof with Alex Hill – it has to snow into the receptacle in front of us for all those Christmas bets to be paid out.

before lunch on the second day, England's opening batsman John Edrich, who was fielding at the side of me at square leg, remarked, 'We're going to get caught on a helluva sticky wicket here. Just look at those rain clouds. They're as black as the ace of spades.'

Sure enough, just as the last man got out the heavens opened, and pretty soon Edgbaston was awash. When the rain eventually abated the groundstaff did a magnificent job in making the pitch playable again by quarter to four. At the close England were 83 for 7 and they never recovered. Australia won easily, and Denness got the sack. Now had Denness known that it was going to rain like that on the afternoon of the second day, I am sure he would have elected to bat first and the outcome could have been so different. He could even have kept his job.

Everyone, of course, remembers those famous television pictures of the weatherman doing forecasts from the Weather Centre roof, so I was determined to go up there, despite not being too fond of heights. It was quite an experience. There were lovely views of London, and I also saw the tipping bucket that collects water and measures how much rainfall there has been. Did you know that when people bet on a white Christmas it does not count unless it snows on the Weather Centre roof?

Princess Anne has been a great ambassador for Olympic sport. Here she has a friendly word with Daley Thompson, the former Olympic Decathlon champion.

*

If East Anglia were to end up under water, I wondered which generation of our royal family would end up bailing out Sandringham. I could imagine the Queen and Princess Anne in their wellies passing the buckets with great efficiency.

I was once asked by a magazine to pick five outstanding people of my time and my nominations included those two. They didn't quite rate with Mother Teresa, who topped the list, but they were right up there.

By that you will gather I am a royalist through and through. Without a shadow of a doubt I reckon we've got it absolutely right with the royal family as heads of state – a figurehead, if you like – and a democratically elected government. None of this republican nonsense for me. The Queen, the Duke of Edinburgh, Prince Charles and Princess Anne are out practically every day on some official duty or another, and I once had the privilege of standing in for the Duke at one of his engagements.

Prince Charles, here meeting Springbok captain François Pienaar, does an enormous amount of good for young people via The Prince's Trust.

It was the Cricket World Cup dinner in London. All the teams, managers, coaches and officials were invited and the Duke was the main speaker. It was a really big do, but a protest march was planned in London for the same day, and so, in the interests of safety, the Duke's appearance was cancelled, and the teams were also told to stay away.

The dinner itself went ahead because at such short notice it was impossible to let everyone know what was happening. When the decision was made, I was already on my way, having set off early by train. It was only when my cab was stopped by police halfway to The Guildhall that I realised something was wrong. We were told we could not go any further because the roads were blocked off.

In a way I was glad about that because I'd already totted up a £50 taxi fare and the blooming meter was still ticking round at an alarming rate of knots. I asked the cabbie for directions and how long it would take me to walk. It must have been another couple of miles, and I dread to think what the bill would have been had I continued by taxi. There should be reduced rates for pensioners.

I managed to skirt round the trouble spots, the protesters having by this time been cordoned off by the police, and eventually arrived at the Guildhall in a rather dishevelled state. I had my dinner jacket on – including dickie bow, naturally – and as this was in the middle of summer, sweat was pouring off me after the two-mile walk.

It was then that I was told that the teams, officials, dignitaries, and the Duke of Edinburgh would not be attending due to the trouble on the streets, but the dinner was going ahead because there were still a lot of people who would be there – and would I stand in for His Royal Highness as guest speaker. I was stunned. I didn't know what to say.

I once stood in at short notice for the Duke of Edinburgh at a Guildhall dinner. He's just like a good Yorkshireman, he says what he thinks.

But I couldn't let all those people down, could I? It was literally a case of 'After the Lord Mayor's Show' because the Lord Mayor spoke first and I followed him. Happily, it was not a dust-cart job. I got a standing ovation.

Shortly afterwards I met His Royal Highness when I presented the Duke of Edinburgh Awards at St James's Palace and he thanked me personally for deputising for him. 'They tell me you did a tremendous job,' he said.

I like the Duke. He has his critics and sometimes he does make some extremely provocative statements, but he's just like a good Yorkshireman. He says what he thinks.

I have been to Buckingham Palace quite a few times, once to receive the MBE, of which I am immensely proud. Having lunch with the Queen will always be another outstanding memory because there were so few people there – Her Majesty, her lady-in-waiting, Prince Edward and one or two specially invited guests. It was a very intimate gathering and a very, very special day.

When I hailed a cab outside the Palace to take me to the station for the trip home, the cabbie asked, 'What are you doing down here, Dickie, in the middle of winter?'

'I've just had lunch with the Queen,' I replied, proud as punch. Do you know, I'm not sure to this day whether he believed me or not.

Below left: Former prime minister John Major and J. Paul Getty have both become personal friends through our mutual love of cricket.

Below right: When Tony Blair invited me to Chequers, I found myself holding baby Leo until he and Mrs Blair returned from church.

I've also had invitations to receptions and lunches from the last three prime ministers. In 1981, I was at Downing Street for a reception put on by Lady Thatcher mainly for showbusiness people, including Eric Morecambe, Ernie Wise, Terry Wogan and Ronnie Barker. Ten years later, I received an invitation from John Major to attend a buffet luncheon at Chequers. Having stayed overnight at a small hotel nearby, I was on his doorstep at nine o'clock next morning. As my luncheon appointment was not until twelve-thirty it dawned on me that the PM might not be quite ready for me – he was probably just finishing breakfast – so I waited in the car for a couple of hours. Even then it was still a bit early, but I was welcomed with a coffee and enjoyed a chat with the Majors before the other guests arrived. There was a similar scenario when I was invited to Chequers by Tony Blair. When I arrived, the Blairs were still at church, and I ended up bouncing little Leo on my lap until they returned.

I have remained friends with both John Major and Tony Blair. Politics don't enter into it. I've mixed with royalty, top politicians and some of the richest men in the world, including cricket-loving Paul Getty, and have forged lasting friendships with them; not bad for a coal-miner's son from Barnsley. I also have so many friends among the

How would that suit me? BMB divisional director Graham Child shows me a length of cloth.

Made to measure – Jim Smith has me taped. BMB do everything from cricket blazers to battledress.

less famous and less well off, and I have cricket to thank for bringing us together.

If you decide to go to Buckingham Palace when it is open to the public, watch out for the guides pointing tourists in the right direction. They will be wearing suits, with a red collar and ERII gold buttons, made by a firm in Goole. Nothing extraordinary about that, you may say, but that firm also makes my suits.

BMB Menswear Ltd has supplied the uniforms ever since the Palace was opened to the public seven or eight years ago, and they are very proud of the fact. They also service all parts of the Royal Household, Windsor Castle, the Queen's Gallery, Clarence House, and Windsor Great Park, with battledress jackets and frock coats, and kit out the Household Cricket Club with uniforms and blazers. BMB also have an overseas business in the United States, servicing American air bases. 'The Yanks just love the royal warrant on our stuff,' divisional director Graham Child told me. 'And it is a terrific source of pride to us that we are selling British products on American air bases.'

I've had quite a few suits made by BMB, and an England umpiring blazer. Graham told me that was a difficult one because I went to them with the crown and three lions badge already embroidered on to a piece of material and asked them if they could put it on to a blazer I

BMB is one big happy family firm, employing generations of the same Goole families, including Jean Bligh and her daughter Mary.

There are ninety-five different pieces in the jacket of a suit, and sixty-five more in the trousers. Not many people know that.

had. But they did better than that. They had a hell of a job finding material that was a near enough match – they went all over the place – but rather than put the badge on to the existing blazer, they put it on a new one and gave me the old blazer back. How's that for service?

The last time I went there to be measured, Jim Smith, who is director for manufacture and distribution, took off my jacket and observed, 'My, but this is a bit heavy, Dickie. What on earth have you got in your pockets? Your bank balance?' The cheek of it.

What I like about the factory is that the workforce all come from within a thirty-mile radius of Goole and is into the second and third generation of families. Mothers, daughters and sisters are employed there. Jean Bligh and daughters Mary and Jackie are a good example of the way the firm is family-orientated.

Incidentally, there are ninety-five different pieces on the jacket of a suit, and sixty-five more on the trousers – a total of 160 different pieces. Not a lot of people know that, either.

Wandering through the factory, I noticed blazers with a fox on the badge pocket and I recognised them at once because I still have a similar blazer – green with a yellow fox. It's shabby now, but still wearable after more years than I care to remember. The colours had changed – these blazers were navy, with a silver or pastel yellow fox – but there was no doubt about it. These were Leicestershire County Cricket Club blazers. When I looked closer, I found that the names of the players were all individually woven on the inside pocket.

Graham told me they also supply the Celebrity Masters Golf competition, in which sports and showbusiness stars such as Gary Lineker, Alan Hansen and Bruce Forsyth join the top golfers. They make a special blazer for the winner, which he admits is a rip-off of the American Masters green jacket. In the summer of 2002 BMB also manufactured the suits worn by the England football team for the World Cup.

The firm takes pride in the celebrities who have had suits made to measure. I was told – and there are photographs to prove it – that magician Paul Daniels actually lay down on the cutting-room table while the lads chalked round him. Now I like that. But not a lot.

I also like to have something comfortable on my feet. What with all the standing around I've had to do, that's essential. And I've found nothing to beat the footwear that I've been supplied with by Barker's shoes of Earl's Barton in Northamptonshire. As a matter of fact I'm still wearing a pair that I got from them thirty years ago. Now that's what I call value for money.

CHAPTER 15

GLORIOUS DEVON

A fishing vessel moored in Brixham's working harbour.

WHEN I retired from county cricket at the end of the 1964 season, I was at a bit of a loose end. But several good opportunities were offered to me, including a post as cricket coach at Plymouth College, the public school in Devon. I had always enjoyed coaching and the idea appealed to me, so for the next three years I helped develop the skills of the youngsters there while playing professionally for Paignton. I enjoyed the new challenge. It was a happy relaxed time for me, and it was the start of a Devon love affair. I have gone back there at least once a year ever since.

It was while playing with Paignton that I first met John Perry, now senior vice-president of the club, and I have always stayed at his hotel, the Livermead Cliff, while umpiring or on holiday. The location was just what I wanted, right at the water's edge, looking out over the bay. If you peer over the seawalls surrounding the hotel, you can very often see shoals of mackerel. On one famous occasion, a former manager of

Right: With my old and trusted friend John Perry outside the Livermead Cliff Hotel, where I stayed on my visits to Torquay for more than thirty years.

Left: Pleasure craft surround a replica of Sir Francis Drake's Golden Hind in Brixham harbour.

Livermead Cliff chef Tim Davenport serves me my breakfast kippers.

the hotel, Jeffrey Poat, took the net from the tennis court, ran down the steps, threw it into the sea and trapped hundreds of them. Game, net and catch. Amazing!

It was lovely to sit in solitude on the promontory by the hotel, look-ing over the sea and playing my favourite Barbra Streisand tapes on my Sony Walkman. When I wanted to go out I would walk into Torquay or Paignton, or sometimes make the longer trek to Brixham and back, which took me all day. I would set off after breakfast and have a stroll on Goodrington Sands on the way. I used to take note of little cafés where I would stop for a cup of tea and maybe a cake or some toast. I found those walks so refreshing, whatever the weather. In my younger days I used to run on the sands to keep fit, but in more recent times I have had to be content with a stroll.

Sometimes I would go down to the Livermead Cliff in the middle of winter and, if it was a bit cold on my walk, I would wear a balaclava helmet that had been given to me by Stan Richards – Seth Armstrong of 'Emmerdale'. I once heard John telling a friend, 'I don't know if he thinks it's a disguise or what, but if you had a million people in Torquay, you'd pick out Harold' – he always called me Harold – 'because of that bloody balaclava.'

It was true. People would spot me from a mile off but I didn't mind. I like to meet the real punters, the people who pay through the turn-stiles. You do get the odd anorak who bores the pants off you with facts and figures, and the know-it-alls, but by and large it is simply a joy to talk to the real cricket enthusiasts who know the game and know what they are talking about. For some reason, I seem to attract a lot of ladies of, shall we say, mature years. Maybe it's the boyish charm of a fellow pensioner that does it.

John was on the board of directors at Torquay United for eighteen years and he finally persuaded me, after much cajoling, to go to watch them. Quite an education, that was. I mean, I'd been used to top-quality football with Barnsley. I told John his team was a load of rubbish, but for a long time I was able to claim that they never lost when I was a spectator. Then came the day they did and I never went back. That was me, finished.

Although John is no longer on the board, he remains a season-ticket holder, and he said to me, 'There is absolutely no way I would not support Torquay United. They are my team.' I feel just the same about Barnsley.

In 2001, John sold the hotel before embarking on a well-earned retirement with his wife Pat. I doubt I'll stay at the Livermead Cliff again. It just won't be the same. So on what could be my last visit, I was determined to take in the places round and about that had given me so much pleasure on my autumn and winter breaks in that beautiful part of the world. First whistle stop was Paignton station for a trip on the steam railway to Dartmouth, at the same time renewing my acquaintance with the station manager, Barry Cogar.

All steamed up at Paignton with station manager Barry Cogar.

Barry has always been interested in transport, and his connection with the Paignton-Dartmouth Steam Railway Company began as a volunteer in 1968, when he was working as a supermarket manager with Fine Fare. A couple of years later, the then managing director of the railway company asked if he would like to become its manager.

Said Barry, 'I was a bit taken aback. I was one of the youngest supermarket managers in the country at the time, so things were going well on that front, but I decided that here was too good an opportunity to miss. I was still young. I wasn't married, I had no family to worry about, so I said I'd give it a try. That was thirty-one years ago and here I am, still giving it a try. But I love it. It's a job and a hobby all in one.

'Of course there are problems. But I never wake up on a Monday morning and think, oh, no, not work again, not another week of this. I really enjoy what I'm doing, and there are not too many people who can say that about work.

'It's demanding, too. In the summer it means working six or seven days a week to take full advantage of the main holiday season. If you don't take the money then, you've got problems. Those six weeks of the school holidays, from the end of July through August, are vital.'

The company runs Christmas specials, which are very popular, but there are no trains in November, January, February or early March. That's the time when they do all the heavy maintenance, repairing the track, checking the tunnels, working on the viaducts, servicing the engines, repainting the coaches and mending the fences.

Barry told me that they carry 320,000 passengers a year on the Paignton to Dartmouth line, which is one of the most popular in the country. They have a permanent staff of just under twenty, with seasonal people in the summer, many of whom have just taken early retirement – he actually offered me a job as a ticket-seller – and volunteers as well.

Unlike some other similar companies, it is not run by volunteers. It is a commercial company out to make a profit. However, the money is ploughed straight back into the company and Barry enthused, 'We're improving things all the time. We intend to turn the cinema, which is currently closed, into a new terminal building, knock the old terminal down and make another platform. Everybody will walk off the street and into the cinema to buy their tickets. They'll go into the auditorium and there'll be a shop on one side and a café on the other where they'll be able to sit and enjoy a coffee in beautiful art deco surroundings, before going through to the new platform. It will be a mini Grand Central, New York, in Paignton.

'We'll be able to run extra trains. The existing platform takes only seven coaches, and although we've got five steam locomotives and three diesel, even at peak times we can run just two trains that cross at

Churston. We need at least one extra train. It would also enable us to do a bit of corporate entertainment.'

Obviously they are aiming high, and all power to their elbow. This is a most beautiful railway. It has so much variety. There is the sea, but also inland areas with picturesque woods and the River Dart meandering its way to Dartmouth. It has everything, viaducts, a tunnel, the lot.

What makes it even more exciting is that the company has bought the river link, so now they can offer a round trip. Passengers start off on the train at Paignton, catch the ferry at Dartmouth, then, subject to the tide, sail up river before being transported back to Paignton by bus. Perhaps the government could learn something from an integrated transport system such as this.

The railway has been the setting for a number of films through the years – 'The French Lieutenant's Woman' at Kingswear and 'The Hound of the Baskervilles' at Churston are possibly the most famous – and it has been featured in documentaries and holiday travel programmes many times.

When I arrived in Dartmouth it was at its best on a glorious Saturday morning, so I decided to follow my usual route – ferry across the river, then small boat to the castle on the headland. That latter trip lasts scarcely five minutes, but it is quite long enough for such a bad sailor as I am. I have been known to chicken out if the water looks a trifle too

One of the most popular lines in the country, the Paignton to Dartmouth steam train chugs along the cliffside track above Goodrington Sands.

A ferry trip across the Dart aboard the reassuringly named 'Y Worry'.

choppy where the river flows into the sea and the boat is bobbing up and down like a cork. But there was no problem on this day. There was hardly any swell at all. When the boatman took my arm to help me on to his craft, I felt as calm as the river for there in front of me, in bold letters across the bows, was the name of his boat – Y Worry. Why, indeed.

Up by the castle it was warm, sunny and so peaceful. I sat on a bench and looked out over the soothing scene. There was the river flowing into the sea; yachts and boats to-ing and fro-ing; the paddle-steamer splish-splashing from one side to the other with its cargo of cars; the trees covering the surrounding hills in their summer greenery; the sun glinting like diamonds on the water below. As you will gather, I felt poetic.

It was less than a fortnight after the terrible terrorist attack in America, when thousands of people had been killed as suicide pilots flew two jet planes into the twin towers of the World Trade Center, and I wondered to myself, 'Why?' Why would anyone want to bring so much evil into such a wonderful world as this? It simply didn't make sense.

Eventually I roused myself out of a state of impending depression. Time, I thought, for a cup of tea. I was tempted into having a Cornish pasty as well, despite feeling a little bit guilty about devouring such an offering in Devon. Maybe a cream tea would have been more appropriate but it was only midday. So Cornish pasty it was.

On the trip back to the harbour it dawned on me yet again just how much I loved Dartmouth. It is another little jewel in the British crown and there are so many places like this dotted up and down this wonderful country that I cannot understand anyone wanting to live anywhere else. There is so much beauty, so much variety.

I wandered round the harbour area before nipping in to my favourite coffee shop, buying a bag of fudge, and catching the ferry that links up with the return steam train back to Paignton. Then it was back to the Livermead Cliff for a shower before the evening meal. It is difficult to imagine a better day.

The following day, after a brief morning visit to an enchanting little spot at Stoke Gabriel, I drove to Cockington village to watch a cricket match. Visitors will know that, in the past, stumps were set up in such a way that the bowlers ran down a steep banking on either side of the ground, so that the fast bowlers often appeared to be more fearsome than they really were as they charged in at full throttle to fire in their express deliveries.

The wish-you-were-here postcard village of Cockington.

I remember on one occasion when I played there for Paignton against Chelston in a Devon Cup tie, this huge bloke – I thought he must be the village blacksmith judging by his size – steamed in to bowl at me. His first ball knocked my cap off; his second sent my middle stump cartwheeling halfway to Brixham and I faced the long tiring trudge past him and all the way up the hill to the pavilion.

Cockington Court overlooks the cricket pitch where I was once briefly on the receiving end of some fearsome fast bowling.

That was thirty-four years or so ago but, blow me, I got into conversation with a chap that afternoon who had actually played for Chelston in that very game. We had not clapped eyes on each other since. Dave Mitchell tried to convince me that the fast bowler in question, a guy called Allan Bearne, had not been a blacksmith after all, but a rep for a local fruiterer. I wasn't having any of that. They were never oranges that he fired at me – more like miniature cannon-balls.

The original pavilion was burnt down by hooligans – yes, they even get them in such idyllic surroundings – and it had been my pleasure to open a new one for them in September 1997. There is a little plaque commemorating that occasion, but it had to be placed inside. They were scared it might be vandalised if they put it on the outside wall. Sign of the times, I suppose.

On that afternoon, the game was between Torquay Conservative

Club and Torquay Social Club – and there was hardly a set of whites between the lot of them. Some were in shorts, others in jeans, some in T-shirts, some in sweaters, some had trainers, some had ordinary shoes – and not a helmet in sight. You couldn't tell the umpires from the players and play kept getting interrupted by people walking across the outfield. One young lad nearly met with a dreadful accident when he flew down the slope on his Bob-the-Builder scooter right across the pitch just as the bowler was about to launch another delivery into orbit – and a dog ran off with the ball.

It brought back memories of when we used to play on any patch of ground that we could find. We probably had one ball, one bat, and one pair of pads between us. The batsmen wore one pad each – on the front leg – and the bat was passed from one to the other, depending whose turn it was to face the bowling. If we hit the ball into the surrounding hedges and lost it, that was the end of play for the day.

Just before that day's enlightening cricket at Cockington, there had been a christening party in the pavilion, and when the people there saw me I was literally left holding the baby while they took photographs for the family album. I was gobsmacked when they told me that four-month-old Jake Harvey Mitchell was the great-grandson of former Surrey and MCC cricketer A.C. Gadsby.

Inside Cockington Church it smelt of harvest festival and there had just been a christening.

Cockington Church, a
house of prayer, a place
of history.

The christening itself had taken place in Cockington Church, one of
the most picturesque churches I have ever seen. It is very old and
steeped in history. I know some visitors are surprised to find that the
church is still in use, but many is the time, when I have been playing,
coaching, umpiring or holidaying in the area, that I have attended the
Sunday morning service.

As I wandered in again on that September day in 2001, I paused to read the words on the plaque on the rear wall: 'This church has stood here for nearly a thousand years in its perfect setting in the countryside as a lasting reminder of the Glory of God amid the changing scenes of history. It has warned the sinner, comforted the mourner, and pointed the way to a happier life beyond the grave. Generation after generation have worshipped here.'

There is another notice which reads: 'This church is visited by more than 100,000 people every year and stands for the Christian faith handed down through the generations. It is a house of prayer; a place for contemplation; a place of history; but, above all, a place of mission.'

You feel so insignificant in a place like that.

I strolled round, reliving old memories, and suddenly realised that this must be the harvest festival weekend. There on the window ledges and perched precariously on the screens, along with the more traditional offerings of fresh fruit and vegetables and the beautiful flower arrangements, were tins of custard, hot-dog sausages, soup and sardines. I had to smile.

I smiled even more on seeing the notice on the back of the door as I prepared to leave: 'Please close the door after you. If the doors are left open, birds do get trapped inside.'

Not this one, I thought, and escaped to my waiting car.

Cockington's beautifully crafted pulpit.

William of Orange landed in Brixham in 1688 on his way to claim the throne of England. So what, thinks the pigeon.

My final port of call, quite literally, was Brixham harbour, which had been the turnaround point for my along-the-cliffs walks from Torquay. The route takes you along Goodrington Sands, passes Sugar Loaf Hill, the attractive and popular Broadsands Beach and the smaller Elbury Cove before skirting Churston Golf Course and eventually reaching the edge of Brixham.

It is here that you have the first of several views of this famous fishing port. The church you can see on the left is All Saints, where Henry Francis Lyte arrived in 1824 to take up the post of curate-in-charge. If you find the name familiar, it is because he is famous for writing those wonderful hymns, 'Praise My Soul, the King of Heaven' and 'Abide with Me'.

On the waterfront is a statue of William of Orange, always, it seems, with a seagull perched on the top of his head, using the poor chap as a point of convenience, if you see what I mean. William landed at Brixham on 5 November 1688, before going on to claim the throne as William III. The statue was erected in 1888, exactly 200 years after he arrived with an army of 15,000 in a fleet of 670 ships. It appears that their presence boosted the local trade to the extent that the pubs were drunk dry.

The tourists are still doing their best on that front, as I discovered when I spoke to harbourmaster Paul Labistour. Said Paul, 'Tourism continues to thrive and comparatively speaking we are doing okay as far as the fishing industry is concerned. The harbour has been here for hundreds and hundreds of years and the fleet has had its ups and downs, but currently we have the biggest fleet in England and Wales – upwards of a hundred boats.'

Paul told me that 10 per cent of the working population of Brixham was tied up with fishing and they were one of the most successful ports in England and Wales in terms of value and volume.

'All these boats,' he pointed out, 'are separate businesses and have their own quotas. We are also well known in the south-west for our support industry. We've got an auction here which sells around sixteen million pounds-worth of fish a year, and we've got other associated industries such as engineering, electricians, the processing business, fish merchants, buyers etc. I do believe that without fishing there would not be a Brixham.'

The port has been able to develop so successfully, Paul explained, because there is a natural harbour which is protected from the predominantly south-westerly gales.

Brixham harbourmaster Paul Labistour originally hailed from Hull. We Yorkshiremen get everywhere.

On reflection, Brixham harbour is as pretty as a picture.

'When we go into the winter months,' he said, 'and it's blowing continuously from the south-west, you can stand on Berry Head with winds of thirty or forty knots threatening to blow you over the edge, and the sea being whipped into a frenzy below, yet it's as calm as can be in the harbour itself.'

The more we chatted, the more I thought there was something familiar about Paul's accent. It certainly wasn't Devonian. It turned out he was born in Hull. We Yorkshiremen get everywhere. He told me that in the early days of the twentieth century, many fishermen from Brixham worked their way round the coast and settled in Hull. He, it seemed, had made the trip in the opposite direction.

'Fishing was something I fell into,' he said, chuckling at the thought. 'But now I'm primarily port manager. I'm responsible for the finances, management of staff, the whole lot, and fishing is a bit of a by-product of what I do. It's a job I enjoy, but one of the difficulties of working in a small community is that I have very much an enforcement of law and order role. There are quite a few local bobbies doing that job in Brixham but there is only one harbour-master – me.'

Having come thus far, I could not leave without making the short drive up to Berry Head, which is now a National Nature Reserve on the site of an ancient fort. The 200-foot limestone cliffs were once the bay's first defence against attack, and the Napoleonic fortifications, which are still visible, are a fascinating reminder of those days.

Berry Head is a bird-watchers' haven and that afternoon it was treated to a visit from another rare species which had flown in from distant Yorkshire. The Torquay Coast and Countryside Trust has a visitor centre there and I discovered that shags, kittiwakes, fulmars, herring gulls and jackdaws breed on the cliffs and in the quarry, while the scrub areas provide shelter for breeding white-throats, linnets and occasionally stonechats. You can even see on closed circuit television, which beams pictures from the cliffs' ledges, the largest colony of guillemots on the south coast as they are nesting.

They've gone batty about bats up there as well. I was told that not only was the endangered species of greater horseshoe bat protected, but pampered. As I walked up the track to the cliff edge, I was puzzled by the sight of several cows among the gorse bushes. It was hardly their natural habitat, and I had this bizarre picture of

Sorting and filleting for a thriving industry. Brixham fish auction sells fish worth £16 million a year.

them running away to Berry Head to escape the awful threat of the foot-and-mouth outbreak and hiding there to avoid slaughter. All was made clear when I learned that the cattle had been brought in deliberately to produce cowpats, which provide the bats' favourite snack of dung beetles. In addition, all the bats were radio-tracked to check up on their feeding grounds, and even their caves had been made less draughty.

Berry Head is also the place to be if you are a butterfly lover. Around twenty-five species can be seen during the summer.

I would have liked to have revisited Buckfast Abbey, but there simply wasn't time, not even to stop off and buy the famous Buckfast tonic wine.

All this serves to emphasise that here is a part of the country that has something for everyone – beautiful inland countryside, woods, hills and valleys with streams and rivers running through them; seaside resorts for the kids, providing traditional family holidays; headlands teeming with wildlife; harbours of great beauty; picturesque villages; steam trains; pleasure and fishing boats; castles, abbeys and churches; and areas of wonderful peace and quiet for the times when, like me after a hard season, you just want to relax and recharge the old batteries. Is it any wonder I went back there year after year?

CHAPTER 16

THE CARERS

Remembrance Day – respecting those who gave up their lives for our country.

Left: The lollipop lady with a lovely smile.

WESTON Park Hospital, Sheffield, specialises in cancer treatment, and people think of it as a place where you go in upright and come out horizontal. Little wonder, really, when you consider that cancer is Britain's most feared disease, which hits one person in three and kills one in four. Yet Bridget Cobbald, the director of the hospital's Cancer Appeal, finds it a very happy place to work.

'I know people will think that's mad,' she told me. 'But this is the best job I have ever had – and certainly the most rewarding. A lot of people come to Weston Park thinking it's the end for them, but we are often able to give them a better and longer life, whether it be six years or six months.

'I was a bit nervous when I first came here, not really knowing what to expect. The first thing that struck me was the lack of that hospital smell, and it's a really friendly hospital. There's so much here that warms the heart. All the letters we get, thanking us and sending donations, say that while people are sad that a relative has died, they have been happy to know that their loved ones have been so well treated.

'We have lots of stories about people across the region who go to their local hospital and are told that they don't know how long – or how little time – they've got left to live. So they ask for a second opinion and are referred to Weston Park. Occasionally, they're cured, which is wonderful, but often the doctors will say, "Look, we can't cure you, but we can give you two more years," or whatever it may be. People often agree to help the doctors by trying out new drugs in liaison with our Cancer Research Department, so while they're prolonging their lives, they're also helping others.'

The Cancer Appeal was established in 1994 to support Weston Park Hospital in the care, treatment and research into the causes of cancer. Since then, there has been a remarkable sequence of successful projects, the first of which was the purchase and financing of a computer driven CT scanner/virtual simulator at a cost of £2 million. Another £2 million funded the building and equipping of the Cancer Research Centre.

The Appeal depends solely on donations and fund-raising, and words cannot express my admiration for all those people who have put in so much time and effort to raise money for this very worthy cause.

There are so many stories that bring tears to the eyes, but at the same time give you a real lift. For example, there was the triathlon runner whose wife had a brain tumour. It was thought that she would die and, even if she did not, she would almost certainly be sterile. Yet she not only survived but went on to have two children. Her husband was so grateful that ever since he has used his triathlon races to raise money, competing in what Bridget described as 'all this weird gear'. That, I learned, usually comprises shorts so skimpy that Weston Park cannot use the photographs for publicity purposes because 'they leave very little to the imagination'. Even so, the appeal has received a lot of publicity as a result of what the couple call their 'miracle babies'.

Talking of skimpy outfits, a clothing firm in Barnsley, S.R. Gent, decided to do something along the lines of the famous WI calendar, but they did it with blokes from their factory instead of the girls. It went down a bomb, especially with the lasses. Then there was the pub that staged an auction of male slaves. The blokes had bare chests and dickie bows up top and very little down below. All the girls put in bids to have them as their slaves for the night. Seeing my raised eyebrows, Bridget was quick to reassure me that there was no hanky-panky involved. It was simply a case of doing some ironing, dusting, hoovering, polishing, washing and all that. Naturally, I believed her. Anyway, it was a good idea, a good night, and very successful in terms of fund-raising.

Twelve-year-old Amy Staniforth is typical of the many schoolchildren who raise funds – but hers is another touching story. Amy's father, Russell, lost his battle against cancer at the age of thirty-eight. He had been a patient at Weston Park and, in recognition of the care he had received, Amy and her friends decided to raise some cash. She and Laura Hinchliffe, Jacob Parker and Sheridan Weston set up a sale of second-hand goods at the end of Amy's drive and they raised £116. Amy's eight-year-old sister, Abbie, did her bit by buying most of the toys.

Sponsored head-shaving, abseiling, modelling, parachute jumping, raft racing, tea dancing and zorbing have all played their fund-raising part, with participants' ages ranging from octogenarian abseiler Joseph Goddard to two-year-old model Georgia Bridges. You don't know what zorbing is? Neither did I. I thought it must be some sort of Greek dance, but no. Apparently you step inside a perspex ball which is then rolled downhill. I dread to think of the mayhem when you get to the bottom. It shouldn't happen to a hamster.

The Teenage Cancer Trust is the most recent success story at Weston Park. This special young persons' unit has five bedrooms, each with a personal computer to enable patients to maintain contact with their friends and keep up with their studies. There is a lounge and a kitchen, facilities for friends and relatives to stay overnight, plus a high-dose chemotherapy bed.

Kelly Denver, from North Derbyshire, was diagnosed with non-Hodgkin's Lymphoma when she was eighteen and she said, 'Despite friendly and open doctors, and mother being able to stay overnight, it was difficult being on a ward. You are constantly with people of all ages and differing levels of illness – something I found particularly distressing. There were private rooms but they were understandably given to the most needy, and not always available to the younger patients. On the few occasions I was lucky enough to have one of those rooms, I found my time in hospital much more relaxing. That's why I'm delighted to see the introduction of the specialised unit.'

Staff at the hospital are invited to submit funding proposals. They are able to apply at any time for small grants of up to £3,000. Projects include relaxation tapes and CDs for use by patients and carers; wall and free-standing mirrors so that radiotherapy patients dressing after treatment can check their appearance; a massage chair; heat pads and fans; iced-water coolers; and an ultrasound gel warmer, which has come as a great relief to those suffering from breast and testicular cancer. At set times, staff can put in their bids for much larger projects of up to £500,000. As a result, in June 2001 it was agreed to fund eight major new projects.

There is no doubt, from what I have seen and heard, that Weston Park has well earned its reputation as a centre of excellence, offering a full range of treatments to young and old patients locally and specialist treatments regionally, nationally, and sometimes internationally. One of only three purpose-built cancer hospitals in the country, it is comparatively small, with about 115 beds. But an awful lot of people are referred as outpatients, so they deal with up to 6,000 people a year.

The Cancer Research Centre in the hospital grounds, opened in October 1999, has a Clinical Test Centre and Bone Metastasis Unit pushing forward the boundaries of cancer research. Clinical trials cover a wide range of conditions, including breast, lung and prostate cancer, often offering patients hope when otherwise there might be none. While it remains the most feared of all diseases, survival rates are improving through research. All those at Weston Park believe that, with the continued help of the public, cancer can be beaten.

A tribute to bravery – Remembrance Sunday 2001.

Cancer doesn't just affect the patient. The whole family, along with friends, become involved in the patient's progress and welfare. I don't think there can be a family untouched by this dreadful disease. That is probably the main reason why the Weston Park Cancer Appeal has been so successful. Long may it continue.

Having to face up to the possibility – and sometimes certainty – of death from cancer is hard, and that is where Macmillan nurses have proved invaluable. These wonderful people – men as well as women – give much-needed support in their own homes to those diagnosed with the disease. I am so proud to be patron of the Macmillan Barnsley Appeal.

Macmillan nurses are trained in a broad range of skills to do with patient care, recognising that emotional and practical support is as vital as symptom control and pain management. They treat the symptoms and manage the pain, but they do not ignore the psychological issues. They try to build up a relationship with their patients so that they can talk with ease about their illness. The nurses have to be good listeners – not like me. I tend to talk too much.

Eileen Higgins set up the Barnsley service in 1987 with a colleague. Now there are five of them and she is hoping to expand further. When I spoke to her, she was hoping to raise enough money to recruit

Eileen Higgins set up the Macmillan cancer nursing service in Barnsley. Now she is planning to expand her team of five: (*from the left*) Sue Jones, Janet Chambers, Joan Greaves, Eileen and Annette Watson. They do a marvellous job, which I am proud to support.

a clinical nurse specialist to work in nursing homes, and also a social worker.

She told me, 'Due to the deprivation in Barnsley, we have lots of social problems. We have been trying to deal with them in cooperation with existing social workers, but we do need one attached to our team so we can have first call on his or her services.'

Eileen says it is an honour to work with the people in Barnsley. 'They are very, very proud. And we are involved, quite intimately. Some of the things they tell us would make your hair curl. I thought I had heard everything as a district nurse but, believe you me, when you sit there open for people to speak to you, some of the things you learn are very humbling. Scary, too, because you know they have trusted you with that information.

'But their pride is remarkable. Imagine a scenario where the bread-winner of the family is very ill with cancer. That person needs a regular change of bed linen and clothes and one day the dryer breaks down. The family is struggling. They can hardly make ends meet. It's pelting down with rain so they can't hang the clothes out. They can't afford a new dryer but they're too proud to ask for help.'

That is where Eileen and her team come in. They say, 'Look, you can't carry on like this. We'll try so-and-so to see if we can get you one.' And they apply for a grant from the Macmillan Cancer Relief charity. That is one of the practical ways in which they can help.

The charity came into operation in 1911, founded by Douglas Macmillan and his family. He had watched his father die from cancer and did not want to see anyone else suffer in the same way, so he and his family set up a Trust fund. One of the main objectives was to give grants to people on low incomes, and that still applies today. Barnsley utilises the system quite a lot. According to Eileen, hardly a week goes by without them receiving an application.

So how, you may be asking, do patients obtain the services of a Macmillan nurse? Well, the referral must come from a professional source. Barnsley is small, made up of villages, and each nurse works in a specific area. If Mrs Brown down the road has had excellent care from one of the nurses, she'll say to someone in a similar situation, 'Oh, you ought to have Joan. She sorted out all that for us.'

'But,' said Eileen, 'that's hardly enough. We need a bit more information than that. We need quite a lot of medical background, and we need to know who are the people who can benefit most from our services. We have criteria for people referred to us, and that's care management, symptom management, pain management and emotional support. We work within that framework.'

The nurse gets in contact with a new patient within two working days of referral, and they always ring first before making a visit. That, as Eileen told me, is important in these days when there are so many people knocking on doors. A visit is arranged, hopefully with the carer there as well. Incidentally, Macmillan nurses don't wear uniforms. Eileen said she had lost count of the number of times when, on a first visit, the patient had asked, 'Are you a real nurse, then?'

Eileen continued, 'Many a time the information that is passed on to us will state that the patient and the carer are both aware of the diagnosis. Yet when we meet them, they say that they have been told certain things but don't really know what it means. So it's our role to explain. We must also explore psychologically what it means to them. That's very important but it's entirely up to the patient how far we go. If they don't want to talk about certain things, that's fine.'

When they see the Macmillan nurse, a lot of people say, 'You're not going to tell me bad news, are you?' If that's what they say, the nurse will not tell them any bad news.

'I just say I'm there to support them,' Eileen continued. 'To work with what they've got. If they want to explore treatment, we explain about it. If they don't want to know about treatment, I suggest that some information can help them to cope. If they try to deal with it without information, it can be very difficult.

'When people go back to hospital, they very often don't know what questions to ask, so our consultants have got used to our patients turning up with a sheet of paper with loads of questions written down. I mean, it is scary for the patient. Going back to hospital they are vulnerable. They get frightened. The doctors seem so busy, and all they want to do is get back home.'

I thought about my recent visit to the Manchester Eye Hospital for an operation to save the sight in my left eye and I had an idea what she was talking about. It is frightening going to hospital and meeting with doctors and surgeons, mostly because you don't know exactly what is going to happen. It must be far, far worse when you are suffering from a life-threatening disease such as cancer.

Eileen went on, 'The doctors are very good at explaining things. They have had a lot of experience, but because patients are fearful of what they are being told, they don't really take it all in. They say, thank you, put on their coats and go home. Then they start thinking, what did he say? So we always visit them after they have been to hospital to make sure that they do understand what has been said. If they don't, we explain it to them.'

Some of the training the nurses have is in breaking bad news.

'Some people,' said Eileen, 'can be extremely angry at first – angry with the consultant, angry with the doctor, angry with the nurses, angry with themselves. When you have been told you've got cancer, probably for the first time in your life you are not in control. Our

Together with Rachel Salt, the area manager (on my left), and other members of the RNIB fund-raising team at their Leeds headquarters. They are very caring people.

philosophy, as a team, is to try to give the patients back some measure of control.

'Basically, that's what we do. We just work with people, give them information, answer their questions, support them through their illness. Sometimes we have people who are cured, but the vast majority are in what we call a palliative state, where there is no cure, only treatment. That treatment can go on for a number of years. Sometimes we see them on and off throughout that time, at any stage when they feel we need to be involved.'

Eileen was not too sure that it needed a special kind of person to be a Macmillan nurse, but you do need life experience and quite a bit of training. They are all registered nurses to the level of ward sister. They have to do a diploma and then a degree in palliative care, which is now a recognised subject. All the nurses are trained up to degree level. Anyone wanting to be a Macmillan nurse must already have had at least five years' experience working in palliative care.

But the learning never stops. There is always something new on the horizon and when you are the senior nurse, as Eileen is, you need to be up to the mark with all the developments. She admitted, 'I have to keep up to scratch, and it's not easy.'

Cancer can trigger family problems. As Eileen said, 'If you are diagnosed with cancer, it can be an emotional time bomb affecting everyone around you. So counselling is vital. Unfortunately, you can get someone complaining that they are doing all the care for their mum while another daughter or son is not doing anything, or maybe one son has given up work while the other has carried on in his job. You've got to try to get them to understand each other. I tend to try to get them to work a rota. That comes from being a prefect at school I suppose. I tell them that a rota is not something they must do, it is something they can do. And if they do all they can, that is good enough. You've got to try to get all members of the family to see the other person's point of view. And that's not easy. So we have to work with families a lot, as well as the patients themselves. It can be very draining. The bereavement service is growing all the time as well.'

People used to say they did not want a Macmillan nurse because that meant they were dying. The nurses have done such a marvellous job and earned such an excellent reputation that you do not hear that so much these days. Eileen summed it up perfectly when she told me, 'The key message is that we help people to manage life – how to live well with their diagnosis, and how to deal with the symptoms. We do not look upon it as dying with cancer, but rather living with cancer.'

*

Another cause close to my heart is the Robert Ogden School for autistic children at Thurnscoe, not far away from where I live. The first time I visited there and saw those kids, I left determined to do as much as I could to help them.

Imagine for a moment that you are not able to communicate, that you are locked in a bubble where no one can hear you, no one can understand you, you cannot speak and you cannot learn – not even the most basic of life skills such as washing, dressing and cooking. To carry out the simplest tasks, you need to be taught each step, then how to link them together.

Then again, maybe you have a fragile communication system based on pictures, which allows you to get across to others your needs and interests. Perhaps, just as you think you are beginning to understand the world around you, everything changes and you find yourself back at square one again, throwing you into a flurry of anxiety and panic. To cope, to feel safe, you may scream, shout, or hit out. Alternatively, you may just withdraw and sink into a state of depression.

You may be particularly good at something – remembering numbers, art, or writing – yet you cannot hold a simple conversation, you cannot understand someone else's point of view, you cannot predict the outcome of your actions or theirs. You might have a strict routine to which you stick rigidly and repetitively so that it becomes almost like a ritual and does not allow you to continue normal living.

Coping with the outside world is baffling. You may find sight, sound, smell, touch and taste becoming too much for you. The unpredictability of life makes you anxious and confused. The most ordinary activities such as going shopping, catching the bus, or handling money are overwhelming.

That was how autism was explained to me. Can you imagine the confusion, the frustration, the isolation, the desperation you would feel in such a situation? Go on, humour me. Think about it. Just for a minute. That is what thousands of people with an autistic-related disorder face every day of their lives.

Did you know that more than 520,000 people in the UK are affected by autism and related conditions, not to mention the families and professionals who care for them? That's four times more than cerebral palsy and seventeen times more than Down's Syndrome.

Claire Strachan, who is the Yorkshire regional fund-raising manager for the National Autistic Society, told me that autism, first formally identified in 1943, is as hard to define as it is to diagnose, but in all cases, communication is the key.

She told me, 'All people with a form of autism have impairments in social interaction, verbal and non-verbal communication, and imagination, commonly referred to as the triad of impairments. These traits are often accompanied by a narrow range of interests, activities and behaviour patterns and a resistance to any unexpected change in routine.'

Since its humble beginnings in 1962, the National Autistic Society has provided an influential voice in society, encouraging a better understanding of autism, spearheading national and international initiatives and pioneering special services in support of people with autism and those who care for them.

President of the society is Jane Asher, who says, 'Autism can be a puzzling, heartbreaking and devastating condition. It affects not only the children or adults with autism, but also – to an enormous extent – their families and friends. It is hard to imagine, even for those of us who have worked with people with autism for many years, just what the stresses, emotional tensions and physical demands must be for the parents of an affected child.'

Getting to grips with the batting. I pass on a few tips at the National Autistic Society's Robert Ogden School at Thurnscoe.

The NAS now has six day and residential schools that provide tailored education and support and the Robert Ogden School is one. After re-locating to new premises at the former Dearne High School in July 2000, it has become the world's largest school for children with

autism and currently caters for 135 children, with the capacity to increase this to at least 165. It caters from primary schooling up to secondary and post sixteen, with the majority of pupils coming from the Yorkshire area although, due to its excellent reputation, the catchment area also includes the north-east, Lincolnshire, Derbyshire, Lancashire, Cumbria and Warwickshire.

But, as with all ventures, finances are an ongoing problem and the school needs to raise £1.4 million. In April 2001, the Yorkshire Post joined forces with the NAS to help raise that sum. It launched the Hidden Disability Appeal and a significant amount has been raised, but there is still a long way to go. They hope to reach their target by the end of 2002.

I went there to help publicise the appeal, and I was delighted to meet up with some of the kids again. One young lad who was particularly keen on cricket asked me who is my favourite cricketer and what is my favourite ground. 'Sobers and Lord's,' I told him, but realising that Gary Sobers played long before his time, I threw in Ian Botham for good measure. He smiled at the mention of his name. 'And David Gower,' he said.

St John Ambulance members of Starbeck and Knaresbrough division at a charity football match between stars of Emmerdale and Harrogate Town FC. They do a magnificent job.

I was asked to sign my name on a Dickie Bird toby jug miniature that somebody produced from nowhere, and then I was asked for my autograph by one of the carers.

'Who is it for?' I asked.

'Darren Gough,' came the reply.

'No, seriously,' I said.

'I am serious,' he replied. 'My name is Darren Gough.' And you thought there was only one, didn't you?

Incidentally, the Robert Ogden School was nominated as charity of the year 2002 by Taylor's of Harrogate, who were aiming to raise between £8,000 and £10,000 for the appeal. The school was hoping to arrange a training course for the children at Taylor's cookery school to help them develop skills for when they leave school. For my part, I promised to help to arrange a charity cricket match.

Talking of schools, whenever I go down into my local village as the pupils are coming and going, I am always impressed by the cheerfulness and helpfulness of the lollipop ladies who make sure that the children can cross the road safely. These people are so often taken for granted, but where would we be without them? They show another side of caring.

In all the years I've been going to watch Barnsley at Oakwell, I can't remember a match when members of the St John Ambulance Brigade haven't been there. There is hardly a public function that goes on without these lads and lasses being around to help if anyone is injured or ill. They do a magnificent job.

I could go on at length about so many people, many of them volunteers, who care so much for the welfare of others that they give up countless hours of their precious time to help. It warms the cockles of my heart. I have a tremendous admiration for them all, especially those people involved with the special charities I support. I am proud to be associated with them.

I am proud, too, that on Remembrance Day we still show that we care about all those people who laid down their lives so that we might be free to live ours in peace. May we go on remembering them.

CHAPTER 17

BOATS, BALLS AND BIRDS

The annual Henley regatta is a great sporting occasion first and foremost – and also a good excuse for socialising. Anyone for Pimms?

Left: Temple Island, a smart vantage point opposite the start line at Henley.

I HAVE always stressed the importance of mental toughness for any sportsman – or team – to be successful, and rower Sir Steve Redgrave has that in abundance. That is why he is one of the greatest Olympians the world has ever seen. In 1996, at the age of thirty-four, he won his fourth successive Olympic gold medal, this time in a pair with Matthew Pinsent, and afterwards declared, 'If anyone sees me getting into a boat, they have my permission to shoot me. I don't want to get in a boat again. Ever.' Just as well no one took him at his word because a year later he teamed up with Pinsent, James Cracknell and Tim Foster to win the world championship. That was remarkable enough, and testament to Redgrave's mental and physical strength, but then came his greatest battle of all, and ultimately his greatest victory. He was diagnosed with diabetes and thought that this time his career really was over. Even he was depressed for a while before becoming more philosophical about the situation. It was no big trauma, he told himself. His career had to end sometime. If it was now, so be it. But his doctor wife, Ann, persuaded him to see the year through, and when a specialist told him that there was no reason why he could not achieve what he still wanted to achieve, that stubborn Redgrave streak surfaced again. It would not be easy. So what? When did anything worthwhile come easily? He decided to give it a go.

After a while, he started to struggle. He said it was like driving a car when the fuel wasn't getting through to the engine. Once again depression set in for a while. He needed regular injections and the diabetes dogged his preparations for the Sydney Olympics in 2000. His sugar levels had to be carefully monitored. They had to be exactly right. Even more sacrifices than before had to be made, both on the water and in his private life. And, despite his tremendous record, his position in the crew for the Olympics was under threat.

He told me, 'I realised I might not make the Olympics after all. I wasn't performing to the levels I used to and that was very frustrating. You don't want to become the weakest link in the unit.'

But Redgrave toughed it out and won his fight for a place in the boat. Even then, however, there was another set-back to overcome. In

Catching up with Britain's record-breaking Olympic rower, five-medal man Steve Redgrave at Henley.

their last big race before the Olympics the British quartet were well beaten by the Italians in Lucerne. It was a big shock and there was not much time to put things right.

But put them right they did and on the day, Redgrave's great mental resolve again shone through. He did not have much sleep the night before the final, and next morning he was as nervous as he had ever been. The build-up was very emotional. The waiting was agony, but just before the race he told himself, 'Look, don't worry, we're going to win this.' He was convinced that victory would be theirs.

There was the merest fraction in it at the finish, but afterwards Redgrave declared that he never had any doubts that he and his colleagues would hold on to win. He said, 'The small margin of victory was irrelevant. It's who crosses the line first. And we crossed first. It didn't matter by how much or how little. We did it.'

It was as the boat crossed the line, the tiniest margin ahead of their great Italian rivals, that the scale of his achievement suddenly hit him. He recalled, 'I was gasping for breath, my lungs were screaming for oxygen, my arms and legs were aching like mad and I was hurting all over. But at the same time I was thinking, that's it, five gold medals. Nobody can take that away from me now. That's it for life. That's never going to go away. The pain will.'

It was a graphic description of what it had taken to make Steve a great Olympic champion with a record that will surely never be bettered, or even matched. He added, 'I knew it was my last Olympic final, and I wanted to enjoy that moment of victory. It really is over now. No more rowing.'

But this, remember, is Steve Redgrave talking. He could not resist a final fling on his home water at Henley in the annual regatta of 2001. As a steward, a committee member and a finish-line official, he had enough on his plate as it was, but the lure of a seat in the Leander Club crew for the Queen Mother Challenge Cup proved irresistible. Despite a minimum of preparation, Redgrave and his team-mates in the quadruple scull proved too strong for their opponents from the London Rowing Club, and he completed yet another successful chapter in a long and memorable story.

I have often wondered what makes Henley so special, so I travelled down to meet Steve and watch the rowing to find out about the unique appeal of this typically English event. The venue is delightful, the competition is keen, there is an opportunity to see the world's best oarsmen in action and the atmosphere is tremendous. It is a shame that the fuss about the lengths of the women's skirts sometimes overshadows what is a great sporting event. Sadly, too many people who are more concerned with socialising than spectating end up prostrate on the lawns, or tottering dangerously near the river bank three sheets and more to the wind – not a pretty sight. But it is a magical day for all that.

Redgrave's Olympic team-mate James Cracknell summed it up perfectly for me.

'Henley is bigger than the stereotypes that surround it – the Pimms-drinking upper class who don't watch the racing. It's a unique event to be at. Winning at Henley, for club and international oarsmen alike, is special, and if you know that people who have come to watch you racing are enjoying themselves, it makes it even better.

'Racing at Henley is as close to being in a stadium that rowing can get. The crowd numbers and noise far exceed any other race – even the Olympics. In the last three hundred metres you cannot hear the calls being given out in your boat. As world champions in the coxless fours, we raced the Australian 1992 and 1996 Olympic champions, "the Awesome Foursome", at Henley, and that remains the most amazing atmosphere in which I have raced. Memories of the roar down the enclosures still make the hairs on the back of my neck stand up.

'But Henley isn't just about internationals. It's the place where every club oarsman wants to win. These are the rowers who get the most out of Henley. We are fortunate enough to race abroad with big crowds, coverage on TV and good sponsorship, so we can train all the time. Club oarsmen train before and after work, every weekday and week-ends as well. They deserve this racing atmosphere. Their love of and commitment to the sport puts professional sports to shame.'

As far as the Sydney crew was concerned, Cracknell thought that the people who had supported them so magnificently deserved the chance to see them race.

'Surprisingly,' he added, 'this can be achieved without the need for a ridiculous blazer, Pimms or money, as eighteen hundred metres of the two thousand three hundred metre course is open to the public.'

For the foursome, particularly Redgrave, it was another chance to get used to the tremendous adulation that had come their way since their Olympic triumph.

Steve told me, 'I couldn't get used to all the praise and recognition when I first returned home from Sydney. I kept looking over my shoulder to see who they were cheering. On the other side of the world you are so wrapped up in what you are trying to do that you don't realise just how special those two weeks are for the people back home. It was said that our victory was a symbol of national pride.'

Steve was voted BBC TV's Sports Personality of the Year for 2000 – and not before time. Receiving the award he reflected, 'I've been coming here for sixteen years, waiting for this moment. It is a very special night, and a great honour.'

I had met him on those previous awards nights and every time I said to him, 'Good luck, Steve, I think it's yours this time.' But it never was until the Sydney success. There would have been something very wrong if he had not received it then. I still feel he should have won it earlier. What he has achieved is remarkable.

It is unbelievable that he completed that nap hand of gold medals after being diagnosed with diabetes. That shows tremendous mental strength, will power and great self-belief, and he has been a marvellous ambassador for this country. No sporting hero deserved a knighthood more than Sir Steve.

After his retirement, Steve and Ann ran the London Marathon. It was part of his programme of de-training. It would have been dangerous to stop immediately after twenty-five years of hard grind. Even then he was competitive. He had a dread that Ann would beat him, and he was determined not to let that happen. However, being the understanding and loyal partner that she is, she ran with him side by side from start to finish. It was somehow symbolic of the unselfish support she had shown throughout her husband's glittering career.

Incidentally, Steve has now launched a charitable trust to raise money for children, with the target of £5 million over five years. He'll make it, you just see.

His final words to me were, 'To be honoured with a knighthood by your country when you have come from a working-class background is something you can only dream about. You can receive only one knighthood. So that's it now. It really is the end of the road.'

As someone whose only rowing experience was going round in ever-decreasing circles on the lake in Scarborough's Peasholm Park as a

They're away. Racing at Henley is as close to being in a stadium as rowing can get.

young Yorkshire cricketer, and subsequently dizzily depositing my breakfast on the bandstand, I have a tremendous respect for anyone who can propel a boat in a straight line, especially at such a phenomenal speed. As a rower, and as a man, Steve Redgrave is someone to be greatly admired.

Steve may have picked up five Olympic golds, but I can boast of a Wimbledon hat-trick. Three times I have been invited by the Lawn Tennis Association to sit in the Royal Box – and three times it has rained.

My first visit was particularly memorable. When the heavens opened – it came down like stair-rods – the president of the All-England Club asked if I would entertain the spectators on a packed centre court until the next patch of blue sky emerged out of the darkness. I had never been in that situation before. Usually when it rained, I scarpered to the umpires' room to put my feet up and enjoy a cup of steaming hot tea. So I was a mite nervous when I looked out at all those people sitting there in the rain, protected only by a sea of multi-coloured brollies. The previous year, Sir Cliff Richard had done his

Gene Kelly impersonation by singing in the rain, and I thought, I can't follow that.

However, I took the mike, told a couple of funny stories, and relaxed as soon as I realised the crowd was laughing along with me. I chattered on for about half-an-hour and we all enjoyed ourselves. In fact, they pleaded with me to go back again, just in case it rained and they needed someone to serve up a racket of a different kind.

Although it rained for my second visit, it was not nearly as bad and my verbal volleys were not required. But there was another problem. Somebody must have set fire to a chip pan or something because suddenly thick smoke puthered out from a nearby building and we could see – and hear – the fire engines in the background. It got so bad that play had to be stopped for a short time. Wouldn't you know it, but some wag in the crowd shouted up at me, 'We expect rain with you, Birdy, but not smoke and fire as well.'

On my third visit, I found myself in extremely distinguished company. How about this for a roll of honour? From the world of cricket there was Darren Gough and Clive Lloyd; from football Sir Bobby Charlton, Sir Alex Ferguson and Sir Bobby Robson; and there were also ten of our Olympic gold medallists from Sydney 2000 – cyclist Jason Queally, five of the men's rowing eight (Kieron West, Simon Dennis, Fred Scarlett, Ben Hunt-Davis and Andrew Lindsay), sailor Shirley Robertson, shooting's Richard Faulds, and Stephanie Cook, the winner of the inaugural modern pentathlon for women.

If I could keep Dennis Lillee in order, I reckon I'd have been a match for John McEnroe in one of his you're-the-pits tantrums.

Right: Today, John McEnroe is one of the best commentators on the game, chatting here with former rival, now great friend, Bjorn Borg.

Below: Sue Barker does a splendid job covering Wimbledon for the BBC, and when it's too wet for her to work, I've been known to take a turn.

On the spectator front, the middle Saturday at Wimbledon is traditionally dedicated to personalities from other sports, and I was very proud to be in such exalted company. After all, these were sporting greats and I'm only an umpire. Of course, trust the crowd to have a go at me when they saw me sitting there. During one on-court altercation they shouted to me, 'How would you have handled this lot, Dickie?'

Well, I'll tell you something. If I could have swapped sports for a while to sit in the Wimbledon umpire's chair when John McEnroe was at his nastiest as a player and throwing his infamous 'you're the pits' tantrums, it would have been some contest. I like to think Mac would have met his match. If I could keep Dennis Lillee in order, I am sure I could tame anyone. 'You cannot be serious?' You bet I can.

Ironically, I think that John has now become a great commentator on the game. He knows tennis inside out and puts his views across well. Sue Barker is very good, too. Indeed, on the whole, BBC coverage of Wimbledon is excellent.

McEnroe, of course, was a great champion, even allowing for his fits of pique and eyebrow-raising outbursts. Many experts claim that Rod

Bjorn Borg tops my list of the greatest tennis players of all time.

Laver was better, maybe even the best, but Bjorn Borg tops my list. I am a great admirer of his. He was a wonderful sportsman, and I am disappointed that I have not had the opportunity to meet him.

There were some memorable contests between McEnroe and Borg. They developed a great respect for each other and forged a lasting friendship. In later years, they played a lot of tennis for charity, including a match at Buckingham Palace.

Wimbledon is to tennis what Lord's is to cricket – a spiritual home. In 2001 there was an overlap between two of the great sporting occasions – Wimbledon fortnight and the first match of an England v. Australia Test series in this country. Needless to say, the Aussies won the Test, but they just missed out in the tennis, with Pat Rafter losing to Goran Ivanisevic in the men's final.

Mind you, it could all have been so different in SW19 had it not rained on the Friday night when British hope Tim Henman was leading Ivanisevic by two sets to one and was ahead in the fourth. I am convinced that, but for the rain interruption, which meant that the semi-final was not finished until the Sunday, Henman would have won

Right: Goran Ivanisevic gets up off his knees to clinch the Wimbledon men's title at last by beating Pat Rafter.

Below: Our Tim – did a semi-final rain delay cost Henman his crowning glory at Wimbledon in 2001?

through to his first Wimbledon final – and who knows what might have happened then?

Naturally, it opened up the debate about fitting the centre court with a retractable roof that could be pulled across in the event of rain, like the Millennium Stadium in Cardiff. Had it been in place in 2001, Britain could well have had a first Wimbledon champion since Fred

Jumping for joy – the power machine that is Venus Williams, celebrating her Wimbledon championship triumph in 2001.

A packed Wimbledon is a very special place. It's the tournament all the players want to win.

Perry in the 1930s. Not only that, it would also come in very handy to cater for my visits. Some say a roof over the centre court might spoil the atmosphere and there could be problems with the grass, but that may be a small price to pay.

In any case, I don't think you would ever lose that buzz at Wimbledon, roof or no roof. What helps make it special is that the spectators are so close to the action. It really is exciting to be there, especially if you have the privilege of being a guest in the Royal Box. On the stairway leading up to the box there are boards upon which all the names of the champions are inscribed, and you feel a great sense of history and tradition when you walk past. Maybe one day Tim Henman will be added to the list. We can but hope.

Trafalgar Square, I suppose, is the place most noted for pigeons, but I have never seen more in one place than I did one afternoon at Trent Bridge, Nottingham. The invasion came when I was standing at a Test match between England and the West Indies. With our lads in their usual spot of bother, John Snow decided to try out a new tactic in a bid

to slow the visitors' galloping run-rate. After lunch he went out with his pockets stuffed with breadcrumbs, which he proceeded to sprinkle all over the ground. Within seconds we were surrounded by a multitude of apparently starving pigeons. It seemed that they covered just about every single blade of grass. It did the trick. Play ground to a full stop. I was not amused. Pigeons and pie were words that immediately sprang to mind. But a good number of years later I came to realise just how beautiful and interesting these birds really are.

Bird meets bird – Kevin Hodgson introduces me to one of his pigeons and explains the unexpected intricacies of the sport of homing.

There are a lot of pigeon breeders and racers around Barnsley, and I decided to get to know a little bit more about the sport of homing. The Keel Inn at Stairfoot is the headquarters of the Barnsley Federation of Homing Societies, and I met up with Kevin Hodgson, who has his lofts there.

We were waiting for some of his young birds to return on their debut flight from Nottingham. It was a stirring sight to see them flying in a big circle before zooming straight into the loft. It begged the question that always springs to mind about homing pigeons – how on earth do they find their way back after being released many miles away, sometimes across the Channel, without a map or a compass or even the wife to navigate? Kevin tried to explain.

'Pigeons,' he said, 'have a homing instinct. Experts reckon it's something to do with the magnetic field. There's no doubt that homing pigeons perform better when it's sunny. If it's cloudy they don't seem to pick up the line the same. It takes them longer to get home. And if the weather is really bad, you can lose them altogether, especially on the Channel trips. For some reason, pigeons don't seem to like an easterly wind either. It affects their navigational senses.'

So a pigeon's ability to find its way back home to its loft remains very much a mystery. Kevin told me of an experiment in which a pigeon with frosted contact lenses over its eyes was released many miles away, and got to within a mile of its home loft – flying blind, as you might say. Well, that certainly opened my eyes although it didn't do much for the pigeon's.

Racing starts every year in April. Old bird races take place until the end of July and then young bird races are staged up to 16 September. Four or five races start in France, and the rest go from such places as Fareham, Southsea and Weymouth. For every race there is a special transporter, financed with money from the clubs in the Federation, to take the birds to the liberation point. With the Channel races it may not be viable to provide their own transport, so the club will contact Christine Gooch at Catterell's Transport in Blackpool, which has a fleet of wagons specialising in continental racing.

Said Kevin, 'Christine will give you a price on baskets, depending on how many you require, and provide a convoyer to go with the driver. The convoyer looks after the birds, feeding and watering them. Some of the birds may be basketed at Stairfoot on the Wednesday or Thursday, but not liberated from France until the Saturday, so they need to be carefully cosseted in the meantime.

'Christine will provide the club with the latest weather report on the Saturday before liberation, give them the line of flight, advise them of wind speeds and directions over the Channel – in fact, every bit of information they need from race point to home area. If the weather report is too bad, the pigeons will not be liberated. If the race goes ahead, they fly back to their home loft where they are clocked in. The clock is then taken to the headquarters where it is checked.'

This was all very well but, while even a simpleton like me could understand that the bird returning first to the Stairfoot Society lofts at the Keel Inn was the winner within that Society, what of the Channel races and other Federation events, in which all the societies in the area took part? After all, the birds have to return to different lofts, up to twenty miles apart. Who wins then, and how do they decide?

Well this is where the clever bit comes in. It was explained to me that every loft has a longitude and latitude location and, with all the birds being liberated from a central point, that is how the velocity – the

Des. res. to suit international racers, while the chart-topping piped music scares away the cats.

rate of the bird's movement – is worked out. And you thought it was all flat caps and feathers, didn't you?

In fact, I did not see one single flat cap. It is hardly a poor man's sport these days, when you consider that Kevin's loft cost him more than £5,000, and that is nothing compared with some. There are those that could easily be mistaken for residential bungalows. Some lofts are heated, not particularly for comfort, but so that, at the beginning of the year, just before the start of the racing season, a constant tempera-ture can be maintained throughout the day and night, leading to what is known as early form.

Said Kevin, 'It gives the birds an edge in the first few races of the season. Pigeons need sun to create form. They need warmth. Cold weather is not good. I have no heating in my lofts, but I have panels in the roof to provide extra light and they also help heat things up.'

So what was the point of the music, I ventured to ask, as the latest chart-topper blasted from within the loft? Did it make the birds more content, and therefore better able to produce their best form? Or did they just enjoy karaoke sessions?

'I'm not sure it has any beneficial effect on the pigeons,' Kevin replied, 'but it helps scare the cats away.'

I'm not surprised.

Kevin confirmed that a lot of people had the wrong conception of pigeon racing. He explained that today it is a specialised sport. 'Basically,' he went on, 'these birds are athletes, and you have to treat them that way. We even have special diets for them. At the beginning of the week in which they are due to race, we feed them light digestible food. Then, come the middle of the week, we put them on a high-protein diet to help build them up for the racing. Again just like an athlete, if you feed them wrong, they peak too early. After racing you give them electrolytes to get all the toxins out of their blood.'

As you will gather, there is more to pigeon racing than the droppings. Nor is the sport confined to the so-called working classes, if we are still permitted to use that term. Her Majesty the Queen has her own lofts at King's Lynn in Norfolk. Of course, she has a manager there, and I don't suppose she nips over to feed the birds personally all that often, but she takes a keen interest and the pigeons are raced in her name.

From what I gathered there is a lot of money to be made at the big events – what they call the classics. If you are lucky enough to win one of those you can make even more money from breeding. I learned one other thing as well. Knowing that, like me, Kevin was a keen Barnsley supporter, I had put on a red jumper specially for the occasion, only to be told that pigeons don't like red. I almost scared them all away. Now if only I'd known that all those years ago at Trent Bridge . . .

The beautiful River Trent, where I often went to relax on my days off when umpiring at Nottingham.

CHAPTER 18

DRIVING FORCES

Colin Montgomerie in a spot of bother.

Left: Overlooking the 18th green at Wentworth.

WHEN I was invited to sit on the panel of 'A Question of Sport' on BBC Television, I arrived early, as is my custom, and got into conversation with the only other occupant of the hospitality room. We talked about cricket, and many other sports, and eventually we touched on golf.

'Whatever happened to the lad who won the Open in 1999 after that Frenchman ended up in the water at the last hole?' I asked him.

'Do you mean Paul Lawrie?' he replied.

'Aye, that's him. The Scotsman.'

He smiled. 'You're looking at him,' he said. 'I'm Paul Lawrie.'

You should have seen my face. It was redder than the new ball on the first day of a Test match. I offered my grovelling apologies.

'Not to worry,' he grinned. 'That's another story I can use in my after-dinner speeches.'

You may think this little episode emphasises my lack of knowledge about golf, and it is true that golf is a sport I have never played and have found little time to watch because of my cricketing commitments. But I have always been interested in it because so many cricketers play the game, and it is so popular worldwide that it has become another British institution.

After my retirement, therefore – and more so after my embarrassing encounter with Paul Lawrie – I decided to find out more about the sport, which is said to have its roots planted firmly in Scotland.

Golf flourished in all classes of the community – kings, bishops, noblemen and folk of every rank were to be seen out on the Scottish links, and the Stuart kings helped make golf fashionable south of the border.

The classlessness of the game, at least in Scotland, is indicated by the story of the caddie who, judging that the spectators were getting too close, grabbed hold of one of them by the ear, and invited him to stick his nose into the hole so that he could feel if the ball was there or not. He just happened to be the local magistrate.

Allan Robertson, the first golfer to beat 80 at St Andrews, was accepted as the leading player of his day. With his assistant, Tom

Morris, he ran a thriving feather-ball business out of the window of his workshop, which doubled as the kitchen of the Robertsons' house. Stuffing a top-hat full of feathers into a leather casing was a job for an expert, and not even the best of them could manage more than three balls a day.

After his death, Prestwick Golf Club put up a red morocco championship belt for competition over three rounds of the club's twelve-hole course in order to find his successor. They must have been disappointed when just eight players turned up for what has gone down in history as the first 'Open' Championship, although the fact that all eight were professional means that it was not technically an Open at all.

However, the event did involve amateurs from the following year, 1861, and it was dominated by Tom Morris, runner-up at the inaugural competition, and his son, who was also called Tom. After Old Tom had won for the fourth time, Young Tom went on to emulate that feat and became the first holder of the present trophy, a silver claret jug, in 1871. The Tom-Toms certainly beat out a remarkable success story in those days.

Although the British Open has been in the doldrums from time to time, it is now recognised as one of the best organised major sporting events in the world. Attendances soar past 20,000 every day. Indeed, at the Millennium Open at St Andrews, when Tiger Woods claimed his first claret jug, more than 200,000 fans poured in during the week. A huge tented village offers golf gear, food and drink, and media coverage is massive.

However, there can still be the occasional hiccup. For example, in 1965 an entry was received from a certain Walter Danecki of Milwaukee, who described himself on the entry form as a professional golfer. As soon as he swung his club on the first tee at St Andrew's, it was obvious that there might possibly have been just the slightest distortion of the facts. He went round Hillside in 108.

The press pounced and Walter was only too pleased to talk to them. He explained that he was, in fact, a mail sorter who had occasionally played golf at his local municipal course over the last seven years. But he explained, 'I wanted the crock of gold, so my conscience made me write down professional on the form. The formalities for joining the PGA were too complicated and protracted, so I hit on the idea of winning the British Open to cut through the red tape. If I won the Open, they would have to let me in.'

Although he had such little experience and admitted to being self-taught, he said he was confident that he could beat Arnold Palmer.

The Royal & Ancient officials nominated a substitute to take

St Andrew's, the historic home of golf, shown from the notorious 17th green.

Danecki's place in the second round, but Walter was having none of that. He reported to the tee, determined to repair the damage of his opening 108. 'I'm no quitter,' he said defiantly. 'I came here to play golf, and that's what I'm going to do.'

He began seven, seven, eight, and then the wheels really came off. He finished with 113, giving him a total of 211 over the two rounds, which meant he had failed to qualify for the Open Championship by a mere seventy-five strokes.

But was Walter disheartened? He was not. In fact, he was quite chuffed. 'I have to say,' he told the clamouring press lads, 'that your small ball is right for this sort of course. If I had been playing our bigger ball, I would have been all over the place.'

Eleven years later, the R & A were caught with their pants down again. Maurice Flitcroft, a forty-six-year-old crane driver from Barrow-in-Furness, had taken up golf eighteen months earlier and his experience was limited to hitting shots on the beach. When he was called to the tee at Formby for the first qualifying round, again after claiming to be a professional golfer on his entry form, he was embarking on the first eighteen holes of his life.

On two holes his marker lost count of the number of shots Maurice took, but gave him the benefit of the doubt, with an eleven and a twelve. By the end of the round, Maurice had knocked Walter's effort into a cocked hat. He had compiled the grand total of 121.

He explained his 'form' as follows. 'At the start I was trying too hard. By the last hole I was beginning to put it all together.'

His scorecard backed up this extraordinary statement. There had been a definite improvement on the back nine. He had gone out in sixty-one and come home in sixty. But, despite this great step forward, he withdrew from the second round because it had dawned even on him that he had no chance of qualifying.

There is a lovely postscript to this story. When the news of his score flashed through to the Open venue at Royal Birkdale, there was a mass media exit as a convoy of cars dashed to the qualifying course at nearby Formby and caught up with Flitcroft in the car park. While he was telling the story, the R & A's press officer George Simms was busy at Birkdale tracking down his home and phone number. Eventually, he got to speak to Maurice's mother. 'As your son has never played a round of golf before, don't you think he had a bit of a nerve in entering for the Open?' His mum replied, 'Well, he's got to start somewhere hasn't he?'

Maurice would, no doubt, have fared better had he called on the advice of golfing guru John Jacobs, who has helped countless thousands of club players through his Practical Golf Schools. He has also

I met up with golfing guru John Jacobs at Wentworth.

Tiger Woods stands head and shoulders above the rest.

given priceless advice to some of the most illustrious names in the game, among them Jack Nicklaus, Greg Norman and Severiano Ballesteros. A fellow Yorkshireman, born at Lindrick, Jacobs went on to become the professional at Sandy Lodge; played in the Ryder Cup; fought to set up the hugely successful PGA European Tour; was a key figure in the mushrooming golf centre boom of the sixties and seventies; and was twice captain of the Ryder Cup team. Just the man, I thought, to put me more in the picture, and I caught up with him at the Cisco World Matchplay Championship at Wentworth in October 2001.

Many professional cricketers play golf, but when I was a young lad at Yorkshire, our coaches would not allow us to play because they thought it might affect our cricketing technique, and they were dead right, as John explained.

'Cricket is largely keeping the ball along the turf, golf is hitting it in the air. Donald Bradman would score three hundred and never hit the ball in the air once. So the technique used in playing golf would be detrimental to young cricketers. However, once they have become established at their own sport, then they can adapt to golf with no adverse effects. In fact, there are some cricketers who have played golf at a high standard, notably Ted Dexter who won the President's Putter at Rye, to add to Sussex and England cricket successes.'

Denis Compton was apparently not one of them. Said John, 'I played with him years and years ago and, while he was a wonderful batsman, he was a terrible golfer. He couldn't hit the ball more than a hundred and thirty yards because he never used the bottom hand.'

John is well aware that golf instruction can easily take ability away if you overdo it, but he has always felt that if he could improve someone's technique, he could also improve their temperament a little. As far as temperament is concerned, he reckoned that Jack Nicklaus was the strongest of the lot. He told me, 'Jack had a relatively poor technique, believe it or not, but I still regard him as the best golfer of the last century. Ben Hogan was probably the best technician. If you put a lot of golf balls in front of him, he could hit them wonderfully. Nicklaus, on the other hand, merely hit them well. But he had the greater mental strength, and that, for me, comes before technique.'

Of today's players, Tiger Woods stands head and shoulders above the rest. From the way he played in 2000, John thought he was already the finished article. 'He was the best driver, the best iron player, the best pitcher, the best chipper, the best putter, the best bunker player – the best of everything.' However, in 2001 he did not play as well, and John's theory for this is that by concentrating on one shot at which he wanted to become even more proficient, the rest of Tiger's game suffered.

Tiger soon put that right when he showed his game was in perfect shape as he won his third US Masters title in 2002.

When top golfers get on the phone to ask John to help them sort out a problem he says to them, 'Don't tell me what you think is going wrong, tell me what the ball is doing.' If they do that, he knows exactly what the club is doing when it strikes. 'Golf,' he went on, 'is what the ball does. If you walked with players such as Norman von Nida or Doug Sanders, you would notice that they never hit a straight shot, but they could cut it both ways to great effect. I was the same. There are, you see, many, many ways of playing golf successfully.'

The same applies to cricket. I've got every coaching qualification there is, but I don't harp on about it because the most important thing in coaching is making people believe in themselves. If what they are doing works for them, you should try to encourage it, not alter it.

There was a time when John coached the German national team and they used to go to the south of Spain for two or three weeks. One year the weather was so awful that they found themselves Morocco bound instead. On the first day he was on the practice tee when this chap told him, 'You're playing with the king this afternoon.' John got the distinct impression that if he did not do as he was told, he and the rest of the team would be on their way back to the Fatherland in quicksticks. So, every afternoon, he had to be available for the king. After his morning stint with the Germans, he would be picked up by the biggest stretch limousine he had ever seen and taken to the king's private nine-hole course at the palace.

The first time he played there he was surprised to find a truck accompanying them round the course, carrying thirty sets of clubs. The king would play a couple of holes with one set, then change to another, and so on all the way round. John would partner the king against two goodish golfers from his entourage – but there was never any doubt about who would win.

Said John, 'Wherever the king hit the ball, it was teed up for him, and when he putted on the green, no matter how far away from the hole he was, his opponents would chorus in unison, "Given, Your Majesty."'

On another occasion, John was on holiday with his wife in Tenerife and was playing a fourball with three friends. There was a single player behind them, so they waved him through on to a par three. They stood behind the green and watched him hit the biggest slice you have ever seen. It finished up fifty yards over the hill. He topped the next shot, but it hit the top of a bunker, flew into the air, and finished dead. He tapped it in and walked on.

When they were having a drink in the bar afterwards, the fellow

Enjoying a chat with the Bedser twins at the Cisco World Matchplay Championship at Wentworth.

walked past and John remarked, 'My word, but we were all very impressed with that three you got on the seventh.'

To John's amazement he replied, 'Oh, yes. I find this course very easy compared to where I play at home.'

Stunned, John asked, 'Where is that, then?'

'Wentworth,' came the reply.

John was convinced that the whizz-kid had never been to Wentworth in his life, so he persisted, 'You play very well. You must have lessons.'

'Oh, yes,' he said. 'I go to the John Jacobs Golf Centre.'

'In that case,' chorused John's three buddies, 'can we introduce you to the grey-haired old buzzard!'

There is good money to be earned in golf and it has become big business. For a lot of people it is a nice little perk to be invited to have lunch in the marquee and watch golf out of the window, as I did that day at the Cisco World Matchplay along with the Bedser twins, Alec and Eric, who have always been very keen golfers. Television has brought in extra revenue, as well as creating a lot of additional interest. The BBC covered the day I was at, but Sky, I was told, had done a tremendous deal with the European tour, paying very big money to cover events.

The BBC, of course, first gave coverage to TV golf, with the incomparable commentary of Henry Longhurst. Then came Peter Alliss, who proved a worthy successor. Both Augusta National and the Royal & Ancient have stayed faithful to them in the continued coverage of the US Masters and the Open Championship.

My old mate Lee Westwood – I would have had a long wait to see him play. He teed off the next day.

I have always thought that the standard of behaviour of golfers is very good and John agreed. 'By and large you are your own referee. You can cheat if you want to because there is nobody around, but thankfully that's very rare – at professional level, anyway.'

John and I have a lot in common. We played to a certain level at our sports, but earned our reputations after we stopped playing. Not many have the privilege, or good fortune, to be able to do that. Now he is on a committee rewriting the teaching manual, still very much involved in the modern game. He was not sure about taking up that particular challenge, but says as long as he is able to keep his sense of humour he knows he can cope.

'You have to make sport fun,' he observed. 'You have to enjoy it.'

Dead right. Once the fun and enjoyment goes out of any sport, you may as well pack it in. After lunch I spotted my old mate Lee Westwood on the driving range.

'Now then, Dickie,' he said, 'and what brings you to Wentworth?'

'I've come to watch you play, mate,' I replied.

'Then you're going to have a long wait,' he countered.

'Why's that, then?' I asked.

'Because I'm not due to tee off until tomorrow.'

Trust me to get the wrong day.

But I caught up with him on television the next day as he beat Denmark's Thomas Bjorn only to be beaten in the next round by a revitalised Ian Woosnam, at forty-three still producing superb golf.

His victory in the final against Irishman Padraig Harrington was well deserved and he was naturally delighted with his winner's cheque for £250,000. As in cricket and indeed every sport, it's winning that brings the greatest satisfaction.

It was quite an experience for me to be in the splendid surroundings of Wentworth and I didn't need telling that it's one of the premier golf clubs of Britain. It has three courses, the most famous being the West course, which became known as the Burma Road because of its testing character. This was where the World Matchplay Championship was being staged. The impressive clubhouse – originally the home of the sister of the Duke of Wellington – is like a five-star hotel, providing facilities for its members and visitors that are in use every day of the year. It certainly has no close season, like cricket. All the world's greatest golfers have played there from the great Triumvirate of Vardon, Braid and Taylor to the Big Three of Palmer, Nicklaus and Player, and following them Tom Watson, Nick Faldo, Seve Ballesteros, Greg Norman, Sandy Lyle and Colin Montgomerie, right up to Tiger Woods.

Former British Open champion Nick Faldo.

CHAPTER 19

CRICKETERS OF
THE FUTURE

There's no doubt about that one.

Left: Enjoying a welcome cuppa during the tea interval with my colleague in the white coat, Bruce Ropner.

BEDALE, in North Yorkshire, is situated in such a lovely part of the country that I was only too delighted to accept an invitation to umpire a schoolboys' match at Camp Hill, close to the village of Carthorpe, in the summer of 2001 – despite suffering from a dodgy shoulder, a bad back, game knee and failing eyesight.

But when further details of the fixture were explained to me, I began to have serious doubts. This was no ordinary encounter. This was to be the first game played on a pitch that had been created from a virtual wilderness in the grounds of a country house, and, as someone more used to standing at Lord's and all the other great venues, I wondered what I was letting myself in for. I had visions of an area more suitable for a ploughing competition than a game of cricket.

However, passing through the gates on my arrival and making my way up the long, curving drive to the main house, I began to sense the remarkable transformation that had taken place. As I glanced to my right through a group of trees, there in the morning sunshine was a welcoming field of the lushest green, in the middle of which was a mighty motorised roller of colossal proportions chugging proudly across the virgin strip – if you'll pardon the expression. A small but handsomely designed pavilion nestled in the shade in one corner, with an adjacent conveniently placed portaloo. Nails were being driven into a newly erected and freshly painted scoreboard. All around people were scurrying hither and thither in excited and enthusiastic preparation for what was, for them, an historic occasion.

When my host, Bruce Ropner, whose son Robert's brainchild all this was, took me down to the ground for a closer pre-match inspection, I was even more impressed. They had even erected nets in the far corner. The only problem was, as Bruce explained, that 'rabbits had been eating the bloody things'.

When I heard the full story of how the pitch had been developed, I was amazed. Six months earlier the area we were standing in had been knee-high in grass, weeds and nettles, with three trees – two lime and a chestnut – branching out to provide further obstacles. The trees had now gone. There was no trace of them. But a telegraph pole had to stay.

There was no way that could be chopped down. In any case, it was pretty much out of harm's way near the boundary edge. In a sense, it even added to the unique charm of the place. It reminded me of Canterbury where a lime tree stands within the playing area. There is a story told of a chap called K.L. Hutchings who thought he had scored a certain six, only to see the ball hit the top of the tree, drop from branch to branch, and eventually fall into the gleeful hands of the fielder waiting below. Thankfully, we were never led up the pole, so there was no call for an official adjudication on a direct hit.

It was almost impossible to conceive that this lovely little ground had been carved out of such an unlikely and inhospitable environment. To be honest, I was staggered, and I told Bruce so. I had been expecting a patch of rough ground little bigger than a sizeable back garden.

It turned out that Bruce and I had a lot in common. We had been born in the same week; both of us had a passion for cricket from a very early age; and both had the good sense to decline an invitation to join the Yorkshire committee. So when he heard that there was a possibility that I could umpire the inaugural match at Camp Hill if facilities were all in place for the 2001 season, he and Robert decided to bring their plans forward by twelve months. They probably thought that, as I was getting a bit long in the tooth, I might peg out if they left it another year.

Taking the bull by the horns, he waded into the project with great gusto. Indeed, his wife told me that he spent four hours a day, every day for four months, clearing the area and creating his own little piece of cricketing magic. We are talking here about a sixty-eight-year-old with two replacement hips.

If all this took me by surprise, a complete tour of my surroundings left me quite breathless – in more ways than one. Robert, who now owns the estate and runs the business, first of all pointed out the conference centre to the left of the main house and then, to the rear of that, what looked like a narrow-gauge railway track. Was this, I wondered, a previously undiscovered offshoot of the famous North Yorkshire Moors line? I half expected one of those wonderful old steam trains to come puffing past at any minute. But, to my astonishment, Robert explained that this was an essential part of the British bobsleigh team's build-up to the Winter Olympics.

'This is where the team trains,' he said. 'They use the track from May to September to build up their starting speed before going on the ice because if you don't get one of the best pushes in the world, you will never win, even if you have the best driver. They go to Norway and Austria in the middle of October to train on ice for the first time.'

Camp Hill, near Carthorpe, where a cricket pitch was created out of a wilderness.

Bruce proudly added that Camp Hill had staged the British Push Championships three years earlier.

Then it was into the woods where all sorts of fiendish management development courses are put on, to help people discover themselves, as Robert put it.

He pointed out what he described as a 'zip wire' stretching from a platform in one of the trees, over a lake, and back down to ground level. He turned and looked at me challengingly. 'It's activities like this that help people see just how far they can go.' As far away as possible from that zip wire, I thought. I must confess that just at that moment I was having a turn of Shane Warne proportions because I honestly thought they were going to ask me to give it a try, and zipping down a wire from the top of a tree wasn't my idea of a pre-match warm-up.

A little further on we entered another clearing and were confronted with a sheer wooden climbing wall forty feet high. If I had known what was to come next, I would have insisted on an early lunch.

'Right, Dickie,' said Robert, 'we thought you might have a go at this.'

I spluttered, 'I'm not going up there, mate. No way. I can't stand heights. I get dizzy going to the top of the stairs.'

They finally managed to persuade me to stand on the first foot-hold, a whopping six inches or so off the floor. Even then I nearly had a nose bleed.

Said Robert, 'There, you see, that's the first step.'

'Aye, lad, and the last,' I gasped.

Robert patiently explained that this was an essential part of the character-building exercise. The idea was to try to get people to do what they were either afraid to do, or thought they were not capable of doing.

He'd got me on both counts.

He pointed out that if someone put on the safety harness and helmet, they would score points. If they climbed as far as letter A on the wall, they would be awarded another point. If they made it to B, it was two points, C was three points, and so on.

'If someone who had never tried this sort of thing before reached C, it would be something to be proud of,' declared Robert. 'It would be much more of an achievement than an accomplished athlete going straight to the top and thinking nothing of it.'

I think I got two points. But, then again, I am occasionally prone to exaggeration.

We had a superb lunch at the Fox and Hounds pub which is Egon Ronay listed and situated in the village of Carthorpe. They served up a delicious duckling, crisply cooked just the way I like it.

Bruce said, 'we would very much like to have youngsters coming here to play cricket and other sports. Until the early 1950s Carthorpe had its own pitch but not now. The large village of Bannerton one and a half miles north of here doesn't have one either. They do have a school so hopefully there will be plenty of demand for matches to be played here'.

Before the game started, I had another look at the pitch. It really was a credit to Bruce and his helpers. To get a square like that – and a track like that – from a rough field of long grass, nettles, weeds, trees – and a telegraph pole – was truly amazing. When the pitch is bedded down and worked on, I am convinced it will be a good one. The more it is rolled and watered the better – roll and water, roll and water. That is the key, especially in a dry spell, and especially very early in the morning and late at night when there's dew on the pitch. That's the best thing. All the old groundsmen used to do that. Up at the crack of dawn they were, and still there at dusk. You don't find too much of that kind of dedication around today.

As for the Camp Hill roller, a few county grounds would benefit from that monster. It would flatten anything. It certainly played a big part in preparing a strip that, although presenting scoring problems for the batsmen because of its low bounce, was in no way dangerous. The ball did not fly about all over the place, which would have been a worry.

So it turned out to be a wonderful day, far exceeding all my expectations. After what I had been told, this was a revelation. I never

Feeling my age on the very first rung of the ladder. I quietly left the younger generation to get on with the Camp Hill character-building exercise!

thought in a month of Sundays that it could be anything remotely like this. I was impressed with every aspect – the pitch, the outfield, the environment, the setting – and my umpiring colleague. I thought Bruce handled the role magnificently. There was one lbw appeal which was very close, but Bruce got it spot on. He thought about it for a long time, but then decided, quite rightly, that it was a fraction outside the leg stump, and the lad had taken a big stride forward anyway. Here was an umpire after my own heart. If he had given that out he would have been guessing. If there is even the slightest doubt, the decision has to be not out as far as I am concerned. Hawkeye can put that in his pipe and smoke it.

The game itself, between two immaculately turned out sides, was a good one. The local team, including Bruce's grandchildren, put up a spirited performance before being beaten by 15 runs playing against strong opposition from Thirsk, who recovered from a shaky start to make 85 in their allotted twenty overs, batting first.

It looked as if Thirsk had decided on their batting order by size. Several strapping teenagers filled the early order. Then, after a bit of a collapse to 9 for 3, a couple of batsmen who were just short of a mere six feet led a revival, stroking the ball around nicely to score 20 each before making a compulsory retirement. After that, the size of the batsmen began to decrease in proportion to the increase in runs. When the last 'man' arrived at the crease, he was just eight years old, hardly bigger than a penn'orth of copper – a smidgeon taller than the stumps – and carrying a sawn-off bat.

Bruce Ropner at the wheel of an impressively heavy roller that would be the envy of a few county grounds I can think of.

He took his guard and proudly told me, 'I played in a match, Mr Bird, when I scored fourteen in one over.'

I replied, 'I don't think this is quite the pitch for big-hitting, son.'

But he was having none of that defeatist nonsense. 'I'm going to hit one over the pavilion,' he declared.

I smiled condescendingly. He didn't look big enough, or strong enough, to knock the ball off the square, never mind clear the pavilion. But I was surprised to discover just how accomplished a batsman he was for one so young, showing really good technique. That is what impressed me about all those youngsters, whether batting, bowling or fielding. I saw some kids there that day who could really play. One or two, I discovered, were already going for coaching at the School of Excellence at Headingley, and some were destined for Ampleforth College where they would be coached by the former Yorkshire and England star, Don Wilson.

It all reminded me of the time when I first set out on my career and the opportunity that I almost missed. One day, after I had left school, I went to Barnsley Cricket Club's ground in Shaw Lane in the hope of getting myself noticed. I had to catch two buses to get there, and even then there was a long walk from the bus station. When I arrived, I asked if I could have a bat. The appearance of this skinny kid from the back streets obviously failed to impress. I was told to clear off.

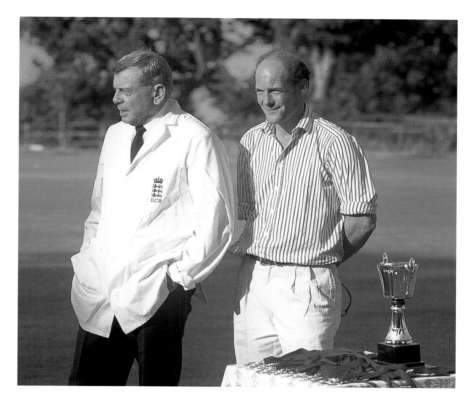

Waiting to present the Dickie Bird Trophy with organiser Robert Ropner.

Heartbroken, I was on my way out of the ground when a chap by the name of Alf Broadhead called me back. He took me into the nets, bowled to me all night, and told me to go back the next day. And I kept going back. He bowled not only to me, but also to Geoff Boycott and Michael Parkinson, for hours on end, giving us vital batting practice. We all eventually made it into the first team. Boycs and I went on to play for Yorkshire – and he for England. Parky, sadly, fell by the way-side. I often wonder what became of him!

But for Alf, cricket might have been lost to me. He gave me my chance. And those youngsters at Camp Hill were being given their chance by Bruce and Robert Ropner. I would like to think, at a time when so little cricket is being played in schools, that other kids from more deprived backgrounds than the ones who so impressed me that day will be given similar opportunities on other occasions.

Meanwhile, wouldn't it be just wonderful if one of those lads who performed with such distinction on that mid-August day in 2001 went on to bigger and better things? And, with the proper advice and encouragement, who knows? A lot of those youngsters certainly had the potential. But would they have the right mental approach? That remained to be seen. What a story it would be if that inaugural Camp Hill match for the Dickie Bird Trophy produced a future Yorkshire cricketer.

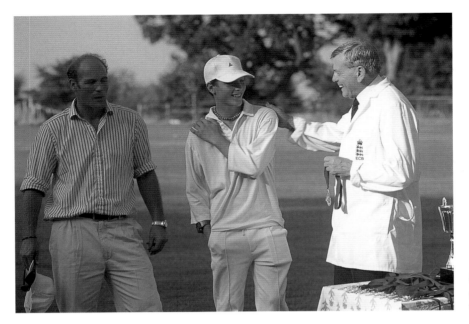

Congratulations are in order at the end of a very good game.

Then I would be able to relax in my rocking chair, content in the knowledge that the Dickie Bird story had come full circle and another aspiring youngster had been given – and had taken – his chance to make a name for himself in this glorious game that has been my life and has enabled me to see for myself so much that is the best of Britain.

What a story it would be if the inaugural Camp Hill match produced a future Yorkshire and England cricketer.